Hindu Rites, Rituals, Customs and Traditions

A to Z on the Hindu way of life

Prem P. Bhalla

HINDOOLOGY
BOOKS

Published by

An Imprint of

Pustak Mahal®, Delhi

J-3/16 , Daryaganj, New Delhi-110002
☎ 0-11 23276539, 23272783, 23272784, 23260518
E-mail: info@pustakmahal.com • *Website:* www.pustakmahal.com

Sales Office & **Branches**
Bengaluru: ☎ 080-22234025, 40912845
E-mail: pustakmahalblr@gmail.com

© Copyright: Hindoology Books
ISBN 978-81-223-1475-5

Edition: 2024

Printed at: SRK Graphics, Delhi

Dedicated to the

Saints and Sages

who made Hinduism great

Preface

Modern youth are in a hurry – to grow up, to acquire education, to work and get married, to own a vehicle and a home and, finally, to arrive. Arrive where? Most youth do not know. Nor do they know their ultimate goal in life.

Those who dare answer will tell you that they are trying to make the best of their life. When asked how, they are not too sure. They are in the run to find happiness. They seek this happiness from the many comforts available in modern society. But soon they realise the things that ensured happiness yesterday do not do so today. The novelty has faded and everything appears ordinary.

The truth is that mankind is driven by desires, both good and bad. When one is achieved, it leads to another. It is an endless game. Every achievement brings temporary happiness. Every failure brings frustration and a feeling of hurt. Ultimately, one realises the futility of chasing happiness through desires of the body, mind and intellect.

There are millions of living beings around the world. Of these, life as a human being is the most precious. Did God grant this form so human beings could fulfil their desires endlessly? Could this really have been God's purpose? Hinduism teaches us that God grants life as a human being as a gift to enable a soul to reunite with Him through faith and devotion. Religious texts confirm this. A human being is specially gifted to be able to think, reason and choose a path of action to achieve this purpose.

Since a human being can think, reason and choose, when confronted with diverse situations one tends to choose what is easy and pleasurable. The fault is in choosing what one sees and feels rather than searching for the eternal happiness that already exists within the individual. The Hindu way of life teaches one to make this happiness a part of life. Activities are prescribed from the time of conception until death. One needs to understand and follow them. This book is an effort to bring simple everyday activities to householders who can make material progress worthwhile by combining it with spiritual guidance and fulfilment.

This book would not have been possible without the valuable research done on the subject by Dr Prakash Chandra Gangrade and the permission by Mr Ram Avtar Gupta, Managing Director, and Mr S.K. Roy, Executive Editor, Pustak Mahal, to use the same in this book. I extend my gratitude to them.

–Prem P. Bhalla

Contents

What is the basis of the life of a Hindu?

A Hindu is a person who adheres to Hinduism – a religion followed by the vast majority in India. It is more about what people do than what they think. Each individual follows a way of life that provides some meaning to it. One comes across many improvisations in Hindu homes. There is no specific objection to deviation or change. The Hindu way of life is liberal in permitting space and liberty to every individual.

The Hindu way of life is principally based upon the teachings in the Vedas. The Rig-Veda, which was recorded in a form of Sanskrit over 3000 years ago, is the oldest of the four Vedas. It has 1,028 hymns to a pantheon of gods. Over the years the teachings have passed on from one generation to another through memorisation and word of mouth. Two other Vedas, the Yajur-Veda and the Sama-Veda, later supplemented the Rig-Veda. The fourth Veda, the Atharva-Veda, was added perhaps a hundred years later.

The Hindu way of life has also been profoundly influenced by the Upanishads – Sanskrit religious scriptures. They came as the final portion of a Veda, and are also termed as Vedanta (*Veda-anta* – end of knowledge). The word *upa-ni-shad* ("sit down near") suggests a personal touch to explaining a religious truth. The earliest Upanishad dates back to about 2,800 years. Others followed chronologically. It is believed that as the first three Vedas split into a number of branches, each branch produced its own Upanishad and is named accordingly. There are about 200 of them. The emphasis is on personal realisation.

Definite thinking emerged from additional knowledge with time. Meditation, belief in rebirth and the existence of an *atman* (soul) in every individual influenced the thinking. Hindus learnt that life is everlasting. An individual does not die. The body dies. When one body dies, the soul moves into another body. The selection of a body depends upon actions performed in a lifetime. From this emerged the importance of an individual's actions or *karma.*

The two great epics the *Mahabharata* and the *Ramayana* were sources of inspiration and direction to the Hindu way of life that followed the Upanishads. Each is narrated in the form of a meaningful classic. Within each there are shorter stories, tales and discourses on subjects that pertain to life and living. The epics date back to over 2,000 years. Over the years their popularity has grown tremendously. Newer versions came about. Translated into many languages, in modern times they have been made into movies and television serials. Their popularity is unmatched as people feel there is something new to learn and be inspired by each time.

The Puranas were composed after the epics. Some of them deal in detail with subjects and characters in the epics. The Bhagavata-Purana describes the life of Krishna. The Puranas elaborate on the hymns of praise, philosophies and rituals. They use iconography as a descriptive tool and praise Shiva, Vishnu, Ganesh and many other gods and goddesses.

Along with the Puranas, the Dharmashastras and Dharmasutras (textbooks on sacred law) provide many guidelines on life and living. Of these, Manusmriti is perhaps the most important. What is significant is that the study of these is restricted to a learned few. The common man believes in the theory of *karma* (action) and has learnt the Hindu way of living through rituals, customs and beliefs passed on by word of mouth from one generation to another.

A ritual can be taken to mean several things. It could be a religious or solemn ceremony that involves a series of actions performed according to a set order. It could also mean a series of actions followed without variation or refer to a system of religious or other rites or observance of set forms in public worship.

Similarly, customs can also be interpreted in different ways. It could mean a traditional way of behaviour that is specific to an occasion, place or time. It could also refer to a habitual practice or a way of acting in given circumstances. The habitual activity could be transmitted from one generation to another. Customs gradually became an established way of doing things. Continued use made them a part of social usage.

A belief is a firmly held opinion or conviction. It may be a trust or confidence in something that cannot be immediately proved. It may come from personal or religious faith through use and experience.

Rituals, customs and beliefs together give direction to individuals to act in particular ways in everyday life, and also in the conduct of certain rites and ceremonies for religious services or on public occasions.

Hinduism has thrived despite a variety of reforms due to urbanisation and modernisation. The country faced foreign invasions and occupation. Changes were then necessary. Yet the rituals, customs and beliefs have survived not only in temples and religious institutions, but also in millions of homes around India. Individuals continue to follow traditional patterns. They derive strength from the confidence the rituals and customs inspire.

The inquiring mind looks for reasons to uphold traditions. Modern youth want facts to decide what they can accept or reject. An effort has been made to trace the origins of many rituals and customs and find explanations for their usage.

Hinduism is the oldest of all religions. No individual or prophet has founded it. While other religions are dated in that you can go back to their origin, Hinduism emerges from the mists of time. It is a synthesis of a variety of religious experiences and offers a complete view of life. It is not rigid in thought and is tolerant of how individuals interpret it in their own life.

According to Swami Chinmayananda, "Love is the very basis of Hinduism. If you know how to love, you are a Hindu. All great people have become great because of their love for others. They gained greatness because they learnt to love."

Hinduism allows great freedom of thought to man. There is no restraint upon reasoning, thinking or the will of man. Hinduism is not theoretical. It is a practical philosophy of life.

If we can call it a religion, then it is a religion of freedom. No Hindu is bound to accept any particular set of beliefs or rituals. They may have been used over hundreds of years. They may even have been misinterpreted or distorted for the personal benefit of a few. Everyone is free to reflect upon them, investigate and inquire about their utility and, finally, accept or reject them.

Your questions answered...

The Vedas date back to over 3,000 years. Are they not irrelevant in modern times?

The Vedas do not pertain to a particular time or place. They pertain to mankind. They contain knowledge pertaining to every field of science. The four Vedas and the four Upa-Vedas include the study of phonetics, the code of rituals, grammar, etymology, literature, astronomy, medicine, archery, music and architecture. They are not irrelevant in the modern context as they touch every aspect of life. What may be lacking is our effort to understand them.

Why do Hindus consider 'Om' sacred?

'Om' is a solemn and sacred exclamation. Chanting 'Om' is a purifying experience for all Hindus. It is a source of great happiness. 'Om' is the most sacred word. Nowadays, it is also written as *Aum*. The three-syllable a+u+m represents and salutes Brahma, Vishnu and Mahesh (Shankar) and invokes their blessings. The three syllables also represent the three Vedas – Rig-Veda, Yajur-Veda and Sama-Veda.

'Om' is the source of all religions and religious scriptures. The syllable 'a' carries mankind like a horse. The syllable 'u' is a pointer to the condition and location. The syllable 'm' is indicative of the rhythm and melody of life. The uttering of the sacred and mystical 'Om' is called Om-kar or On-kar. It is the melody of life. It is the sound of Brahma. It is the predominating force and power. For this reason chanting 'Om' before every auspicious activity is essential. It is considered both mystical and powerful. Since time immemorial, devotees have had great reverence for 'Om-kar'. There is much in praise of 'Om' in all the religious books.

In the **Kathupanishad**, 12/15, Yamdev tells Nachiketa:

सर्वे वेदा यत् पदमामनन्ति तपांसि सर्वाणि च यद् वदन्ति।
यदिच्छन्तो ब्रह्मचर्यं चरन्ति तत्ते पदं संग्रहेण ब्रवीम्योमित्येतत् ॥

Nachiketa, I will tell you of the power of the word that has been praised in the Vedas and repeated in love by devotees. The word is the essence of the Vedas. It is the speech of devotees and the experience of the learned. It is 'Om' and 'Om' only.

Again, in the **Kathupanishad**, 1/2/16-17, it is said that 'Om' represents Brahma – the creator. It came even before Brahma. With the knowledge of the word 'Om' a person attains whatever is desired. It is the finest foundation and the last resort for all. Knowing this all devotees find dignity in Brahmalok (the abode of Brahma).

The **Mandukya Upanishad**, Agam Prakaran, **25** advises:

युंजीत प्रणवे चेतः प्रणवो ब्रह्म निर्भयम् ।
प्रणवे नित्ययुक्तस्य न भयं विद्यते क्वचित् ॥

The mind must concentrate on 'Om'. 'Om' is fearless liberation. Those who concentrate on it shall never be afraid anywhere.

In the **Bhagavad Gita**, 8/13, Sri Krishna has said:

ओमित्येकाक्षरं ब्रह्म व्याहरन्मामनुस्मरन् ।
यः प्रयाति त्यजन्देहं स याति परमां गतिम् ॥

Whoever controls his mind and knowing that the soul resides in the forehead repeats the word 'Om', knowing it as representing Brahma, and thinking of Me his soul leaves the body, that person shall attain the supreme goal.

Again, in **Bhagavad Gita**, 17/24, Sri Krishna says that all distinguished persons know that when chanting Veda mantras and performing religious ceremonies or acts of charity one must begin by remembering the Supreme Spirit and chanting 'Om'.

In the **Gopath Brahman** it is said that without using the prefix 'Om', chanting a mantra does not bring any results. Chanting 'Om' before the mantra enhances the power of the mantra. 'Om' represents Shiva, and the mantra represents Shakti. When chanted together the purpose is achieved. All the Upanishads, the Dharmashastras, Gayatri mantra and all the mantras used when performing a yagya or in reverence to gods begin with 'Om'.

'Om' must be chanted in a high and prolonged note with great devotion. Chanting produces a quivering sensation and power within. It affects every part of the body. The mind experiences unity and strength. The voice becomes gentle. Negativity in the mind is destroyed. The body feels buoyant. One forgets worldly thoughts. The dormant inner strength is aroused. Self-confidence grows. Since the life force move vertically, by chanting 'Om' 7, 11, 21 or 51 times, sadness and disappointments vanish and contentment grows. When chanted in a group, the beneficial influence is much greater. To ensure physical and emotional health one must chant 'Om' with a tranquil mind for some time everyday.

Even scientists agree that chanting 'Om' is beneficial. Yogasana and exercises do not fully influence the functioning of the brain. Chanting 'Om' influences the whole brain. The electrifying effect of 'Om' cleanses unwanted deposits in the brain and promotes well-being. Chant 'Om' and be happy.

Think it over...

The Upanishads are the solace of my life. They will be a solace to me after my death also.
–Arthur Schopenhauer, German philosopher (1788–1860)

Why do Hindus offer prayers to Sri Ganesh before a special occasion?

Sri Ganeshaya Nama! Sri Ganesh is the most revered of Hindu gods. Before any special ceremony or auspicious occasion prayers are first offered to Sri Ganesh. He is *vighanharta* and master of *Riddhi-Siddhi*. This simply means that he removes all obstacles confronting devotees. A prayer, an offering or penance made for him ensures success. It brings wealth and prosperity.

He is easily pleased. Before any ceremony or special occasion all one needs to do is chant 'Sri Ganeshaya Nama' followed by the mantra:

वक्रतुण्ड महाकाय कोटि सूर्य समप्रभः ।
निर्विघ्नं कुरु मे देव सर्व कार्येषु सर्वदा ॥

Sri Ganesh is the God of learning and knowledge. Through devotion to him one learns to be responsible, to differentiate between good and bad and develop farsightedness. He teaches discipline. It is for this reason that offerings are first made to Sri Ganesh before a ceremony or auspicious occasion.

Two popular stories illustrate the importance of this custom.

In **Padanpurana**, it is narrated that when mankind was established the question arose as to who should be considered the most revered. To find an answer all the gods went to Brahmaji. To settle the issue Brahmaji declared that whoever went around the world and returned first would be the revered most.

On hearing this all the gods set out on the journey in their respective modes of transport. Sri Ganesh was plump and pot-bellied. Besides, he had a mouse as his mode of transport. How could he go around the world swiftly? He consulted Narad, who suggested that he should write 'Ram' on the ground, and go around it seven times.

After completing the seven rounds, Sri Ganesh went to Brahmaji. When asked how he had completed the journey in such a short period he explained what he had done. He explained that Sri Ram's name was an embodiment of the Supreme Spirit. Not only this earth, but the entire universe also depended upon him. On hearing this explanation, Brahmaji had no other option but to declare Sri Ganesh the most revered of all gods.

In **Shivpuran**, another story narrates that once all the gods went to Lord Shankar to inquire as to who should be the chief amongst them. In response, Lord Shankar proposed that whoever went around the world thrice and returned to Mount Kailash first would be the most revered of all and declared as the foremost amongst gods.

Sri Ganesh's mode of transport was a mouse. Surely it was too slow to undertake the journey. Using his ingenuity, Sri Ganesh went around his father Lord Shankar and mother Parvati thrice. With folded hands, he then stood humbly before them. His silence and humility indicated that he had completed his mission. Delighted at his son's ingenuity, Lord Shankar smilingly told him that none could be as clever and crafty as he was. By going around his parents thrice he had achieved more than he could by going around the world three times.

Pleased, Lord Shankar blessed Sri Ganesh and declared that whoever offered prayers to him before a ceremony or an auspicious occasion would never face obstacles. Since then all mankind has been offering prayers to Sri Ganesh before an auspicious occasion.

Sri Ganesh is easily pleased. Just by offering him a little *durva* (also known as *dub*) grass (Cynodon dactylon) with 3 or 5 nodes, he is pleased to grant one's heartfelt desires. For this reason, religious texts commend offering of *durva* grass to him. The Puranas confirm this.

At one time a ruthless demon named Anlasur created havoc around the world. Even the gods in heaven were not spared. He would swallow saints, sages and innocent people alive. There was terror all around. The chief of gods, Indra, tried to control Anlasur several times by engaging him in battle. However, there was no respite. Anlasur was beyond Indra's control.

Panic stricken by Anlasur's terror, all the gods went to Lord Shankar for help. He revealed that only Sri Ganesh could help them. Sri Ganesh was pot-bellied and could swallow Anlasur. There was enough space in his belly to accommodate the demon.

The gods offered prayers and pleased Sri Ganesh, who agreed to help them. He chased Anlasur, caught and swallowed him whole. But this created a great burning sensation in Sri Ganesh's stomach. Many remedies were tried. None worked. Sri Ganesh was in great agony. When sage Kashyap heard of Sri Ganesh's plight, he went to Mt Kailash, collected 21 stems of *durva* grass, and offered them. The moment Sri Ganesh ate this grass the burning vanished.

Sri Ganesh is also very fond of *modak* or *ladoos* (sweetmeats). Without *ladoos*, any offering to Sri Ganesh is incomplete.

In **Vinay Patrika**, Sant Tulsidas says:

गाइए गनपति जगबंदन। संकर सुवन भवानी नंदन ॥
सिद्धि-सदन गज बदन विनाय। कृपा-सिंधु सुंदर सब लायक ॥
मोदकप्रिय मुद मंगलदाता। विद्या वारिधि बुद्धि विधाता ॥

From this, Sri Ganesh's love of sweets is evident. All devotees offer a variety of *ladoos*. Some are made of wheat flour, dried milk and sugar. Others are made of gram flour and sugar. Whoever offers *ladoos* to Sri Ganesh with love and devotion has his/her desires fulfilled.

The word *modak* – derived from two words, *mode* meaning *pleasure* and '*k*' denoting a small *bit* – literally means something that gives pleasure even when it is in a small quantity, or when one sees it. When tasty sweets are offered to Sri Ganesh his pleasure in accepting them is reciprocated to the devotee by way of great pleasure and happiness.

In another narration it is said that just as knowledge is symbolic of a *modak*, which is sweet, the blessing of knowledge too is sweet.

In **Ganpati Athvarshirsh** it is narrated:

यो दूर्वाङ्कुरैर्यजति स वैश्रवणोपमो भवति ।
यो लाजैर्यजति स यशोवान् भवति स मेधावान् भवति ॥
यो मोदक सहस्रेण यजति स वांछित फलमवाप्नोति ॥

Whoever offers durva *grass to God becomes like Kuber, the God of Wealth. Whoever offers rice and paddy achieves success and fame. Whoever offers a thousand* ladoos *to Sri Ganesh finds fulfilment of personal desires.*

Sri Ganesh is known to be very fond of jaggery (brown sugar). In **Padampuran**, there is a story that narrates his love for *ladoos.*

It is said that once when all the gods came to meet Sri Ganesh and his brother Kartikeya, they were extremely pleased with them. In appreciation, they presented a divine *ladoo* to their mother Parvati.

Describing the *ladoo* Parvati said, "This *ladoo* smells of the elixir of immortality. Without doubt whoever smells its fragrance or eats it will become most knowledgeable on the religious texts, science and art, writing and culture."

Both brothers eagerly asked for it. However, she could not decide who deserved it more. To settle the issue she said, "Whoever of you can prove your superiority through sincere and honest action shall get this *ladoo.*"

On hearing his mother's directions Kartikeya immediately left for a round of the universe seated on Mayur, his swift mode of transport. Within a short period he visited all the places of pilgrimage. On the other hand, in all sincerity and devotion Sri Ganesh went around his father and mother. Standing before them with folded hands he said, "Fasting, making offerings or visiting places of worship and pilgrimage does not equal one-sixteenth of the devotion for one's father and mother. Therefore, I rightly deserve to get the *ladoo.*"

Content with Sri Ganesh's reasoning, Parvati gave him the *ladoo* with the blessings that because of his love and devotion for his mother and father he would forever be revered and the first offering would always be made to him.

Think it over…

God's intentions are codified and indicated in the great textbooks on *dharma*, which preach the higher values of life, that is, the ethical and moral rules of life. Live well. Live in kindness, love and understanding.

—Swami Chinmayananda

Why do Hindus say God is omnipresent?

All Hindus believe God is omnipresent. One cannot see a tree hidden within a seed. The butter cannot be seen in milk. One cannot see the oil in mustard. The fragrance cannot be seen in the flower. One can feel pain, but cannot see it. We cannot see the ills within us. In the same way, though God is omnipresent, we cannot see Him.

Just as the soul resides within the body, God resides within the whole universe. We cannot see Him because of our ignorance. With knowledge and devotion we can experience our proximity to Him. Just as there is water everywhere underground, but we can source it only through a well, in the same way, although God is everywhere, we can reach Him only through devotion and prayer.

In the **Bhagavad Gita**, Sri Krishna says, "I am present in perfect form everywhere. However, everyone perceives Me in harmony with the devotion in his or her heart. One can perceive Me only through the heart."

In the **Bhagavad Gita**, 13/13, it is said:

सर्वतः पाणिपादं तत् सर्वतोऽक्षिशिरोमुखम् ।
सर्वतः श्रुतिमल्लोके सर्वमावृत्य तिष्ठति ॥

God is everywhere. He can touch and feel everything. He can see everywhere. He can hear everything. No place is without Him. He can understand everything. There is nothing that He cannot see. There is nothing that He cannot accept. He can reach everywhere.

20

In the **Yajur-Veda**, 40/1, it is said:

ईशावास्यमिदं सर्वं यत्किञ्च जगत्यां जगत् ।

In this world God resides in all things.

In the **Swateshwar Upanishad**, it is said:

एको देवः सर्वभूतेषु गूढः सर्वव्यापी सर्वभूतान्तरात्मा ।

There is one God. He resides within everyone. He is universal. He is present as the soul in every living thing.

Everyone must have deep faith in the existence of God. He meets all His devotees. We must meditate with belief to reach Him. He resides within everyone. Whoever desires Him, will attain Him.

In the **Naradpuran**, Purvkhand, 11/57-64, it is said that God resides in the hearts of all those who give up attachment, maliciousness and hypocrisy in devotion to Him. Even those who are free from jealousy, are honest and sincere, hold their parents, teachers and learned people in respect, are kind and hospitable to guests, enjoy the company of good people, visit holy sites and offer food and charity always keep God within their heart.

Sunlight falls evenly everywhere. However, in the presence of a mirror it reacts differently. With a magnifying glass the same sunlight can create fire. In the same way, a knowledgeable person who is clean and pure can see God within the heart.

In the **Bhagavad Gita**, 13/15, it is said:

बहिरन्तश्च भूतानामचरं चरमेव च ।
सूक्ष्मत्वात्तदविज्ञेयं दूरस्थं चान्तिके च तत् ॥

The true supreme spirit resides within the body and the mind always. However, it is so subtle that it cannot be perceived by the senses. It is close at hand, and yet far away.

Just as moisture captured within rays of sunlight cannot be seen by everyone, only those can perceive God who have faith and devotion. For the ignorant and those without faith He is far away.

In the **Mundak**, 2/2/11, it is written:

ब्रह्मैवेदममृतं पुरस्ताद्ब्रह्म पश्चाद्ब्रह्म दक्षिणतश्चोत्तरेण ।
अधश्चोर्ध्वं च प्रसृतं ब्रह्मैवेदं विश्वमिदं वरिष्ठम् ॥

Like the nectar of immortality the eternal spirit faces you. It is behind you. It is on your right and to your left side. It is below you. It is above you. This whole universe is filled with the universal spirit of God.

With God around every Hindu knows that His secret hand is guiding the world we live in. We need to live life with faith and devotion.

What is the Hindu belief about the life cycle of the world?

According to Hindu religious thought, the life cycle of this world is divided into four definite eras, or *yugs*. It is believed that when mankind was created it was totally pure. With time life degenerated. This degeneration can be seen in the four eras.

The first era, **Satyayug** or **Krityug**, was the golden age during which all the gods lived. It lasted 4,800 divine years or 1,728,000 human years.

The second era, **Tretayug**, was the silver age during which incarnations came to this world and rid it of evil people. Parshuram and Ram were born in this period. This lasted 3,600 divine years, or 1,296,000 human years.

The third era, **Dvaparyug**, was the copper age when the later incarnations and religious leaders lived. This lasted 2,400 divine years, or 864,000 human years.

The fourth era, **Kalyug**, is the iron age, or the era of the machine. In this era mankind has degenerated very rapidly, as can be evidenced in everyday life. This era is said to have started in the year 3,102 B.C. Lesser incarnations and religious leaders have influenced mankind. It is expected to last 1,200 divine years or 432,000 human years.

Just as there is much sin and degeneration in this era, it is equally possible to attain God-realisation. One just needs to remember Him in whatever way is suitable. This is what the average householder needs to know and follow. God can be realised.

At the end of this era the world will come to an end. There will be a new beginning. Then there will be a new cycle of four eras – beginning with the golden age.

Think it over...

Let noble thoughts come to us from all directions.

−Rig-Veda

What is the Hindu view on the many gods and goddesses they pray to?

No other religion has as many gods and goddesses as Hinduism. Many times people are at a loss in keeping count of them. Does this not create doubt in the mind of a Hindu? Is it not difficult to choose one god from another? Are some gods easier to please than others? Are they all equally benevolent?

To answer these questions one needs to comprehend the Indian scenario. India is a vast country. The language, food and habits vary from one region to another. With all Hindus being god-abiding there are innumerable temples spread all over. Each one has its importance. In a different language, the god may appear to be different. But this may not be so in reality. We need to comprehend the situation correctly and understand how Hindu beliefs originated.

Whatever we may have heard or learnt from others, there is only one Supreme Spirit we call God. He created the universe. He sustains it. He destroys it, and then regenerates it again. He created all living beings. He is the living force within all living beings. He created mankind. The only way He made mankind different is that He gave mankind a mind with the power to reason and choose. This makes mankind superior to all living beings. But this is also the unmaking of mankind. Basking in its superiority over other living beings, mankind forgets that the life force driving it to success and achievement is a gift of God. Mankind does not possess the ability to create anything.

Why did God bless mankind with special abilities? This is not easy to answer. Our religious texts tell us that it is only after passing through innumerable births that one attains the body

23

of a human being. God desires that after a long journey through innumerable births a human being should be able to return to Him through good actions. Since a human life is too short to experiment with, one needs to draw upon the wisdom and experience of all the saints, seers and sages who have tried to make it possible to realise God within the span of a lifetime.

It is interesting to note how the gods, the planets, the environment around us and even great people who came to this world influence our thoughts, reasoning and choice to attain a better life.

Your questions answered...

No other religion has as many gods and goddesses, stories, rituals, philosophies and scriptures as Hinduism. Why?

What you say is just an opinion. When you gain knowledge, you begin to see the real picture. There is only one God. He is manifested in three forms as the Creator, Preserver and Destroyer to repeat the cycle once again. There is only one God, but known by many names. He has one abode. We are all a part of Him, a part of His family. The stories help us to understand life better. The rituals help give direction to life. This is how Hinduism has survived thousands of years.

What is the basis of Hindu religious thought?

Hindu religious thought is based upon the triad Brahma, Vishnu and Mahesh. The three are together responsible for creating the universe, preserving it and destroying it.

Brahma is the first member of the Hindu triad. He is believed to have taken birth from a golden egg. Some believe that a lotus appeared from Vishnu's navel, and Brahma was born from the lotus. He created the universe and all things in it. He is also known as *Prajapati*. The word *praja* means *populace* and *pati* denotes *master*. Together they mean *master of the populace*, or king. It is also believed that he created ten *Prajapatis* who helped in creating the earth.

It is said that Brahma had five heads. Shiva cut off one. The four heads are symbolic of the four Vedas, of the four *yugs* (ages or eras) and the four castes amongst Hindus. Brahma uses a swan as the mode of transport.

Vishnu is the second god of the Hindu triad. He has a thousand names. He has several incarnations, but there are ten that hold special significance. The last one, Kalki, has yet to come. Vishnu has Garuda, the king of birds, as his vehicle.

Mahesh is the third god of the Hindu triad. Mahesh is another name for Shiva, the destroyer. He represents both, death that destroys, and reproduction that follows destruction. He destroys and disintegrates. After destruction, he helps in reproducing again. He is also known by many names. As a benevolent god he is known as Shankar, Mahadev and Vishwanath. As one who destroys he is known as Rudra, Mahakal, Virbhadra and Bhairav. Shiva is symbolised by the *Ling*, or phallus, that enables reproduction. He has three eyes, the third one in the middle of the forehead. With these he can see the past, present and future. His weapon, the *trishul*, a three-pronged trident, is symbolic of the abilities to create, destroy and regenerate. His mode of transport is the bull, Nandi.

Equality for women has always been a subject of heated discussion. However, it is not so for Hindu gods and goddesses. If the Hindu triad is revered, the wives are equally revered.

As the creator Brahma created **Saraswati**. So she is the daughter. He then married her and, therefore, she is revered as his wife. She is the river Saraswati personified. She is the goddess of speech, learning and knowledge. Those who pursue learning hold her in high reverence and always seek her blessings. She uses a swan as her vehicle.

Vishnu's wife **Lakshmi** is revered as the goddess of beauty, good fortune and prosperity. She went through several incarnations in order to be with Vishnu. Almost every Hindu home has her picture. All businessmen specially revere her. She uses a lotus as a seat and an owl for a vehicle.

Parvati is an incarnation of Sati, daughter of Daksh, and could marry Shiva only after severe penance. All Hindu women aspire to have a married life like that of Parvati. For good partners and a happy married life, unmarried youth, particularly women, pray to Shiva and Parvati. Just as Shiva changed forms by being both, benevolent and destructive, Parvati too changed forms. She is also called Durga as she killed the demon Durg. As the divine universal power she is called Shakti. In her destructive form she is Kali. Shiva and Parvati had two sons, Kartikeya and Ganesh. She uses a lion or tiger as a vehicle. Twice a year during *Navratris* (nine nights) that last ten days each time, people fast and offer prayers to her all over the country.

Brahma's role was that of a creator. After he created the universe and mankind, the role of preserving it was that of Vishnu. He fulfilled this role by taking several forms through incarnations. Shiva fulfils the role of destruction and regeneration. In everyday life mankind seeks the favours of Vishnu and Mahesh along with the three goddesses – Saraswati, Lakshmi and Parvati.

An important temple dedicated to Brahma stands alongside the lake at Pushkar near Ajmer in Rajasthan. Saraswati occupies a place of reverence in all institutions of learning. There are innumerable temples dedicated to Vishnu and Lakshmi, and Shiva and Parvati all over the country and abroad.

After the writing of the two great epics, *Ramayana* and *Mahabharata*, attention shifted to Ram and Sita and Krishna and Radha. Although the names and forms are different, the object of reverence has always been the same. Their idols and pictures can be found in almost every Hindu home. Thousands of temples dedicated to them attract millions of Hindus daily.

Think it over...

In those Three Persons the one God was shown –
Each first in place, each last – not one alone;
Of Shiva, Vishnu, Brahma, each may be
First, second, third among the Blessed Three.

–Kalidas

26

What is the Hindu belief about the *Navgrah*?

At a religious ceremony after making the first offering to Sri Ganesh, all Hindus make the next offering to the *Navgrah* or the nine planets. With the Hindu belief that God resides in all things, places and people, it is evident that everyone is connected to each other through God. We are all children of the same God. Brothers and sisters influence each other in a home. Similarly, as children of God we influence each other.

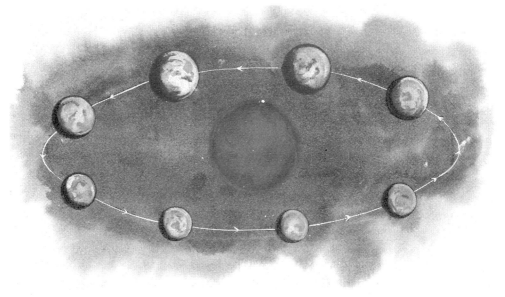

According to Hindu belief, the greatest influence upon everyone is that of the nine planets. They are in constant motion and their influence varies with their position. They influence the destinies of nations and people. They influence the life of every individual. An individual's horoscope is cast on the basis of the time and place of birth. A horoscope predicts the destiny based upon the configuration of the nine planets at the time of birth and the changes that will occur from one year to another.

Does this mean that once the destiny of an individual is cast it cannot be changed? This is not so. The position of the planets is indicative of their influence at a particular time and place. This indication is not a compelling force. It is at best a suggestive guidance. On the contrary, human effort is a definite force. Through positive actions the influence of the stars can be altered. According to Hindu belief, each of the nine planets is personified, and exerts a definite influence. This influence can be altered through appropriate activities. The purpose of making offerings to these planets is to keep them content and happy. One must get to know the nine planets well.

The first and foremost of the nine planets is ***Surya***, the Sun. He has two arms, and carries lotus flowers in each hand. On his head he has a beautiful golden crown. A gem-studded necklace adorns his neck. He sits on a lotus throne and rides a chariot drawn by seven horses.

According to **Markandeypuran**, Surya is like Brahma. The world arises from it and resides within it. Like the elements it is eternal. It is like Brahma, Vishnu and Mahesh. Like them, it creates, protects and destroys. To please Surya, one must make an offering to him everyday, read or listen to **Harivanshpuran**, and wear ruby in a ring. One must give wheat, jaggery, copper, gold and red fabric in charity.

The second of the nine planets is ***Chandrama***, the Moon. The clothes, the chariot and the seven horses that pull him are spotlessly white. There is a golden crown on the head. A pearl necklace adorns the neck. Chandrama sits on a lotus throne and holds a mace in one hand and blesses everyone with the other.

Lack of blessings from Chandrama causes mental and breathing problems. To please him one must fast on Mondays, pray to Shiva and wear a pearl in a silver ring. One must give rice, camphor, white clothes, silver, conch shell, white sandalwood, white flowers, sugar, curds and pearls in charity.

The third of the nine planets is ***Mangal***, the planet Mars. Mangal wears red clothes and a golden crown. Red necklaces adorn his neck. He has four arms and carries a trident in one of the right hands and a mace in one of the left hands. With the left hand he assures protection and with the right he conveys his blessings. He rides on a male sheep.

To please Mangal one needs to fast on Tuesdays and offer prayers to Shiva or Hanuman. One should read the *Hanuman Chalisa*. One must wear coral in a ring. Wheat, copper, gold, red clothes, jaggery, red flowers, saffron and land may be given in charity.

The fourth of the nine planets is ***Budh***, the planet Mercury. Yellow is symbolic of Budh. His body is like bright oleander flowers. He wears yellow clothes and adorns a garland made of yellow flowers. He has four arms. He carries a sword in one of the right hands, a mace and a shield in the left hands, and blesses with the right hand. He wears a golden crown and adorns beautiful jewellery around his neck. He rides a lion.

To please Budh, one must fast on the first day of the new moon. One should wear an emerald in a ring. One should give ivory, green clothes, coral, emerald, gold, camphor, a weapon, fruits and a variety of foods in charity.

The fifth of the nine planets is ***Brihaspati***, the planet Jupiter. He wears a golden crown and is adorned with beautiful jewellery. He wears yellow clothes and sits on a lotus throne. He has four arms. In the two left hands he carries a shaft and a vessel. In one of the right hands he carries a *rudraksh mala* (rosary) and blesses with the other.

Brihaspati is a benevolent planet. Pleased with his devotees he blesses them with prosperity and wisdom. He motivates them to follow the righteous path. He protects them from dangers.

To please him one must fast on Thursdays and on the first day of the month. One should wear yellow topaz in a ring. One should give yellow clothes, gold, turmeric, ghee, yellow foods, topaz, a horse, a book, honey, salt, sugar, land and an umbrella in charity.

The sixth of the nine planets is **Shukra**, the planet Venus. A guru of the demons, he is very fair. He wears a beautiful crown. He adorns beautiful jewellery around his neck. He has a white lotus throne to sit on. He has four arms. He holds a shaft and a vessel in his two left hands and a *rudraksh* in one of the right hands. He blesses everyone with the other.

To appease Shukra, one should wear diamonds and offer prayers to a cow. One should give silver, gold, diamonds, rice, ghee, curd, sugar, white clothes, white sandalwood, white horse, white cow and land in charity.

The seventh of the nine planets is **Shani**, the planet Saturn. His complexion is like that of a blue sapphire. He adorns golden jewellery and wears a golden crown. His clothes are blue. He has four arms. He carries a bow and a trident in the two left hands and an arrow in one of the right hands. He blesses with the other. His vehicle is a vulture. His chariot is built of steel. He draws inspiration from Brahma, the creator, and Yama, the god of death.

To appease Shani, one should chant the Mrituanjay mantra, and offer sesame seeds, black peas, iron vessel, oil, black clothes, black umbrella, black shoes, black cow, sapphire and gold in charity.

The last two of the nine planets are **Rahu** and **Ketu**. Rahu, son of Kashyap, is a demon. When the gods had obtained *amrit* (nectar), the elixir of immortality, by churning the ocean, Rahu assumed the form of a god, entered their stronghold and drank some of it. When Surya and Chandrama discovered him amongst them, they informed Vishnu, who immediately cut off Rahu's head with his *Sudarshan Chakra*. Since some of the elixir had already gone down Rahu's throat, he did not die. The head and the body remained alive. The head is known as Rahu, and the body as Ketu. Brahma transformed the two into planets. It is believed that to settle scores with Surya and Chandrama, who had reported to Vishnu, they are known to sometimes swallow them to cause a solar eclipse or a lunar eclipse. Since the head and the body are separate, Surya and Chandrama always manage to escape their wrath.

Rahu looks dreadful. He adorns golden jewellery and a golden crown on his head. He wears black clothes. He has four arms. In the two left hands he carries a trident and a shield. In one of the right hands he carries a sword. The other is free to bless people. He uses a lion as a vehicle.

To appease Rahu, one must chant the Mrituanjay mantra, and wear an amethyst in a ring. One must give mica, iron, copperware, sesame seeds, blue clothes, black peas, seven grains, oil, blanket and a horse in charity.

Ketu has a smoke-like complexion. He wears black clothes and has a golden crown on his head. He has two arms, carries a mace in the left hand, and blesses with the right. He uses a vulture as his vehicle.

To appease Ketu, one must chant the Mrituanjay mantra. One should also wear cat's eye, a precious grey-coloured stone, in a ring. One must give *Vaidurya* (a gem), oil, sesame, a blanket, weapon, musk and blue flowers in charity.

Astrology aims at studying the effects of the planets in general and of these nine planets in particular on human beings. Each of the nine planets has been studied in great detail. The capability of the astrologer depends upon the study and analysis of the effect of each of the planets upon one another and how it affects an individual. The malefic effects can be changed through prayers and offerings.

Your questions answered...

If the destiny of a person is predetermined based on the position of the *Navgrah*, where is the use or need for personal effort?

The position of the *Navgrah* determines the influences affecting individuals in specific situations. These are only an indication of what to expect. However, man's actions are a definite force that can transform any situation. For example, if the sun is very hot and bright, one can still protect oneself by using an umbrella to provide shade and sunglasses to cut out the glare.

What is the significance of the many incarnations of Gods?

When God created mankind and this world, His work did not end there. It is true that He gave man a mind to think with and to chart a course that would be most suitable. He knew that like little children in a class without a proper teacher, man too would create chaos. There would be some degeneration. To keep control over the degeneration He decided to be personally present to direct mankind.

In the **Bhagavad Gita**, 4/7-8, Sri Krishna says:

यदा यदा हि धर्मस्य ग्लानिर्भवति भारत ।
अभ्युत्थानमधर्मस्य तदात्मानं सृजाम्यहम् ॥
परित्राणाय साधूनां विनाशाय च दुष्कृताम् ।
धर्मसंस्थापनार्थाय संभवामि युगे युगे ॥

O people of Bharat, whenever there is degeneration of thought and an increase in sin, I shall incarnate in different forms... I will protect and support the honest and virtuous people, and destroy those who live in sin. I shall incarnate era after era to establish righteous thought.

Since the beginning of mankind there have been many incarnations of gods. Of these, 108 incarnations hold special significance. The ten incarnations of Vishnu are important since they have influenced present-day thought and life of millions of Hindus worldwide.

The first incarnation of Vishnu was in the form of a fish – **Matsya**.

At the end of the first era when Brahma was reciting the Vedas, a demon Haygriv stole them. He took them to the bottom of the sea and hid there, where he felt nobody could reach him. Vishnu then took the form of a fish – Matsya. One day when Manu Vaivasvat was taking a bath along the bank a small fish leaped into his hands. The fish pleaded for protection from the bigger fish in the sea. In compassion, Vaivasvat took the fish home and put it in a jar. Soon, the jar was too small for the fish. So he changed the jar. Very soon, this jar too was small for the fish. Vaivasvat changed several jars. But the fish continued to grow. Then the fish requested him to put it back into the river.

Just when it was leaving, the fish warned Vaivasvat that soon there would be a deluge that would destroy everything. The fish asked Vaivasvat to collect the seeds of all plants and pairs of all other living beings in a boat to protect them from the deluge. He also told him that a fish would appear at the time of the deluge. He should tie the boat to the fish using the serpent Vasuki as a rope.

When the deluge came, Vaivasvat followed the instructions. He tied the boat to the horn of the fish. The fish dragged the boat to the top of the mountain

1. Matsya
2. Kacchap
3. Varah
4. Narsinh
5. Vaman
6. Parshuram
7. Ram
8. Krishna
9. Buddha
10. Kalki

Naubandh. When the floodwaters receded, the boat came sliding down. Everything had been destroyed except the life forms in the boat. Once again, the process of creation began.

The second incarnation of Vishnu was in the form of a giant tortoise – **Kacchap** or **Kurm**.

As the gods grew old and diseased they felt anxious about their condition. When they consulted Vishnu about the problem, they were advised to churn the ocean. He said that by doing so they would find *amrit*, the elixir of immortality, and a lot of other valuable things too. Vishnu's suggestion was appealing, but the work seemed difficult.

To make the work easier the help of the *asuras* (demons) was sought. The mountain Mandar was to be the churning rod and the serpent Vasuki would serve as a rope. The gods took hold of Vasuki on one side, and the *asuras* on the other. However, it did not work as the mountain kept sinking into the ocean. So the churning could not be done. It was then that Vishnu took the form of Kacchap – a giant tortoise. He got into the water and held the mountain on his back as the gods and *asuras* churned the ocean. Finally, the great treasures, including *amrit*, were found.

The third incarnation of Vishnu was in the form of a boar – **Varah**.

Hiranyaksh and Hiranyakashipu were twin brothers born to Kashyap and Diti. Hiranyaksh offered great sacrifices and prayers to Brahma, and as a reward received a boon from him. Thus armed, Hiranyaksh grew overconfident and oppressed the three worlds. He dragged Bhumi (Earth) to the depths of the ocean. Enraged at this action, Vishnu decided to intervene in the incarnation of Varah. He jumped into the ocean, and lifting Bhumi with the tusks brought her to the surface of the water. Bhumi then assumed her beautiful form. Varah then fought Hiranyaksh and killed him.

The fourth incarnation of Vishnu was in the form of the half-lion half-man – **Narsinh**.

Hiranyakashipu was enraged at Vishnu for having killed his twin brother Hiranyaksh. To avenge his brother's death Hiranyakashipu offered great penance, sacrifices and prayer to Brahma who had earlier granted a boon to his brother. Pleased with him, Brahma granted him a boon too. Hiranyakashipu asked that he must be so protected that no god, man or demon should be able to kill him.

Having received this boon from Brahma, Hiranyakashipu became bold and arrogant. He felt that the time was right to avenge his brother's death at the hands of Vishnu. He forbade others from praying to Vishnu. No one was even to take his name. However, Hiranyakashipu's son Prahlad was a great devotee of Vishnu. He refused to heed his father's orders. Hiranyakashipu tried all methods to compel his son to refrain from praying to Vishnu. He asked the teachers to explain matters to the boy. He used wild force. He threatened him with wild elephants and poisonous snakes. Even fire could not frighten Prahlad. He survived all attempts to kill him.

Exasperated at the failure to convince his own son not to offer prayers to Vishnu, in court one day he asked Prahlad where Vishnu was. Prahlad replied simply that Vishnu resided in everything. He could be found in all animate and inanimate things. Enraged at his son's response, he asked Prahlad to summon him from a pillar in the court. Suddenly, Vishnu emerged as Narsinh after breaking the pillar. He looked fearful as a half-lion half-man. Before Hiranyakashipu could react, Narsinh got hold of him, flung him on the ground and tore his body apart – heart, intestines and all. That ended yet another evil period.

The fifth incarnation of Vishnu was in the form of **Vaman**, a son of Kashyap and Aditi.

Bali was a demon king. Through penance and sacrifices he had attained a special power. With this power he defeated Indra and other gods, and gained control over the three worlds. Unable to regain their kingdom from Bali, all the gods sought Vishnu's help. Vishnu then incarnated as Vaman, a dwarf.

One day the dwarf Vaman approached Bali and begged that he be granted as much land as he could cover in just three steps. Bali laughed when he saw the small feet of the dwarf. He generously agreed to grant the request. As soon as Bali had agreed, Vaman began growing. Soon, he became huge. In one step he covered the whole earth, and in the second he covered the heavens. There was no place left for the third step. Bali bent his head down so that Vaman could place his third step over it. Vaman pushed his foot down and sent Bali to *Patal* (the nether world) to rule there. With Vaman's help, Indra again began to rule the universe.

The sixth incarnation of Vishnu was in the form of the sage **Parshuram**, who destroyed the Kshatriya race.

Parshuram was the fifth son of Jamdagni, a devoted student of the Vedas, and Renuka, the daughter of King Prasenjit. One day when Jamdagni was very angry with his wife Renuka, one by one he ordered all his sons to kill her. The four elder sons refused. Parshuram beheaded his mother. Later, when Jamdagni's anger cooled he asked what boon Parshuram desired for having followed his father's orders. Parshuram asked for his mother's life. Renuka was once again brought back to life.

On another occasion, when King Kartivirya and his party visited Jamdagni's hermitage seeking food and water after hunting in a nearby forest, Jamdagni offered hospitality through his cow. The king and his party were deeply impressed with the cow. The king offered to buy it, but Jamdagni did not agree. The king offered ten million cows in exchange for that one cow. He even offered half his kingdom. But Jamdagni did not budge. Finally the king and his party forcibly carried away the cow and its calf.

Enraged, Jamdagni asked Parshuram to get the cow and calf back. There was a fierce battle between the king and Parshuram. In the battle King Kartivirya and many of his sons died. Parshuram brought back the cow and calf.

Yet another time, when Parshuram was away, some of King Kartivirya's sons attacked the hermitage and killed Jamdagni. When Parshuram returned his mother Renuka told him what had happened. She beat her chest 21 times and jumped into her husband's funeral pyre to end her life. Enraged at this action of the king's sons, Parshuram vowed to go around the world 21 times and destroy the Kshatriya race.

It is believed that wild animals and evil people cannot be corrected just by overpowering them, or through education or forgiveness. Therefore, Parshuram felt their destruction was the only way to end evil on earth.

The seventh incarnation of Vishnu was in the form of **Ram**. He is referred to as *Maryada Purushottam* Ram – the Supreme Being with the highest moral conduct. The son of Dashrath and Kaushalya, Ram is a household word not only in India, but in other countries too. The rendition of the *Ramayana* through Ramlila (stage show of the epic *Ramayana*), television serials and films has added to his popularity.

Just when he was to be crowned king of Ayodhya, on the intervention of his stepmother Kaikeyi, Ram went into exile for 14 years. At the end of this period, he killed Ravana for kidnapping Sita, which the demon king did in revenge for Lakshman having insulted his sister by cutting off her nose. Ram was a very capable and just king, who established Ram Rajya. Sage Valmiki has recorded his life in the epic *Ramayana*. Made up of 24,000 verses, it is a classic example of the conquest of evil by good.

The eighth incarnation of Vishnu is **Krishna**. Born as the eighth son of Vasudev and Devki, He was brought up by foster parents Nand and Yashoda along with His half-brother Balram in Gokul. Kansa, who then ruled at Mathura, made several attempts to kill Krishna, in vain. Ultimately, Krishna killed Kansa.

As the central character of the epic *Mahabharata*, Krishna always leaned towards the Pandavas, particularly Arjun. Just before the great battle when Arjun laid down his bow and refused to fight his own kith and kin, Krishna gave a discourse on the duties and responsibilities of human beings, and how to choose the correct course of action. This discourse is recorded in Sanskrit in the form of a dialogue between Krishna and Arjun in 700 verses divided into 18 chapters. It is one of the most sacred Hindu scriptures. Krishna is known for the moral guidance He provided. He linked moral conduct not only with actions, but also with one's objective in life.

After the great battle when all the Kaurava sons of Gandhari were killed, she blamed Krishna for the war and cursed that after 36 years the Yadav race would be destroyed, and He would meet an unsung death. Krishna Lila, serials and films on His life, besides innumerable temples dedicated to Him around the world, keep alive the memory of this vibrant incarnation of Vishnu.

The ninth incarnation of Vishnu was in the form of **Buddha**. He is also known as Gautam Buddha. Son of King Shudhodan, he spent his childhood under great protection and care. But the first time he saw suffering and death, he renounced the world, later attained enlightenment and then spread the message of love, peace and compassion. The purpose of this incarnation was to spread the message of peace and non-violence. Buddha preached that to be free from all worldly problems one must search for inner peace, and practise non-violence. His teachings gave rise to Buddhism that is not only popular in India but has spread to other parts of the world.

The tenth incarnation of Vishnu has yet to emerge. It will be in the form of **Kalki**, who will emerge when degeneration peaks. With the emergence of Kalki the world would come to an end. Only good souls will survive. Once again, a new world cycle will commence with *Satyayu*.

What is the significance of making offerings to Shiva and the Shivaling?

Shiva is another name for Mahesh, the third god of the Hindu triad. The Shivaling symbolises the phallus, which is worshipped as a symbol of Shiva. All people aspire to have a married life like that of Shiva and Parvati, therefore, the great emphasis on making offerings to them.

Mercury is known as *parad* or *para* in Hindi. It is also known as *Shivdhatu*, literally *Shiva's metal.* In reality, it refers to Shiva's semen. Mercury has been equated with this, and is especially revered. Shivalings made from a variety of stones are held in great reverence. However, religious writers have equated a Shivaling made of mercury with Shiva. It is said to possess divine qualities. Whenever a deity is made ceremoniously with a combination of mercury, it is said to be very effective. It is believed that whoever offers prayers to the mercury Shivaling will be blessed and considered as having offered prayers to all Shivalings in the universe.

These blessings are equivalent to those from hundreds of *Ashwamedh yagyas.* Even the blessings gained from giving millions of cows in charity cannot equal this. Giving gold in charity also does not qualify one for as many blessings. In homes where prayers are offered regularly to the mercury Shivaling, all kinds of comforts are available. Success reigns there as Shiva resides in these homes. In such places, *vaastu* shortcomings will be overlooked. Offering prayers every Monday to the mercury Shivaling can also ward off tantrik spells.

In **Shiv Mahapuran**, Shiv has said:

लिंगकोटिसहस्रस्य यत्फलं सम्यगर्चनात् ।
तत्फलं कोटिगुणितं रसलिंगार्चनाद् भवेत ॥

36

ब्रह्महत्या सहस्राणि गौहत्यायाः शतानि च ।
तत्क्षणद्विलयं यान्ति रसलिंगस्य दर्शनात् ॥
स्पर्शनात्प्राप्त मुक्तिरिति सत्यं शिवोदितम् ॥

Whatever blessings are showered upon you on making offerings to millions of different Shivalings, these can be multiplied manifold when you personally offer prayers to the mercury Shivaling. By a mere touch of the mercury Shivaling one can achieve salvation.

Your questions answered…

Why are the Vedas considered eternal?

The Vedas are knowledge. And knowledge is eternal. It has no beginning or end. It has always existed and will continue to exist. Jagdish Chandra Bose discovered that plants are living beings. This fact was only a discovery. Plants were always living beings and will continue to be so. They are unaffected by the scientist's discovery. When you view the Vedas as knowledge, you understand why they are said to be eternal. The Vedas were not composed by anyone. They are revelations that were recorded.

What is the significance of Shalgram for Hindus?

On the banks of the river Gandki in Nepal one comes across smooth, shining, black, egg-like stones that may have a hole, or be like a shell, or have round white lines or designs on them. These are known as Shalgram. These are black stones with fossil ammonite. Devotees of Vishnu consider these stones sacred, believing that Vishnu resides in them. These are considered to be stones of great value by devotees. Religious texts mention that a home is not complete without a Shalgram.

In the **Padampuran**, it is said that in whatever homes you find a Shalgram, that home is better than places of pilgrimage. Just by looking at a Shalgram serious sins are absolved. Those who pray to it are specially blessed. Shalgram is symbolic of the universal Vishnu.

In the **Skandpuran**, Shiva has narrated the importance of Shalgram. Every year in the Hindu Kartik on the twelfth day of the lunar month women conduct marriages between Shalgram and Tulsi and offer new clothes and other items. Amongst Hindus the marriage season starts thereafter.

In the **Brahmvaivartpuran**, Prakritikhand, chapter 21, it is said that wherever one finds Shalgram, Vishnu resides there. After completing several pilgrimages Lakshmi also joins him. All kinds of sins are absolved. Shalgram has the ability to bless one with important positions, property and prosperity. However, one must avoid keeping defective and damaged stones that are sharp, malformed, yellow or discoloured. Such stones bring bad luck and create problems and must be thrown away.

It is also believed that whoever sprinkles water that has been in contact with Shalgram shall be blessed as though he had visited places of pilgrimage and bathed in holy waters. By offering prayers one is blessed as though one has read the Vedas. Whoever bathes the Shalgram with water everyday is blessed as though he has offered great charities. He is then free from the shackles of life and death. At the time of death it absolves one of all sins and one becomes worthy of living in Vishnu's company. It is believed that whoever looks after Tulsi, Shalgram and the conch shell shall always be dear to Vishnu.

Your questions answered...

What is *dharma*? And *adharma*?

Dharma is the practice of righteousness. *Dharma* upholds and sustains the world on a moral order. *Adharma* is the opposite of *dharma*.

Why do Hindus specially revere Hanuman?

Lord Ram's greatest devotee was Hanuman, who was the son of Vayu, the wind god, and Anjana.

It is said that as a child once when Hanuman was hungry he thought that the sun was a fruit and flew towards it to pluck and eat it. But Indra grew concerned about the safety of the sun and hurled his Vajra at Hanuman, who was injured and fell down, breaking his jaw. The injury to his son made Vayu very angry. He carried him to *Patal*. With the wind god gone, everyone began feeling breathless and suffocated. Realising their mistake, all the gods went to Vayu and pleaded mercy. They blessed Hanuman. Brahma and Indra granted him several boons. He was blessed that no weapon could slay him and also that he would die at his own will.

It is believed that Hanuman is an incarnation of Shiva, who had come to help Ram achieve his objective of ridding the earth of the terror created by demons. Hanuman played a crucial role in tracing the whereabouts of Sita, and then helping Ram to rescue and get her back. He is often addressed by using the prefix *Sankatmochan – one who liberates from crises*. He is humble and easily pleased. However, he is forgetful and needs to be reminded of his strength and prowess. Prayers are offered to him by reading *Hanuman Chalisa* (40 verses) that forms a part of the *Ramayana*.

Temples devoted to Hanuman can be found all over the country. Wherever there is a temple devoted to Ram, Hanuman is always there. In temples where Hanuman is the principal deity, he is coated with vermilion. When prayers are offered it is customary for the priest to put a dot of the vermilion on the devotee's forehead as blessing. The use of vermilion can be traced back to the *Ramayana*.

One Tuesday morning when Hanuman felt hungry he went to Sita to ask for something to eat. On seeing the vermilion in the parting of Sita's hair, he inquired, "Mother, what red colour do you have in the parting of your hair?"

Smiling, Sita responded, "Son, this is *sindoor* (vermilion). This is symbolic of a married woman. It is auspicious for a happy married life. A woman seeking the long life of her husband applies it throughout life. It symbolises the husband's contentment."

Hanuman wondered that if a pinch of vermilion could ensure long life for his master, would not applying it on his entire body make his master immortal? Yes, it would, he thought. So, he applied vermilion all over his body and went to Ram's court. Everybody in the assembly laughed. This embarrassed Hanuman. Even Ram smiled at what Hanuman had done, but chose not to laugh at his show of unstinted devotion. Ram knew Hanuman was humble, simple-hearted and obsessed with devotion for his master.

Ram said, "Whoever offers vermilion and oil on Tuesday to my dearest Hanuman shall always be dear to me. Such people shall receive my blessings and all their desires will be fulfilled."

Hanuman was most pleased with his master's response. For a moment, he thought of what Sita had told him. After Ram's blessings, Hanuman's faith in Sita's advice grew firmer.

Since then, remembering the deep relationship between Ram and Hanuman, vermilion dissolved in oil is offered to Hanuman. The ceremony of coating Hanuman's idol with vermilion is literally called 'offering clothes to Hanuman'.

Why do Hindus pursuing music and learning revere Ma Saraswati?

Saraswati is the goddess of speech, learning and knowledge. Those who pursue learning, music and knowledge hold her in great reverence, seeking her blessings and guidance.

In the **Devipuran**, Saraswati is referred to by names like Savitri, Gayatri, Sati, Lakshmi and Ambika. In other ancient texts, she is called Vagdevi, Vani, Sharda, Bharti, Veenapani, Vidyadhari, Sarvmangla and many more names. She is the goddess who dispels all kinds of doubts and imparts correct perception.

She receives great reverence from all musicians. She manifested rhythm, tone and melody. She is remembered through the seven notes – *sa, re, ga, ma, pa, dha, ni.* She is also known as Svaratmika – the soul of music. She is known as Saraswati for having given the knowledge of the seven musical notes. She plays the Veena, the Indian lute. She motivates one to the delights of music. The playing of Veena instils stability in the mind and body. It sends waves of soothing rhythms through every part of the body delighting one to experience peace as though in meditation. The tranquillity of music is focussed in the Veena.

In the **Markandeypuran**, it is stated that Ashvatara (Naagraj) and brother Kambaal learnt music from Saraswati. Vaku emerged in the form of virtuous Saraswati.

Saraswati is fair and charming. She has four arms. She holds a book in one of the right hands and a lotus in one of the left hands. She holds a Veena in the other two hands. She is an embodiment of virtuous intellect. Everyone cherishes this ability. The lotus is a symbol of modesty and morality. It motivates one to live a life of detachment. With a book in the hand she motivates one to learn about people and things.

In the **Devi Bhagwat**, it is said that Brahma, Vishnu and Mahesh hold Saraswati in great reverence. Whoever makes offerings and prays to Saraswati is blessed with thorough knowledge just like her vehicle, the swan. Every year in the Hindu month Magh when *Basant Panchmi* is celebrated, it is customary to offer Saraswati special rituals and prayers.

Writers, poets and musicians make special offerings to goddess Saraswati. It is believed that by doing so inspiration and creative energy are generated within. Besides, with blessings from Saraswati one is freed from sickness, grief, worry and emotional tension.

There are detailed accounts of offerings and prayers to Saraswati in the **Yagyavalkya Vani Stotra** and **Vashisth Stotra** enunciated by the sages Yagyavalkya and Vashisth.

It is said that once Brahma asked Saraswati to reside as poetic ability within a capable man. Saraswati left home in search of an appropriate individual. When she heard Valmiki utter the following verse on seeing an injured bird, she halted:

मा निषाद प्रतिष्ठां त्वमगमः शाश्वतीः समाः ।
यत् क्रौञ्चमिथुनादेकमवधीः काममोहितम् ॥

Impressed by Valmiki's extraordinary ability she decided to reside within him. Through her blessings he received acclaim all over the world and came to be known as 'Aadikavi', meaning one who is a poet eternally.

In the **Ramayana**, there is a mention that when Ravana's brother Kumbhkaran offered great penance and offerings to Brahma, and the time came for Brahma to grant him a boon, Brahma was worried. He knew that even if this demon did no other harm but simply sat down to eat, he could still bring the world to ruin. He then asked Saraswati to create confusion in his mind when he asked for a boon.

Kumbhkaran had intended to ask Brahma that he should keep awake for six months in a year and sleep for one day only. When Saraswati created confusion in his mind, he asked for the opposite – sleeping for six months and waking up for one day. This was the death knell of Kumbhkaran.

In the **Markandeypuran**, there is a reference that once when the sage Jaimini was passing through the forests of Vindhya, he heard birds reciting the Vedas. Their narration and recitation was perfect. He watched them with delight. He immediately understood that the birds were suffering a curse. However, it was with Saraswati's blessings that they were reciting the Vedas.

> ## Think it over...
> In Hinduism, there is one God or Supreme Reality, which manifests or expresses itself through various powers represented by the forms of different gods and goddesses.
>
> —Swami Tejomayananda

Why do Hindus working with machinery revere Vishvakarma?

Vishvakarma is the engineer amongst gods. Since a lot of machinery and equipment is used in factories and even homes, it is customary to seek the blessings of Vishvakarma before starting any work that involves machinery and equipment. This helps prevent accidents and untoward incidents.

The name Vishvakarma is formed from two words. *Vishva* means *the world* or *universe*, and *karma* denotes *deed* or *action*. Together the words mean *the builder of the world or universe*. Son of Vasu Prabhas and wife Varastri, Vishvakarma was married to a celestial nymph Ghritachi. They had three daughters and several sons. Two daughters were married to King Priyavrat, and the third, Sanghya was married to Surya. Since Sanghya could not bear the heat of Surya, Vishvakarma reduced Surya's radiance by one-eighth.

It is believed that with the energy taken away from Surya, Vishvakarma built the Pushpak *viman* (aeroplane), the *Sudarshan Chakra*, a trident for Shiva, and the weapon 'Shakti' for Kartikeya. Likewise, he built innumerable weapons, beautiful ornaments and other useful things for the gods. He built a beautiful castle for Kuber at Lanka. For Indra he made the thunderbolt. He is also known to have built a special steel chariot for Shiva. So, the gods acknowledged him as their engineer.

Vishvakarma's son Nala helped Ram build the bridge to cross the ocean at Rameswaram. His other sons specialised in carpentry, masonry, metals, artistic etching, minerals and other engineering fields. To this day the successors continue in these fields. Many workers use the surname Vishvakarma after their first and principal name. Vishvakarma was a great craftsman, but through his association with the gods he too came to be acknowledged as a god.

It is customary to offer prayers to Vishvakarma on the next day after Deepavali. Many do so on Vishvakarma's birth anniversary. The machinery and equipment are cleaned, tools put together at the place of prayer and formal group prayers organised to appease Vishvakarma. Those who work with machinery everyday seek his blessings as part of the morning prayers.

Think it over...

When two or more are gathered together in *sankirtan* to chant *sabdas* (hymns) and sing *Hari Naam* (the name of the Lord), there is generated a gentle force which, as you take it in, more and more helps your growth in the God-life.

−T.L. **Vaswani**

Why do Hindus fear the influence of Shanidev in their lives?

Shanidev, the seventh of the *Navgrah*, is the son of Surya and Sanghya Devi. Symbolic of the planet Saturn from the *Navgrah*, he is feared most by people. He interacts with other planets for periods of two and half and seven and a half years. The influence of Shanidev is the most malefic when compared to other planets. The influence moves slowly and extends over long periods. This slowness is attributed to Shanidev being lame.

The cause of this lameness is narrated in the **Suryatantra**.

Unable to bear the great heat generated by Surya, his wife Sanghya Devi created a clone of herself. She named the clone Swarna and directed her to look after the children in her absence, and also tend to her husband Surya just as a wife would do. She then left to live in her father's home. Swarna conducted herself so well that even Surya could not detect the difference. Swarna was blessed with five sons and two daughters through Surya. As would be expected, Swarna paid greater attention to her children than those of Sanghya Devi.

One day when Shanidev felt very hungry he asked Swarna for food. Swarna asked him to wait. She said that she would first make offerings to God, and thereafter feed the younger brothers and sisters. Only then could she give him food. This enraged Shanidev and he tensed his leg to kick her. Immediately, she cursed him that his leg would get fractured. On hearing the curse, Shanidev got frightened and narrated the incident to his father.

Surya immediately understood that something was amiss. No mother would curse her child with such dire consequences just for asking food. She could not be his wife. She had to be someone else. When Surya shouted at her in anger and inquired who she was, frightened at the rising heat, she told him the truth. Then Surya explained to Shanidev that Swarna was not his mother. She was only like his mother. Since her curse could not be nullified, it could only be modified. He would not lose his leg but he would walk with a limp, hereafter.

Why do Hindus offer oil to appease Shanidev?

It is customary to bathe Shanidev in oil. There is a story related to this practice in the **Anand Ramayan**.

When the bridge to cross the sea was constructed for Ram's army from Rameswaram to Lanka, Hanuman was entrusted the responsibility of looking after the security of the bridge lest the enemy damage it. One evening as he sat quietly lost in thought, offering prayers to Lord Ram, Shanidev showed up in his dark ugly form and said, "Amongst the gods, I am the powerful Shanidev. I wish to know whether you are strong and brave. Open your eyes and fight me. I want you to test your might with me."

In response, Hanuman opened his eyes and humbly said, "At this time I am meditating upon my lord. Please do not disturb me in my prayers. I respect you. Please leave me alone."

But Shanidev was adamant on picking a fight. At this Hanuman elongated his tail and started coiling it around Shanidev. Slowly he tightened the coiled tail. Shanidev tried to free himself. He could not. Hanuman gradually tightened the coil much to Shanidev's discomfort and pain. Hanuman stood up and walked around the stone bridge. After a few steps, to rid Shanidev of his pride, he moved his tail up and down hitting him against the stones. Shanidev started bleeding. His pain increased immensely. He was in agony. So Shanidev offered apologies, and begged forgiveness. He said he had been punished enough and assured Hanuman that he would not commit a similar mistake again.

Hanuman responded, "I will let you go only if you promise that you shall never pester Ram's devotees. If you ever break this promise I shall punish you."

In great pain Shanidev pleaded, "I promise you that I shall never interfere in the destiny of those devoted to you and Ram. I shall never hurt them. Not even by mistake. Please let me go."

After Shanidev made the promise, Hanuman slowly released Shanidev from the iron grip of his coiled tail. Shanidev felt relieved. Humbly, he asked Hanuman if he could have some oil to relieve his wretched pain. When Hanuman gave the oil to Shanidev, his pain was relieved instantly.

Since then it is customary to offer oil to Shanidev. It is symbolic of soothing his pain. He feels contented and this makes him benevolent towards the devotee.

> ## Think it over...
> Prayer has saved my life; without it I should have been a raving lunatic. Prayer must be the very core of the life of man. The spirit becomes unclean if the heart is not washed with prayer.
>
> **–Mahatma Gandhi**

How did Lord Mahavir influence Hindu thought?

A large number of Hindus follow a system of life popularly called Jainism. Vardhaman Mahavir was the 24th and last *Tirthankar* (prophet) of the Jains who codified this system of living, founded by Rishabh, the first *Tirthankar*. In 599 BC, at Kundpur, Bihar, when a child was due to be born in the home of Siddharth and Trishila, auspicious omens gave signals of a miracle. The child was born on Chaitra Sudi Teras (13th day of the moonlit fortnight of Chaitra) according to the Hindu calendar, now celebrated every year as Mahavir Jayanti.

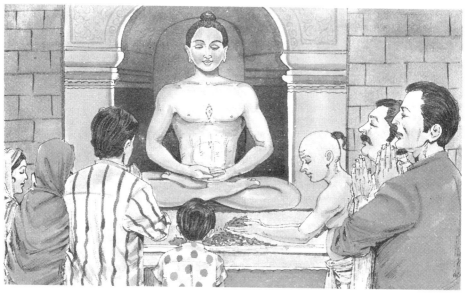

Even as a child people could gauge his greatness. Saints and sages would come to him to clarify their doubts. Because of his humility and wisdom he came to be known by many names – Sanmati, Mahavir, Vardhaman, Ativir, Arihant, Tarvagya, Tirthankar.

Like the many incarnations of Hindu gods, followers of the faith assert that there are 24 Tirthankars. Jainism is based upon the teachings of the Tirthankars. A Tirthankar is a noble person who helps others cross the vast ocean of life. Rishabh Dev was the first Tirthankar. He is believed to have lived around the time the Rig-Veda was written.

As Mahavir saw the society around him, he felt greatly distressed. There was restlessness and violence all around. People were oppressed. Women were treated badly. There was lack of education. Falsehood, stealing and cheating were common in everyday life. Mahavir liked solitude. So, at the age of 30, he left home to become a *sanyasi*.

The next 12 years were spent in penance and austerity. He ate whatever people gave him. He developed complete control over himself. He could also control his sleep. He was steadfast in his search for a solution to the problems of the world. It was on Baisakh Sudi Dasmi (the tenth day of Baisakhi) in Jhumbi village near the Rishjukula River, as Mahavir meditated under an Ashoka tree that he saw how layer by layer the veils were lifted from ignorance, greed and selfishness. He saw life in a new perspective. He had attained *kevala-jnana* (Enlightenment). He was now ready to meet the world and share with everyone whatever he had attained.

It is believed that the opening words of his first discourse were:

उप्पणेदू वाविणस्सेद्र वा धुवेर वा ।

Everything has three attributes. It emerges in several forms. It is indestructible. It appears to be stable or permanent.

Mahavir delivered discourses in the then popular language Prakrit. All kinds of people came from long distances to hear him. Wanting to serve mankind, he travelled from one place to another to benefit hundreds of thousands of people.

Mahavir revealed five important truths for mankind to follow:

1. *Ahimsa* (non-violence).
2. *Satya* (truth).
3. *Asteya* (non-stealing).
4. *Aparigraha* (non-possession).
5. *Brahmacharya* (celibacy).

He disclosed that amassing wealth was the foundation of worry and tension. All problems emerged from it. His principal message was to practise non-violence and thoughtfulness for others. For 30 years, Mahavir travelled long distances to deliver his message through discourses. He returned to his heavenly abode in 527 BC. A temple is established where he left his worldly body. The followers of Jainism believe that Diwali is celebrated in his memory on his death anniversary. It is estimated that over four million Hindus follow Jainism.

After Mahavir, there were several divisions in thought amongst followers of Jainism. The two important sects are the Swetambers, who wear white clothes, and the Digambers, who wear no clothes. Followers of Mahavir do not pray to conventional Hindu gods and goddesses, but have similar temples with the idol of Lord Mahavir. Like all other Hindus, they offer prayers, flowers and sweets and have discourses on special occasions. Many pray everyday.

Besides other festivals, one of the most important occasions for Jains is *Puryushan Parv.* This is celebrated every year for eight days beginning with Bhadon Sudi Panchmi (the fifth day of the moonlit fortnight of Bhadon). This can be equated with Navratris celebrated by a large section of Hindus. *Puryushan* literally means *controlling problems of the mind. Parv* means a *festival, holiday* or *ceremony.* During this period, along with fasting, prayers, charity and religious ceremonies there is an effort to develop control over anger, selfishness, greed and jealousy.

Once a devotee asked Lord Mahavir, "Bhagwan, is it better to sleep or to keep awake?"

Mahavir responded, "Sleeping is good. So is keeping awake good."

The devotee was confused. He asked once again, "Bhagwan, how could both be the same? One must be better than the other."

Lord Mahavir smiled, "For a sinner it is better that he sleeps. For a good man it is better if he keeps awake. A sinner benefits the world by sleeping. A good person benefits it by keeping awake. When a sinner is awake he will promote bad activities. A good person will benefit everyone. Therefore, never let a sinner wake up. Never let a good person sleep."

Think it over...

The most precious thing in life is the self. One who has attained control over it has attained the most precious thing in life.

–**Lord Mahavir**

How did Gautam Buddha influence Hindu thought?

In 563 BC, a son was born to Mahamaya and Shudhodan, the ruler of a small kingdom on the Indo-Nepal border. Mahamaya was on the way to her father's home when she delivered the baby boy. She passed away a week later, and the upbringing of the infant was entrusted to the second queen Prajapati. The child was named Siddharth.

Astrologers predicted that Siddharth would one day either be an emperor, or an ascetic who would renounce worldly pleasures and show the way to mankind. This prediction perturbed King Shudhodan. So he decided to provide a completely protected life of comfort and luxury to his son. The prince was educated within the palace. To further involve him in worldly affairs, he was married young. Renunciation is born out of indifference and aversion to worldly things. The king wanted to keep his son away from this.

However, what is not to be shall never be. One day when the prince wished to drive outside, the king arranged for him to visit the best places and bring back happy memories. Despite strict instructions to the charioteer, the prince persuaded him to change the route. Along the way, for the first time the prince saw a sick man, an old man and a dead person being carried away in a funeral procession. Life was never the same again for Prince Siddharth. Shaken to the core by the misery and suffering he witnessed, he decided to renounce princely life. One night, he left home when everyone was fast asleep.

Siddharth was in search of the truth. He visited the wise and the learned, going from one place to another. He met saints, seers and sages. But his questions remained unanswered. Along with five other friends, he decided to undertake severe penance. This went on for six years, without success. The physical hardships were so severe that his body became emaciated and he appeared a living skeleton. He swooned. Then he realised that fasting and penance were of no avail. When a farmer's daughter offered him rice porridge, he accepted it. This offended his friends and they left him.

With some rest he felt better. Sitting by himself, he meditated under a Peepal tree. On the 29th day, as he sat meditating in the evening, he experienced the presence of a divine light. He suddenly understood the cause of all suffering and found answers to his questions. He was enlightened. Siddharth Gautam was now Gautam Buddha – the Enlightened One.

He proclaimed that there were four eternal truths:

1. There is suffering in life.
2. Sufferings arise from attachment to desires.
3. Sufferings cease the moment attachment to desires cease.
4. There is a middle path to avoid suffering.

Furthermore, he explained that to move on the middle path, there were eight essentials:

1. **Right vision:** One must be able to see the reality.
2. **Right resolve:** One's thoughts must be based upon truth.
3. **Right speech:** One's speech must be free from abuse, falsehood, blame, slander and gossip.
4. **Right deeds:** One's deeds should not harm or hurt others or oneself.
5. **Right livelihood:** One's vocation must be based upon ethics and morals.
6. **Right exercise:** One must maintain physical and emotional health.
7. **Right memories:** One's happy memories promote happiness and lead to divinity.
8. **Right meditation:** One must be able to concentrate and look inwards to find peace.

Buddha began preaching about human suffering and how it could be avoided. He preached the need for love, peace and non-violence. He did not deny existing religious knowledge or speak against the prevalent Hindu way of life. He only spoke about what had been revealed to him. He addressed followers in the language they could understand – Pali. As he travelled far and wide his followers grew. Hindus acknowledged him as the ninth incarnation of Vishnu.

For sometime, the influence of Buddhism grew, particularly when Emperor Ashok too adopted the message of love and non-violence. It spread to several countries in the south-east and east, where Buddhism could be easily adopted along with existing local religious and cultural beliefs. When Gautam Buddha left his mortal remains, his ashes were divided into eight portions to establish eight stupas. Buddhist temples have idols of Buddha.

It is estimated that there are more than 350 million Buddhists around the world. However, despite having been founded in India, Buddhism did not capture the imagination of the majority of orthodox Hindus.

What was the influence of Guru Nanak Dev and his successors on Hindu thought?

Born in Talwandi near Lahore (Pakistan) in 1469, Guru Nanak Dev ushered a change amongst the Hindus of that time. The Mughals ruled over India then. The condition of the people in general was bad. Guru Nanak had a religious temperament by birth, and people were astonished at his faith, devotion and knowledge about spiritual matters.

Guru Nanak was opposed to both the Hindu and Muslim clergy at that time. His teachings were simple. There is only one Supreme God. He is an embodiment of truth. He is the creator of all things. He is present in all things. He is without fear or hatred. He is eternal. He is beyond birth and death. He is beyond the reach of human intellect. A relationship with God can be created only through truth and the divinity within the self.

At the age of 40, he was an acknowledged religious leader and his disciples were called Sikhs. This was the birth of Sikhism. Presently, there are over 24 million Sikhs worldwide. Guru Nanak taught via verses. It is believed these came to him through divine inspiration. Later, these verses formed a part of the holy books *Japji Sahib* and *Guru Granth Sahib*.

Despite opposition from the Hindu and Muslim clergy, he travelled widely in India and the Middle East, addressing both Hindus and Muslims. When he died in 1539, Hindus and Muslims claimed they had disposed of his mortal remains according to their own customs.

Guru Angad took over as the second Guru. He created the Gurmukhi script, meaning *from the Guru's mouth*. He served from 1539 to 1552.

Guru Amar Das was the third Guru and served from 1552 to 1574. He founded Goindwal.

Guru Ram Das was the fourth Guru. He served from 1574 to 1581. He founded the Darbara Sahib, the religious seat of the Sikhs, in Amritsar.

Guru Arjan Dev was the fifth Guru who served from 1581 to 1606. Sikhism developed during his time. He compiled the *Guru Granth Sahib* from the teachings of the Gurus.

Guru Hargobind was the sixth Guru. He served from 1606 to 1644. Considering the political scenario, he built a fort around Amritsar, and also established the Akal Takht opposite the Darbara Sahib.

Guru Har Rai served as the seventh Guru from 1644 to 1661. Due to the prevailing political climate under Mughal rule at that time, he preferred to maintain a low profile.

Guru Har Kishan as the eighth Guru served from 1661 to 1664, and like his predecessor also maintained a low profile.

Guru Teg Bahadur was the ninth Guru. He served from 1664 to 1675. He died a martyr's death.

Guru Gobind Singh was the tenth and last Guru. He served from 1675 to 1708. There was growing conflict between the Sikhs and the Mughal rulers at that time. Guru Gobind Singh established the Sacred Order of the Khalsa in 1699. The Khalsa is distinguished by the 5 Ks: *kesh* (uncut hair), *kachha* (short drawers), *kirpan* (steel dagger), *kara* (steel bangle) and *kanga* (a small comb). Those who followed the Order of the Khalsa were given the second name, Singh. Women were given the second name, Kaur. They were ordained to follow the *Rehat Maryada*. With long hair, all Sikhs wear turbans. Guru Gobind Singh had said that there would be no Gurus after him. The *Guru Granth Sahib* – the compilation of teachings of the Gurus – would be the only Guru.

Sikhs do not visit temples or have any idols in the gurudwaras, where they pray. They pray to the *Guru Granth Sahib* for all rites, rituals and customs, including marriage and death. For all practical purposes, the *Guru Granth Sahib* is personified as the eternal Guru.

A large number of Sikhs are farmers. They celebrate Baisakhi with great fervour as it coincides with the harvest season. The birth and martyrdom anniversaries of the Gurus are also celebrated. Sikhs hold important positions in business and industry, and have travelled and settled in countries around the world.

Think it over...

Impurity of the heart is greed, impurity of the tongue is falsehood, impurity of the eyes is gazing on another's wealth, his wife and her beauty; impurity of the ears is listening to slander. Nanak, even the pretended saint who practises such things shall go to hell.

–Guru Nanak Dev

What is the difference between the national and Hindu calendars?

The national calendar is based upon the solar year of 365 days. The Hindu calendar is based upon the lunar-solar system. With the new moon appearing after every 29½ days, the 12 lunar months take 354 days. The difference of 11 days is adjusted every three years when an additional month called *adhik-mas* is added. The difference between the two calendars explains why the dates of Hindu festivals vary from one year to another.

The names of the 12 months are Chaitra, Vaishakh, Jyeshth, Ashadh, Shravan, Bhadrapad (Bhadon), Ashvin, Kartik, Margashirsha (Agahan), Poush, Magh and Phagun. Hindus sometimes use abbreviated forms for some months.

Since nations worldwide use the Gregorian calendar, the national calendar is adjusted to synchronise it with this, so that Chaitra 1 would always fall on March 22 of the Gregorian calendar.

What is a Panchang? Why do Hindus consult it to fix dates for auspicious occasions?

Panchang is formed from two Hindi words, *panch* and *ang*. *Panch* means five, and *ang* means limbs. Therefore, *Panchang* means *five limbs*. Panchang is a book of tables that lists the days of every month along with astronomical data and calculations. On the basis of this data, the days of Hindu festivals are fixed. It also mentions the auspicious days for marriages and special ceremonies.

Astronomers from all over India compile data in the Panchang based on their astronomical readings. They assemble once a year to finalise it. The Panchang is a complicated document. Astrologers use it to calculate the position of the planets and make predictions accordingly. Everyone relies upon Brahmin priests to interpret the data and announce auspicious days for special ceremonies. Professional Brahmin priests maintain a copy of the Panchang from earlier years.

Why do Hindus hold Yama in fear and awe?

Yama is the God of Death. He lives in Yamlok (abode of Yama). Since he is the master of Yamlok, he is also known as Yamraj. He who is born must die. That is the law of nature. Yet everyone is afraid of death. Because of this morbid fear of death, everyone is afraid of Yamraj. When a person has lived his mortal life Yamraj takes away the soul from the body.

Yamraj is the son of Surya and Sanghya. He uses a male buffalo as a vehicle. Amongst his messengers of death are the pigeon, owl and crow.

Yamraj has a mace as his weapon. In his hand, he also has the *kâlsutra* or *kâlpash*, which he uses to extract the soul of a person. Yamlok is also known as Yampuri. Two ferocious four-eyed dogs guard it. Seated on his throne of judgement he summons every individual one by one. Chitragupta presents the account of their good and bad deeds. Yamraj passes judgement on the basis of this account. Finally, he is the judge of an individual's good and bad deeds.

Yamraj had several wives. Of them Sushila, Vijaya and Hemnaal are best known. Of his many sons, Dharmraj Yudhistra is believed to be best known. Both Yamraj and Yudhistra possessed the attribute of being extremely fair in their judgement of right and wrong, and are addressed as Dharmraj – king of justice. It is believed that the personified river Yamuna is his sister. Prayers are offered to them on the day of Raksha Bandhan.

To enable individuals to get rid of past sins, in ancient times Yamraj established pilgrimages through Yameshwar and Yamaditya temples where one could fulfil one's desires through severe penance. The 14th day of the lunar month that falls on a Tuesday is considered most auspicious to embark on this pilgrimage. It is believed that bathing and offering prayers in these temples spare one from punishment in hell. One is also spared from going to Yamlok.

It is also believed that after a pilgrimage to these temples when one offers *shraddh* to forefathers and prayers to Yameshwar and Yamaditya, one is free from the bond of debt to forefathers. Many people offer a light to Yamraj a day before Diwali and also on other occasions to gain his blessing.

Yamraj is known for his righteousness and justice. In the Puranas there is mention that at one time Mandav Rishi was enraged at Yamraj and cursed that he would be born as a human being. For this reason, Yamraj was born through a maid as Vidura.

Think it over...

One may live as a conqueror, a king, or a magistrate; but he must die a man. The bed of death brings every human being to his pure individuality, to the intense contemplation of that deepest and most solemn of all relations – the relation between the creature and his Creator.

–Daniel Webster, US politician and orator (1782–1852)

Why do Hindus hold Nature in great reverence?

Hindus have always shown great reverence for Nature. Their places of pilgrimage are situated deep in the hills and mountains, alongside rivers, lakes or near the sea. They pray to the sun, the moon and the planets. Hindus believe that the *Navgrah* (nine plants) hold sway over the destinies of individuals, communities and nations.

What may seem just natural phenomena to most people is the will of God for Hindus. Good or scanty rainfall, floods and drought, storms and hurricanes are natural phenomena. However, Hindus see God Indra controlling these to their benefit or detriment. For the modern scientist, the sun is just a source of light, heat or energy. But for Hindus the sun is a god – Surya. The moon too is a god – Chandrama. The other planets are also personified – Mars as God Mangal, Jupiter as Bhagwan Brihaspati or Saturn as God Shani. Others are no different. Just like the planets, the hills, mountains and rivers are all personified. There is the quiet hand of God to support these. The rivers are goddesses giving magnanimously like a mother. When angry they punish children harshly. Fire too is a god – Agni. Without it most Hindu ceremonies cannot be conducted and would remain incomplete. Like other gods, Agni provides mankind energy. It controls the balance in nature. However, when angry Agni causes great damage.

The animal world is a part of the evolutionary process for the modern scientist. But Hindus hold an altogether different perspective. For them the animal world is as important as mankind because the dynamic spirit in animals is the same as in mankind. God decides whether one would be born a man or animal depending upon one's deeds. Animals too are revered. The gods use them as vehicles. When animals are so dear to gods, why would they not attract the reverence of mankind?

The plant world is no different. It is a recent discovery that plants have life just like animals. But Hindus have believed this since ancient times and religious texts affirmed it repeatedly. The plant world has always been revered not because it provided us food, shelter or shade, but because Hindus saw the hand of God directing the destiny of mankind as much through the plant world as through other means.

Your questions answered...

Why do Hindus call the land, 'Mother Earth'?

Many cultures revere the land as 'Mother Earth'. This is because land, like a mother, provides all our needs. It feeds us, clothes us and provides us shelters. It fulfils all our needs. The earth has seen good times, but has also been a witness to all kinds of atrocities. Like a mother, the earth teaches us patience, tolerance, generosity and humility. It is for this reason that Hindus offer prayers to it and seek blessings.

Why do Hindus consider the Ganga holy and worthy of reverence?

Emerging from the serene atmosphere of Gaumukh deep in the Himalayas and flowing over 2,500 kilometres to join the Bay of Bengal, the bountiful Ganga is a river of reverence to all Hindus. Not only has it been a source of great prosperity and happiness wherever it flowed, but on its banks are situated great centres of learning and pilgrimage that have always been dear to the gods and mankind. The water of the Ganga is believed to hold magical properties.

The Goddess Ganga wears white garments that are pink-tinged. She holds a water pot in one hand and a white lotus in the other. She sits on a crocodile in a Himalayan lake. There are many stories about her emergence in this world. The most popular one is about King Bhagirath.

There was a king named Sagar who had 60,000 sons. These sons went looking for the horse of the Ashwamedh sacrifice. The horse had been stolen by Indra and released near a place where a sage, Kapil, was in deep meditation and penance. When the sons found the horse grazing here, they thought the sage had stolen it and raised objections. Enraged at being disturbed in prayer, Kapil reduced them to ashes with his wrath.

Successors were told that the sons of Sagar could gain salvation only if the Ganga flowed over their ashes. Ganga being in heaven, they were unable to bring her to earth. Later, a descendant, King Bhagirath undertook penance, living in the forests in great discomfort. When Brahma was convinced of Bhagirath's sincere penance, he granted him a boon.

"Lord! I have all that I need," King Bhagirath said humbly. "All that I now desire is that Ganga should flow on earth, granting salvation to the 60,000 sons of King Sagar."

"So be it," Brahma said. "I am willing to grant your wish. I have Ganga in my *kamandal*. However, when I release her and she reaches the earth, the land will be flooded, houses destroyed and many people will lose their lives."

King Bhagirath was disappointed. Although he had achieved his goal, a proper solution still eluded him. So, he requested Brahma to suggest a possible solution. Brahma said that Shiva could help him.

King Bhagirath again underwent penance, this time seeking the favour of Lord Shiva. Eventually, Shiva appeared before Bhagirath and said he was willing to help out. He would let Ganga fall on his tresses and not on the ground. In this way, the shock of the cascading Ganga would be absorbed and there would be no destruction on earth.

When Brahma released Ganga from his *kamandal*, she thought that the force of her fall on Shiva's head would push him into *Patallok*. When Shiva realised this, he was enraged. To humble Ganga, Shiva hid her in his tresses so that none could see her.

Once again disappointed, King Bhagirath sought the help of Shiva and persuaded him to release Ganga from his tresses. When Shiva let loose Ganga, three streams went eastwards and another three westwards. The main stream followed King Bhagirath, who rode in his chariot from the Himalayas to the Bay of Bengal. Thus Ganga was able to grant salvation to the sons of Sagar, and to millions others who followed.

In the **Mahabharata**, Vanparv, 85/89-90-93, it is said:

यद्यकार्यशतं कृत्वा कृतं गंगाभिषेचनम् ।
सर्वं तत् तस्य गंगाम्भो दहत्यग्निरिवेन्धनम् ॥
सर्वंकृतयुगे पुण्यं त्रेतायां पुष्करं स्मृतम् ।
द्वापरेऽपि कुरुक्षेत्रं गंगा कलियुगे स्मृता ॥
पुनाति कीर्तिता पापं दृष्टा भद्रं प्रयच्छति ।
अवगाढा च पीता च पुनात्यासप्तमं कुलम् ॥

Just as fire burns the fuel, in the same way if one were to bathe in the Ganga even after hundreds of forbidden deeds, the water of the Ganga would cleanse them all. In Satyayug all pilgrimages produced results. In Tretayug Pushkar, in Dwaparyug Kurukshetra and in Kalyug, Ganga would be most important. The very name of Ganga purifies a sinner. The sight of it is auspicious. Bathing in it or drinking a few drops purifies seven generations.

In the **Bhagavad Gita**, Sri Krishna says:

'स्रोतसामस्मि जाह्नवी'

Amongst the rivers, I am Ganga.

In other religious texts it is said:

औषधिः जाह्नवी तोयं वैद्यो नारायणोः हरिः ।

The medicine for spiritual ills is the water of Ganga. The doctor who cures these ills is none other than Lord Vishnu.

In the **Padampuran**, it is said that with the influence of Ganga the sins of several births are washed away. Much virtue is gained and one finds a place in heaven.

In the **Agnipuran**, it is said that Ganga blesses one with salvation. Those who bathe in it or drink from the Ganga everyday then cross hurdles and sail smoothly in life. Those who chant the glory of Ganga gain many virtues. There is no pilgrimage on a river holier than the one on Ganga.

In the **Skandpuran**, Kashi p., 27/49, it is said:

अनिच्छयापि संस्पृष्टो दहनो हि यथा दहेत् ।
अनिच्छयापिसंस्नाता गंगा पापं तथा दहेत् ॥

Just as fire burns on touching it even though one does not want to be burnt, in the same way Ganga washes away the sins of mankind even when it is not so intended.

Research has confirmed that water from the Ganga does not deteriorate on storage. With its health promoting qualities, Ganga water can be compared to celestial nectar or *amrit*. It is sweet, rich in a variety of minerals and destroys disease. Some people have reported extraordinary cases of revival when Ganga water was given to a dying person. The experience has been described as similar to a fountain of life bursting inside to revive the person. Many people believe that at the time of death a few drops of Ganga water and pieces of tulsi must be administered to a dying person.

Faith and devotion are important to gain the full benefits of bathing in the Ganga.

Once Parvati asked Shiva, "Do people who bathe in the Ganga get absolved of their sins?"

Lord Shiva responded, "Whoever has faith and devotion benefits from it. Others are more interested in the fun and frolic."

When Parvati was not satisfied with Shiva's response, he asked her to accompany him as she could then witness the truth for herself. Lord Shiva assumed the body of a leper and sat near the Ganga. Parvati assumed the body of a beautiful woman and sat besides him. Crowds of people were coming and going for a bath. When they saw a beautiful woman sitting next to a leper they talked about it and were attracted to the woman. Many suggested that she go with them. Both watched the proceedings quietly.

After a while a man came, looked at them and complimented the woman for the devotion to her husband. He told her how impressed he was and offered to help her husband take a bath in the Ganga. Just then Lord Shiva assumed his real form and said, "Here is one who is truly devoted and faithful. He is the only one entitled to the virtues of bathing in the Ganga."

Your questions answered...

• **What should be the goal of a human being?**

The goal of a human being should be to attain oneness with the infinite. This is possible only through the knowledge of the spirit – *Brahma vidya*. This knowledge is available only to human beings.

• **Does the reading or recitation of religious texts make a person learned?**

The reading or recitation of religious texts and scriptures alone do not make a person learned. One must put to practical use whatever one reads and learns. Knowing about a medicine does not cure a patient. The medicine must be used to cure the patient.

Why do Hindus greatly revere the sun?

Of all heavenly bodies, the sun is most important. Everyone needs its benevolent favours. At the same time, everyone is afraid of its malefic influence. It is therefore natural for many people to hold it in high reverence.

In the **Suryopanishad**, it is said that the gods, Gandharvas and sages reside in the rays of the sun. Irrespective of who you are, without reverence to Surya nothing can be attained.

In the **Skandpuran**, it is said that eating without offering libation to Surya is like eating in sin. Without reverence to Surya one is not authorised to undertake any kind of auspicious work. It is important to offer special reverence to Surya on Sankranti (entering of the sun or a planet into a new sign of the zodiac) and Surya Shashthi (the sixth day of a fortnight). Otherwise, it is customary to offer prayers to Surya on all Sundays. Many observe a fast too.

Many Hindus make an offering to Surya every morning. For this, water is taken in a copper vessel and red sandalwood, rice, red flowers and kusha are mixed into it. Kneeling down outdoors, devotees face the sun and hold the vessel near the middle of the chest, offering the water slowly while chanting the Surya mantra or the Gayatri mantra. In all offerings devotion is key. Concentrating on the copper vessel and the sun, devotees visualise the round rim of the sun and then see the rays splitting to display a rainbow.

In the **Shivpuran**, 6/39-40, it is said:

सिन्दूरवर्णाय सुमण्डलाय नमोऽस्तु वज्राभरणाय तुभ्यम् ।
पद्माभनेत्राय सुपंकजाय ब्रह्वेन्द्रनारायणकारणाय ॥
सरक्तचूर्ण ससुवर्णतोयं सकुंकुमाढ्यं सकुशं संपुष्पम् ।
प्रदत्तमादायसहेमपात्रं प्रास्तमर्घ्यं भगवन् प्रसीद ॥

O Master! You look beautiful with the colour of sindoor. Adorned with diamonds and other gems, your eyes are like lotus flowers. Holding the lotus in your hand it appears that you are the cause of Brahma, Vishnu, Indra and the entire creation. O Aditya! Please accept my salutations. O God! Please accept from this golden vessel the mixture of sindoor, kusha and flowers mixed with red water as a libation and be pleased.

Pleased with the offering, Surya blesses one with good health and long life, wealth and prosperity, sons and friends. He also blesses one with knowledge, intelligence, wisdom and fame. One attains entry into *Surya Lok* (abode of Surya).

In the **Brahmpuran**, it is said:

मानसं वाचिकं वापि कायजं यच्च दुष्कृतम् ।
सर्व सूर्यप्रसादेन तदशेषं व्यपोहति ॥

Whoever prays and makes offerings to Surya attains whatever they desire. Surya comes close to them and fulfils desires. With his blessings all physical, oral and mental sins are absolved.

In the **Rig-Veda**, it is said that prayers to Surya free one from sins, disease and poverty, and bless one with happiness and long life. They also bless one with vigour, strength, virility and divinity.

In the **Brahmpuran**, chapter 29-30, it is said that Surya is the most outstanding god who lends lustre and brightness to other gods. Whatever is offered to Surya comes back manifold to the devotee.

In the **Skandpuran**, Kashi Khand, 9/45-48, there are details of attaining wealth and prosperity, good health and children, and other things through *Savita Surya Aradhana* (prayer or adoration of Surya).

In the **Yajur-Veda**, 13/43, it is explained that the *Savita Surya Aradhana* is done because Surya is witness to all the good and bad deeds of people and nothing is hidden from him.

In the **Agnipuran**, it is said that Surya is pleased when the Gayatri mantra is chanted during prayers.

65

Why do Hindus hold the moon in special reverence?

Next to the sun, the moon has always attracted great attention and reverence. In **Chandogya Upanishad** it is said that whoever prays to Chandrama (the moon) lives a good life. All sins and bad deeds are absolved. One is free of problems and sorrow. With good health one lives a complete life and finds happiness in this world as well as the next.

Chandrama is a god of the mind. Since the mind is very fickle and wavering, Chandrama keeps it under control. It is a symbol of special powers. In the body Chandrama resides on the forehead between the two eyebrows. This is where tilak is applied. Chandrama appreciates this. The support of Chandrama is essential in Hatha Yoga. Even in Tantra, Chandrama has special importance. On the head of Lord Shiva one finds the half moon. This is symbolic of Shiva being a great yogi. Being a symbol of hope, the half moon is offered prayers. Lovers have always drawn great inspiration from the moon. Women offer prayers to it for happiness in their married life and for the welfare and long life of their husbands.

In **Brahmvaivartpuran** it is said that Chandrama married the daughters of Daksh Prajapati. When Chandrama failed to look after Daksh's daughters, they returned disappointed to their father's house. Enraged at Chandrama's behaviour, Daksh cursed him to suffer a debilitating disease. Chandrama immediately sought the help of Lord Shiva. To protect him from the curse Shiva took him on his forehead. Frustrated, Daksh asked Shiva to send Chandrama back to him. Otherwise, Shiva would have to bear his wrath through a curse. Shiva went to Lord Vishnu for advice. To set right the dilemma Vishnu gave Chandrama two forms. He gave one to Daksh, and the other was placed on Shiva's forehead. In this way, the curse of Daksh did not lose its validity, and Chandrama too remained free from the curse. Because of the curse Chandrama wanes for 15 days, and then grows again in the next 15 days.

Why do Hindus revere trees?

Hindus have always had great reverence for trees and other plants because they are the foundation of life. In the Puranas and other religious texts, great importance has been accorded to trees and plants, equating them with gods. It is recommended that they should be treated as members of the family.

With confirmation by scientists that plants are living beings, the credibility of religious texts has been strengthened. This has also strengthened belief in the effects of good and bad deeds on rebirth. The special status granted to some plants is now easier to understand.

According to religious texts, when people plant trees and care for them, those plants are reborn as their children. Whoever gives trees and plants in charity pleases the gods through flowers on the trees. In sunny and rainy weather trees serve as umbrellas to passers-by desiring refuge and rest. By offering droplets after the rain, they please forefathers. Those who offer flowers attain affluence and prosperity.

In the **Rig-Veda**, 6/48/17, it is said:

मा काकम्बीरमुद्वृहो वनस्पतिमशस्तीर्वि हि नीनशः ।
मोत सूरो अह एवा चन ग्रीवा आदधते वेः ॥

Do not be like the devilish buzzard that troubles other birds by grabbing their necks and killing them. Do not trouble the trees. Do not uproot or cut them. They provide protection to animals, birds and other living beings.

In the **Manusmriti**, it is said that trees bring with them the fruits of their deeds from the last birth. They are living beings and experience sorrow and happiness. God has created them for the welfare of living beings. They face the sun and the heat, but protect those who come under their shade. They provide refuge and residence to birds and insects. They bear flowers and fruits. One cannot estimate the number of saints and sages who offered prayers under the shade of trees. It is characteristic of the trees to give and keep giving.

During 'Vat Savitri' ladies offer prayers to the *bargad* (the Banyan tree – *Ficus indica*). On Thursdays, prayers are offered to the banana plant. The use of banana leaves for serving food is considered pure and clean. Prayers are offered to the Parijat tree (the queen of the night – *Nyctanthes arbor-tristis* – one of the five trees said to exist in paradise) as though it were the Kalpavriksh (the wishing tree obtained during *Samudramanthan*).

On *Ashok ashtmi*, prayers are offered to the Ashok tree (*Saraca indica*) to end sorrow and usher in hope. Special prayers are offered to the Amla tree (*Emblica officinalis*) during the month of Kartik, as it is believed that Lord Vishnu resides in this tree. Ladies circumambulate the tree asking for a happy married life. The leaves of the mango, its bark and the wood are used for a variety of prayers, ceremonies and yagyas.

It is believed that Brahma, Vishnu and Mahesh reside in the Peepal tree (the Bo tree, *Ficus religiosa*). By offering prayers and water to it one is blessed with children. Ladies also circumambulate and tie threads around the Peepal tree. Hindus consider Tulsi a sacred plant and give it a special place in the household.

> ## Your questions answered...
> **What is immortality?**
> Immortality does not mean to live forever. That would be against the laws of nature. To become immortal, means to be remembered for what you have done in this life. It is the positive influence you leave behind in the hearts of other people.

Why do Hindus consider the Peepal tree holy?

Of all trees, the Peepal holds special significance amongst Hindus. In **Taittriya Samhita**, the Peepal tree is included amongst seven most important trees in the world. The importance of the tree is also attested in the **Brahmvaivartpuran**.

In the **Padampuran**, it is said that the Peepal tree is a form of Lord Vishnu. Therefore, it is accorded special importance for religious purposes. Often described as a divine tree, it is an object of prayer. On several occasions around the year prayers are offered to it. It is believed that Lord Vishnu and Goddess Lakshmi reside in the Peepal tree on *Somapati Amavasya* (the dark night of the month that falls on a Monday).

In the **Skandpuran**, Nagar, 247/41-44, it is said:

मूले विष्णुः स्थितो नित्यं स्कन्धे केशव एव च ।
नारायणस्तु शाखासु पत्रेषु भगवान् हरिः ॥
फलेऽच्युतो न सन्देहः सर्वदेवैः समन्वितः ॥
स एव विष्णुर्द्रुम एवं मूर्तो महात्मभिः सेवितपुण्यमूलः ।
यस्याश्रयः पापसहस्रहन्ता भवेन्नृणां कामदुधो गुणाढ्यः ॥

Vishnu resides in the root of the Peepal tree. Keshav (another name for Krishna) resides in the trunk, Narayan in the branches, Lord Hari in the leaves and all the gods reside in the fruits. This tree is like the idol of Vishnu. All good people serve the virtues of this tree. This tree is full of all kinds of virtues and has the ability to fulfil desires and absolve the sins of people.

In the **Bhagavad Gita**, 10/26, Lord Krishna says:

'अश्वत्थः सर्ववृक्षाणाम्'

Amongst trees I am the Peepal tree.

In the **Padampuran**, it is said that by offering prayers to the Peepal tree and circumambulating it one attains longevity. Whoever offers water to this tree is absolved of all sins and attains heaven. It is believed that our forefathers find comfort in the Peepal tree and, also, that all pilgrimages reside in the tree. Therefore, when one cannot go on pilgrimage for a religious ceremony, it is customary to conduct the same under the shade of a Peepal tree.

Many Hindu women believe that by regularly offering prayers and watering the Peepal tree and by circumambulating it, they will be blessed with good children, particularly a son. This is because unknown souls residing in the tree are pleased and enable such blessings to bear fruit. For fulfilment of desires it is also customary to tie threads around the trunk of the tree. Putting a little oil in the root of the tree and lighting a lamp near it on Saturdays helps get rid of a variety of problems. To reduce the malefic effect of the seven and half years of Shani it is customary to offer prayers and circumambulate the Peepal tree. The shadow of Shani resides in the tree.

The bark of the tree is used for religious ceremonies. The leaves are auspicious and used to make buntings on special occasions. Since the tree is hardy, unaffected by disease and pests and because it cleanses the air, it is considered divine. Devotees ensure there is at least one Peepal tree within the precincts of a temple. Before sunrise, the influence of poverty hovers over the tree. But after sunrise, Lakshmi takes over. Therefore, prayers to the Peepal tree are forbidden before sunrise. Cutting or destroying a Peepal tree has been equated with the murder of a Brahmin.

The Peepal tree converts carbon dioxide into oxygen round the clock. Those who live nearby obtain more oxygen. It is interesting to note that during summers the shade of the tree is cool. During winter there is warmth in the shade. The leaves and the fruits of the tree are used for medicinal purposes.

Think it over...

"Within the body resides the Unknowable One;
But those who are foolish and proud know not the truth,
And search for Him without."

–Guru Nanak

Why do Hindus consider Tulsi the most sacred plant?

According to ancient Hindu belief, it is essential that at least one Tulsi plant exists in the courtyard of every home. It is customary to plant Tulsi in the month of Kartik. The **Skandpuran** says that one gets rid of the sins of as many lives as the number of Tulsi plants one grows. The **Padampuran** asserts that wherever there is a garden of Tulsi plants that place is like a pilgrimage. Representatives of Yama, the God of Death, cannot enter this home. Homes plastered with soil in which the Tulsi grows are free from disease.

Ancient religious texts have praised the Tulsi in many ways. Air that carries the fragrance of Tulsi benefits people it comes in contact with. Planting and caring for Tulsi helps people get rid of their sins. Even if one Tulsi is grown, the presence of Brahma, Vishnu, Mahesh and other gods is assured. Benefits of pilgrimages like Pushkar and that of rivers like Ganga are also available there. By offering prayers to Tulsi, one automatically prays to all gods and it is akin to a pilgrimage, therefore, the benefits accrue accordingly.

During the month of Kartik, when prayers are offered to Tulsi, or new plants are grown, the accumulated sins of many births are absolved. Tulsi affords auspicious opportunities generously. Simultaneously, it removes worries and tension. By offering Tulsi leaves to Lord Krishna one achieves salvation. Without Tulsi religious ceremonies remain incomplete. When charity is given along with Tulsi, it ensures great benefits. And when *shraddh* is offered to forefathers near a Tulsi plant, it pleases them immensely.

Tulsi leaves have excellent qualities and whoever consumes them thrice daily achieves purity and benefits of the *chandrayan fast* (related to the waning and waxing of the moon). Whoever bathes in water in which a few Tulsi leaves have been added is considered to have bathed at all important pilgrim centres. Whoever adds Tulsi leaves in the *charanamrit* offered

71

in prayers and consumes it gets rid of all sins and attains salvation. Such people are protected from ill health and sudden death. The addition of Tulsi leaves protects water from deterioration. At the time of death, it is customary to mix Tulsi with Ganga water and put this in the mouth of the dying person.

It is customary to offer prayers to the Tulsi plant in the evening and light a lamp. One attains the blessings of Sati Vrinda and Lord Vishnu. It is believed that the penance of Vrinda and her surrender and devotion to Lord Vishnu became a part of the fragrance and leaves of the Tulsi. It is customary to circumambulate the Tulsi plant 108 times on *Somapati Amavasya* (Monday that coincides with the dark night of the month) to get rid of insufficiency.

In the **Brahmvaivartpuran**, Prakritikhand, 21/40, it is said:

सुधाघटसहस्त्रेण सा तुष्टिर्न भवेद्धरेः ।
या च तुष्टिर्भनेवेन्नृणां तुलसीपत्र दानतः ॥

Lord Hari is not so pleased after bathing with thousands of pots filled with celestial nectar, as he is when even a single leaf of Tulsi is offered to him.

It is also said that whoever offers even a single Tulsi leaf to Lord Vishnu and prays to him daily attains the benefits of a hundred thousand *Ashwamedh yagyas*. And, at the time of death, even if a single drop of Tulsi water enters the mouth of a dying person, Vishnu Lok (abode of Vishnu) is attained definitely.

The **Padampuran** says that whoever bathes with water in which Tulsi is added attains the virtues of having bathed in the Bhagirathi Ganga.

It is said that in its last birth Tulsi was Vrinda, married to an *asura* named Jalandhar. To gain victory over him, Lord Vishnu persuaded Vrinda to give up devotion to her husband. Pleased with her, Vishnu gave her his blessings. Through his blessings she became Tulsi and is worshipped by people all over the world.

A similar explanation is found in **Brahmvaivartpuran**.

From the scientific point of view, Tulsi is excellent for physical and mental health. It is known to cure very serious ailments, improves the immune system, and promotes vigour and vitality. It is extensively used in Ayurveda.

Think it over...

If we do not return quickly to a state of harmony with the earth and reverence for all life, then we will in all likelihood perish.

—**Bob Hunter, Co-founder of Greenpeace**

Why do Hindus consider the cow sacred?

Amongst Hindus, the cow is specially revered and equated with a mother and the gods. It is believed that all the gods reside within the body of a cow. It is therefore the responsibility of every person to accord it respect and do one's duty by it. For most religious ceremonies the cow is essential.

The cow has been important since ancient times. Maharishi Vashisth once played with his own life for Kamadhenu, the celestial cow. Maharishi Chyavan preferred a cow to a kingdom. Such was the importance of the cow. Like a mother, the cow is known for the good it does mankind. It helps promote good health and long life.

Religious texts say:

गावो विश्वस्य मातरः ।

The cow is a universal mother.

The **Agnipuran** says that the cow is a pure, auspicious animal. Looking after a cow, bathing it and making it eat and drink are commendable acts. Cow dung and urine are said to have medicinal qualities. The milk, curd, butter and ghee are all used in religious ceremonies. Whoever offers a morsel of food to the cow before eating attains salvation. Whoever gives a cow in charity benefits the whole family. Wherever a cow lives the place becomes pure. The touch and care of cows absolves one of sins.

73

In the **Atharva-Veda**, it is said:

माता रुद्राणां दुहिता वसूनाम् । स्वसा आदित्यानाम् अमृतस्य नाभिः ॥

The cow is the mother of Rudras; she is a daughter of the Vasus; she is the sister of Surya. She is a storehouse of ghee that is like the celestial nectar.

In the **Markandeypuran**, it is said that the welfare of the world depends upon the cow. The back of the cow is symbolic of the Rig-Veda, the body of Yajur-Veda, the mouth of the Sama-Veda, the neck of the household deity and the good deeds and the soft body hair are like the mantras. Cow dung and urine give peace and good health. Wherever a cow lives the virtues are never wasted. A cow always promotes contentment.

In the **Vishnusmriti**, it is said that the land on which cows live is pure. Cows are pure and auspicious. They promote the welfare of mankind. They help make a yagya successful. By serving cows one gets rid of sins. Their dwelling is like a pilgrimage. One becomes virtuous through reverence of cows.

In the **Skandpuran**, it is said that cow dung purifies the courtyard and temple.

In the **Atharva-Veda**, it is said that cow's milk helps overcome debility and regain lost physical and mental health. It promotes intelligence.

In the **Bhagavad Gita**, Sri Krishna said, "Amongst cows, I am Kamadhenu."

In the **Mahabharata**, it is said that a cow given in charity becomes like Kamadhenu through its virtues and returns to the donor in the next birth. Through her virtues the cow protects the donor from the darkness of hell just as air protects and guides a boat from sinking and helps it steer through the vast ocean of life. Just as a mantra acts like a medicine to destroy disease, in the same way a cow given in charity to a good person protects one from all sins.

In the **Mahabharata, Kurmpuran, Yagyavalkya Smriti** and several other religious texts, it is said that whoever gives a cow in charity shall always be happy and content and attain heaven after death. It is believed that after death, before heaven one reaches Vaitarni River. To cross it one can hold the tail of the cow and finally reach heaven.

> ## Think it over…
> There is an Indian legend, which says that when human beings die they must cross a bridge to enter heaven. At the head of that bridge they meet every animal they encountered during their lifetime. The animals, based upon what they know of the persons, decide which humans may cross the bridge… and which should be turned away…
>
> —**Anon**

What is the Hindu attitude towards animals?

If the cow is the most sacred of animals to Hindus, the other animals too are worthy of their reverence. Lord Shiva uses the bull as his vehicle just as Durga rides a lion or tiger. Lord Vishnu's vehicle is Garuda, just as Lakshmi's vehicle is an owl. Saraswati's vehicle is the swan. Sri Ganesh rides a mouse. Yamaraj's vehicle is a buffalo. With animals so dear to the gods, Hindus hold them in equally high reverence.

The reverence to animals comes from a simple fact. When God created them, there was a purpose. To accept this purpose is to revere the animal. The animals have given mankind much for its progress, both physical and emotional. If the cow is revered for the many things it gives mankind, the male of the species has helped till the land of farmers for thousands of years. Without them good crops would not have been possible. In reverence, each year farmers celebrate Govardhan pooja the day after Deepavali, when prayers are offered to bullocks that are specially decorated for the occasion.

Many animals have provided a mode of transport to mankind. Elephants, horses, mules, camels, yak, reindeer and even the simple donkey have helped mankind in their own way. The sheep gave mankind wool. The silk worm provided silk thread. The bee gives honey. Even the pig did not refrain from providing bristles used in many ways. Living in harmony with animals is an essential part of the Hindu way of life.

One of the most important qualities of animals is to give their masters love. Just as mankind utilised animals for their development and welfare, animals have responded with love and devotion. Sages and saints could live deep in the solitude of thick forests because of the company of animals like the deer, cows, goats, sheep and even smaller animals like squirrels. Even birds provided love and care for the little they would eat.

What is the Hindu belief about the animal world within the earth?

If there is a world with mankind and animals that they can see, Hindus believe there is yet another place known as heaven where the gods reside. They look forward to go there after death. There is yet another world deep within the earth that one cannot see. In the **Shrimad Bhagwat Mahapuran** it is described as Patallok. Sheshnaag is the master of this world. Within Patallok there are other abodes known as Ataal, Vitaal, Sataal, Talataal, Mahataal and Rasataal. Within these abodes there are smaller cities known as *puris*. Like heaven they have their residences, gardens and parks. Since gods like Surya and Chandrama do not reside here, there is no light, or differentiation as in day and night. Just like on earth, one finds qualities like passion, enjoyment, splendour, contentment and magnificence. Within these abodes reside demons, ogres, insects and reptiles. It is here that the master of Naaglok, Vasuki resides.

According to Sri Sukhdev, deep within Patallok, Sheshnaag of a thousand heads resides. On the heads of Sheshnaag the earth rests. Whenever Sheshnaag is disappointed or irritated, he opens his three eyes and appears with 11 Rudra tridents causing havoc on earth.

In the **Mahabharata**, Bhisma, 67/13, it is said:

शेषं चाकल्पयद्देवमनन्तं विश्वरूपिणम् ।
यो धारयति भूतानि धरां चेमां सपर्वताम् ॥

The Supreme Spirit created godlike Sheshnaag who is omnipresent and eternal. On his head rests the whole world along with the mountains, the sea and the atmosphere.

The thousand-headed snake Sheshnaag is the king of snakes. He reclines to provide a bed to Lord Vishnu who finds great comfort sleeping there. Sheshnaag is most faithful and devoted and has taken incarnation with Lord Vishnu whenever necessary. Lakshman and Balram are said to be incarnations of Sheshnaag.

In the **Bhagavad Gita**, 10/28, Sri Krishna says:

अनन्तश्चास्मि नागानाम् ।

Amongst snakes, I am Sheshnaag.

What is the significance of prayers offered by Hindus when laying the foundations of new buildings?

With the Hindu belief that the earth rests upon the head of Sheshnaag who resides deep within, and disasters occur when he is displeased, to appease him it is customary to bury a silver snake in the foundation whenever a new house is built. It is believed that the house rests upon the head of the snake.

Since Sheshnaag resides in Kshirsagar, during foundation laying prayers are offered to him in a *kalash* (vessel) that contains milk, curd and ghee. He is invited for the ceremony and prayers offered so that he may bear the weight of the house on his head and protect it from calamities. Since the *kalash* is symbolic of Lord Vishnu, it is customary to drop a coin (symbolic of Lakshmi) into it. In this way the blessings of gods and the animal world are invoked for happiness and contentment.

Thus, one can appreciate the Hindu view of holding not only the gods and mankind, but also the entire universe in reverence.

Your questions answered...

Why do most Hindus prefer vegetarian food to non-vegetarian fare?

The human body is evolved to live better on vegetarian food. Those with Rajguna and Tamguna attributes prominent among them are attracted to non-vegetarian food. We cannot overlook that non-vegetarian food involves violence – the killing of animals. With killing of animals the concept of thoughtfulness of others ends. This halts spiritual development. Besides, with animal flesh one consumes a variety of chemicals. This is harmful for the human body.

Why do Hindus consider the human form of life most valuable?

Life as a human being is the greatest gift God could give anyone. Saints and ascetics, thinkers and the intelligent common man have confirmed this repeatedly. To waste this life is the greatest folly anyone could make.

It is believed that one takes on the body of a human being only after 84 lakh births. There are 30 lakh births in plant life, 27 lakh in the insect world, 14 lakh as birds, 9 lakh as fish and 4 lakh as other animals. Religious texts confirm how difficult it is to be endowed with the human form.

In the **Chanakya Niti**, 14/3, it is said:

पुनर्वितं पुनर्मित्रं पुनर्भार्या पुनर्मही ।
एतत्सर्वं पुनर्लभ्यं न शरीरं पुनः पुनः ॥

If wealth is lost, it can be recovered. Friends who are angry or away can return to you. New friends can be made. If the wife is away or leaves you or dies, one can marry again. Land, a home, your homeland can be regained again and again. But one cannot attain the form of a human being again.

Sri Ram explains the importance of the human form by saying:

बड़े भाग मानुष तन पावा । सुर दुर्लभ सबग्रंथन गावा ॥

It is great fortune to attain the human form. All religious texts confirm that the human form is difficult to attain even by the gods.

नरक स्वर्ग अपवर्ग नसेनी । ग्यान विराग भगति सुभ देनी ॥

The human form is a steppingstone to hell, heaven or eternal salvation. Through it one can attain knowledge, detachment and devotion.

नर तन भव वारिधि कहुं बेरो । सन्मुख मरुत अनुग्रह मेरो ॥

The human body is a ship in the vast ocean of life. My favours are like the breeze that pushes the boat.

साधन धाम मोच्छ कर द्वारा । पाइ न जेहिं परलोक संवारा ॥

The human body is a medium to carry one to the gateway of salvation. If one is unable to utilise the opportunity to attain the higher self, it can only be termed unfortunate.

The form of a human being is considered outstanding because it is only in this form that one can find salvation from rebirths. This can be achieved through devotion to God and good actions.

Think it over…

The good is one thing, the pleasant another; these two, having different objects, chain a man. It is well with him who clings to the good; he who chooses the pleasant, misses his end.

The good and pleasant approach man: the wise goes around them and distinguishes each. The wise prefers the good to the pleasant, but the fool chooses the pleasant through greed and avarice.

–Upanishads

How are Hindus expected to make their life worthwhile?

To live a holistic life one needs both faith and devotion. Faith is having complete trust or confidence. It is a strong belief in religion. Devotion is love and loyalty. It is religious worship of the Supreme Spirit that guides the world and us. With this guidance we can make the best of our human form.

There are many references to faith and devotion in religious texts.

In the **Chanakya Sutra**, 234, it is said:

धर्मेण धार्यते लोकः ।

This world rests upon the religion of righteousness.

In the **Vaishoshik Shastra**, 1/1/2, it is said:

यतोऽभ्युदयनिःश्रेयससिद्धिः स धर्मः ।

The conducting of rituals and customs that take us towards our cherished goals in this world, and the next, must be faithfully adopted.

In the **Rig-Veda**, 8/3/13, it is said:

सुगां ऋतस्य पंथा ।

The path of faith and devotion brings happiness and protects one from grief.

In the **Mahabharata**, Vanparv, 263/44, it is said:

धर्मनित्यास्तु ये केचिन्न ते सीदन्ति कर्हिचित् ।

Those who have faith and devotion shall always be protected from misfortune.

In the **Chanakya Sutra**, it is said:

सुखस्य मूलं धर्मः ।

Faith and devotion are the price for happiness.

धर्मो माता पिता चैव धर्मो बन्धुः सुहृत्तथा ।
धर्मः   स्वर्गस्य   धर्मात्स्वर्गमवाप्यते ॥

Faith is the mother. Faith is the father. Faith is the brother and faithful friend. Faith is the path to heaven. Through faith alone heaven can be attained.

धारयते जनैरिति धर्मः ।

Whatever a person adopts and practises is faith and religion.

In the **Chanakya Niti**, 13/9, it is said:

जीवन्तं मृतवन्मन्ये देहिनं धर्मवर्जितम् ।
यतो धर्मेण संयुक्तो दीर्घजीवी न संशयः ॥

A person without faith is like a dead person. One who has faith lives after death. There is no doubt about it. Fame and glory survive death. Such people are long lived.

In the **Mahabharata**, Shantiparv, it is said that faith is the price one pays for being a human being. Faith, like the celestial nectar, grants immortality to gods in heaven. Those who practise faith find eternal happiness even in death.

In the **Mahabharata**, Swargarohan, 5/63, it is said:

न जातु कामान्न भयान्न लोभाद् धर्मं त्यजेज्जीवितस्यापि हेतोः ।
नित्यो धर्मः सुखदुःखे त्वनित्ये जीवो नित्यो हेतुरस्य त्वनित्यः ॥

At no time in life should one sacrifice faith on account of work, because of fear, greed or even the risk of life. Faith is eternal. Happiness, sorrow and grief are not. A human being is eternal. Life is not.

In the **Manusmriti**, 6/92, it is said:

धृतिः क्षमा दमोऽस्तेयं शौचमिन्द्रियनिग्रहः ।
धीर्विद्या सत्यमक्रोधो दशकं धर्मलक्षणम् ॥

Patience, forgiveness, control over the mind, righteousness, purity of body and mind, control over the senses, wisdom, knowledge, truth and control over anger are ten symbols of faith. Their practise makes an individual healthy and happy. Their practise also keeps the family and society happy.

In the **Valmiki Ramayan**, Arunyakand, 9/30, it is said:

धर्मादर्थं प्रभवति धर्मात्प्रभवते सुखम् ।
धर्मेण लभते सर्वं धर्मसारमिदं जगत् ॥

With faith one attains wealth. With faith happiness grows. With faith one can attain everything. In this world faith is the essence of life.

In the **Mahabharata**, Anushasanparv, there is a story related to faith.

In the Himalayas, once when Shiva was in meditation, Parvati approached him and inquired, "Lord, what is the best form of faith? How can those people who have no religion practise it?"

Shiva responded, "Devi, not killing living things, being truthful, having compassion for all living things, having control over the mind and the senses, giving charity according to one's ability, together these comprise the religion of a householder. Being faithful to one's wife and family, keeping away from a woman who is not the wife, looking after what is in your trust and protecting women, not stealing, avoiding meat and liquor, these are the five secrets of faith. One attains happiness through them. Those who have faith must practise these things."

Your questions answered...

Why is it difficult to develop faith and devotion even when we know it is good for us?

Human nature is such that we accept what we like, and find faults with what we do not like. Our likes and dislikes depend upon inherent tendencies brought from our last life. When we give in to these easily, they get strengthened. Only when we think and analyse what is good and what is not, and decide upon a line of positive action, can we overcome our inherent tendencies and rise in life.

What role do rites and rituals play in the Hindu way of life?

A rite is a formal or ceremonial act or procedure prescribed or customary in religious or other solemn use. It can also be referred to as a customary observance or practice. On the other hand, a ritual is a religious or solemn ceremony that involves a series of actions performed according to a set order.

Hindu traditions aim at developing individuals who follow good habits, people who practise rites and rituals that promote happiness. From the social point of view, personal welfare, happiness and recognition are important in life. The purpose of human life is not restricted to eating, drinking or being merry. Sages and saints have described material progress as secondary. The real purpose of life is spiritual knowledge and growth. To achieve this aim, one should prepare to learn rites and rituals that have stood the test of time.

In the Vedas, Puranas and other religious texts, rites and rituals are described pertaining to life from the time a child is conceived, born, grows into an adult and finally dies. Through these rites and rituals an individual is able to understand life better, as well as overcome obstacles and problems. One develops Hindu *sanskars*, a magnetic personality and finds contentment in life.

In the **Gautam Dharmsutra** it is said that rites and rituals help overcome weaknesses and develop strengths.

In the **Brahmsutra Bhasya**, 1/1/4, Shankaracharya has said:

संस्कारो हि नाम संस्कार्यस्य गुणाधानेन वा स्याद्दोषापनयनेन वा ।

The actions that project one's strengths and eliminate weaknesses are termed sanskars, rites and rituals.

According to Maharishi Charak:

संस्कारो हि गुणान्तराधानमुच्यते ।

Sanskars aim at the addition of abilities and virtues in individuals and things.

In the **Sanskar Vidhi**, it is written:

जन्मना जायते शूद्रः संस्काराद् द्विज उच्यते ।

By birth everyone is crude and ignorant. Through sanskars one takes up responsible positions.

According to saints and sages an individual is influenced by deeds, misdeeds and unfulfilled desires in earlier births. The person who takes rebirth selects parents through whom unfulfilled desires can be attained. Even the activities one selects are in harmony with the influences and desires of earlier births. In this way every individual is a slave to past actions.

According to the **Meemansa Darshankar**:

कर्मबीजं संस्कारः ।

Sanskar is the seed of action.

तन्निमित्ता सृष्टिः ।

The beginning of the world depends upon it.

The behaviour of every individual is influenced by *sanskars* of earlier lives. Besides these, one is also influenced by *sanskars* of the family in this life.

One is more easily attracted towards what is pleasurable than what is good. Due to this human weakness, mankind is often overcome by physical, mental and emotional distress. This results in lack of culture and character. Mankind has great capacity to rationalise or cover up shortcomings. Therefore it is important that good habits be developed through adoption of appropriate rites and rituals.

Traditional rites and rituals have a definite influence upon individuals. The activities involved while performing rites and rituals may include yagya, chanting mantras, special offerings and group participation, which are based upon scientific principles. Scientists acknowledge the influence of sound and music, colour, magnetic vibrations and learning to concentrate. There is no doubt about the effect of rites and rituals. Good actions promote good habits. Even psychologists admit that a person learns good things quickly when directed by good people in the correct environment.

The conscious mind controls the bulk of everyday activities. The unconscious mind looks after the more subtle and finer activities. The conscious mind collects impressions and influences from the outside world. However, the unconscious mind sorts the information and builds memories. Depending upon the kind of impressions and influences one gathers from the environment, the subconscious mind gradually transforms itself accordingly. A skilful and efficient mind renders the best support and service to the soul. It is not possible to awaken the soul without a knowledgeable and pure mind.

During rites and rituals a priest invokes the blessings of deities. When individuals experience the kindness of gods and are emotionally touched during the yagya and other activities, the mind gets charged with religious feelings gradually. The importance of the occasion, the enthusiasm, the purity of the place, an emotional oath by the individual, the presence of the family, relatives and friends together add up to create a special kind of mental state. Activities during rituals leave an indelible impression upon the individual. This impression specially influences and educates the mind.

The effect of the ceremonies depends upon the atmosphere on the occasion and the way it is conducted. The many activities during a marriage ceremony may individually mean nothing. But when the bride and the groom experience them and take oaths to stand by each other, the many activities together bind the couple to a lifelong union.

Hindus observe a variety of rites and rituals. The **Gautam Smriti** mentions that there are 40 rituals. Some religious texts place this figure at 48. According to Maharishi Angira, there are 25 rituals. As per the **Dus Karma Padhati** there are 10 rituals.

Maharishi Vedavyas has described 16 important rituals in **Vyassmriti**, 1/13-15.

गर्भाधानं पुंसवनं सीमांतो जातकर्म च ।
नामक्रियानिष्क्रमणेऽन्नशनं वपनं क्रिया ॥
कर्णवेधो व्रतादेशो वेदारम्भक्रियाविधिः ।
केशांतः स्नानमुद्बाहो विवाहाग्निपरिग्रहः ॥
त्रेताग्निसंग्रहश्चेति संस्काराः षोडश स्मृताः ।

The **Karma Mimansha Darshan** in the Vedas recognises 16 rituals. Modern scholars have tried to simplify these and make their observance inexpensive so that more people can benefit. Of these, eight pertain to worldly affairs and the other eight to the path of salvation. Each ritual has its own importance and influence. When these rituals are conducted according to specific procedures on the right occasion and in an appropriate atmosphere, they ensure extraordinary results. So their importance can well be appreciated.

Think it over...

Good nature is the beauty of the mind, and like personal beauty, wins almost without anything else – sometimes, indeed, in spite of positive deficiencies.

–Jonas Hanway, English traveller and philanthropist (1712–1786)

What attributes influence the Hindu way of life?

According to Hindu belief, every individual is possessed of three attributes or *gunas* – *Satogun, Rajogun* and *Tamogun*. These are the driving forces within an individual.

Satogun is synonymous with being virtuous and denotes the qualities of goodness and purity. Rajogun is fondness for sensual enjoyment or pleasure. Tamogun represents qualities of darkness and ignorance. The religious texts explain that while Satogun is represented by the colour white, Rajogun is represented by red and Tamogun by black.

The **Bhagavad Gita** elaborates on the three gunas. In Chapter 18 it explains that those possessed with Satogun are free from attachment, firm, vigorous and not affected by either success or failure. They have control over their ego. Those possessed with Rajogun are attached to enjoyment and seek the fruits of whatever they do. Greedy and aggressive, their conduct is not always virtuous. Both joy and sorrow influence them. Those possessed with Tamogun lack self-control, are arrogant, deceitful, uncultured and given to procrastination.

The **Bhagavad Gita** explains that these three gunas affect every aspect of a person's life – thoughts, feelings, actions, knowledge, intellect, joy and even renunciation. Every individual reacts in harmony with the gunas possessed. No one is free from this. Not even the gods.

It is also explained that everyone possesses a mixture of the three gunas. If there is more of Satogun in comparison to the other two gunas, one is referred to as Satoguni. In the same way one could be Rajoguni or Tamoguni. It is said that in Lord Vishnu, Satogun prevailed. In Brahma, Rajogun prevailed, just as Tamogun prevailed in Shiva.

When one is able to interpret one's temperament on the basis of the knowledge of the three gunas, one can learn how to live a balanced life. One thereby understands why he/she behaves in a particular manner and can then gradually grow emotionally and spiritually.

Why is the Hindu caste system often criticised?

Due to misinterpretations and wrong guidance there are many misgivings about caste and community amongst Hindus.

In the **Bhagavad Gita**, Sri Krishna has said that mankind is divided into four castes (categories) according to their abilities and activities. This has been misinterpreted by dividing individuals according to their lineage and family, which is wrong. People in the same family can be endowed with different abilities. The activity too is a matter of choice, not of birth. One must be included in a caste on the basis of ability and activity. Doing otherwise is wrong.

In order to organise the world so that each individual does what is in harmony with personal capabilities, society has been divided into four castes – Brahmin, Kshatriya, Vaish and Shudra. Each is based on the kind of work done by an individual.

In the **Mahabharata**, Shantiparv, 188/11–15, it is said that the division is not based upon any physical differences between individuals. They have the same kind of body and blood. They eat the same kind of food and inhale the same air. Even their excretions are not different. When Brahma created mankind, everyone was made a Brahmin. Everyone was virtuous.

With time and degeneration of the mind and activities people moved into other castes. A Brahmin who is princely, passionate, courageous and intelligent but has a sharp temperament that gives in to emotions like anger has been described a Kshatriya. A Brahmin who

88

protects the cow, but earns a livelihood from agriculture or business is Vaish. Those who love violence, falsehood and are greedy and selfish, and live by doing menial jobs are called Shudra.

In this way, on the basis of differences in abilities, activities and temperament, Brahmins have been classified into castes. Noble actions and activities based upon religious thought are prescribed for all castes. None are prohibited from them. All the four castes have free access to knowledge.

In the **Mahabharata**, Shantiparv, 188/10, it is said that since all castes have their birth in Brahma, it would be wrong to make differentiation about any being higher or lower.

When a father is blessed with four sons, all of them belong together. In the same way, when the four castes are born of the same father, Brahma, all have equal importance. Any differentiation on the basis of caste is wrong and must be condemned.

In **Manusmriti**, it is said:

जन्मना जायते शूद्रः संस्कारादु द्विज उच्यते ।
वेदाभ्यासी भवेद्विप्रः ब्रह्म जानाति स ब्राह्मणः ॥

All are born pure. They are differentiated on the basis of their sanskars, their abilities and activities. One who follows the Vedas is a Brahmin. One who knows Brahma is also a Brahmin.

In the **Rig-Veda**, 5/60/5, it is said that there is no difference amongst people at birth. None is big or small. All are equal. All must be united in pursuing their goals. Any differentiation on the basis of caste is groundless. There is no religious sanctity. Any kind of untouchability between castes is a slur on humanity. God is influenced by one's action, not by caste.

Bhagat Rae Das has said:

जाति-पांति पूछे नहीं कोई । हरि को भजै सो हरि का होई ॥

God belongs to whoever is devoted to Him. He does not belong to any caste.

Your questions answered...

Why do good people suffer?

It is only the good and noble people who have the capacity to suffer. Most people break down under adversity. Suffering is a way to balance one's good and bad deeds. Once the account is balanced, the suffering ends.

Why do Hindus accord great importance to good and bad deeds?

Amongst Hindus great significance is attached to *karmphal*, the fruit of one's deeds. It is believed that whatever one achieves is the fruit of the person's deeds. The basis of profit and loss, success and failure, happiness and sorrow are one's deeds.

In the **Brahmvaivartpuran**, 37/16, it is said:

नाभुक्तं क्षीयते कर्म कल्पकोटिशतैरपि ।
अवश्यमेव भोक्तव्यं कृतं कर्म शुभाशुभम् ॥

Even with the passing of endless years an individual cannot be free from the fruits of deeds. Whatever be the deeds, good or bad, one has to face the consequences definitely.

In the **Yogvashisth**, 3/95/34, it is said:

ऐहिकं प्राक्तनं वापि कर्म यद्रुकिचं स्फुरत ।
पौरुषोऽसौ परो यत्नो न कदाचन निष्फलः ॥

The effect of deeds of the previous and the present birth definitely bear fruit. No effort made by mankind goes without bearing fruit.

In the **Ramayana**, Ayodhyakand, Devguru Brihaspati referring to the ethical acts of Sri Ram tells Lord Indra:

कर्म प्रधान विस्व करि राखा ।
जो जस करै सो तस फल चाखा ॥
काहु न कोउ सुख-दुख कर दाता ।
निज कृत करम भोग सब भ्राता ॥

In this universe deeds are of paramount importance. Whatever a person does, one is rewarded or punished accordingly. In this world no one can give sorrow or happiness to another. Everyone experiences the fruits of one's own deeds.

Eminent sages and saints, the devoted and the knowledgeable, emperors, kings, capable persons, the brave and courageous have all had to experience the fruits of their own deeds. Sri Ram was exiled to the forest for 14 years. Ravana kidnapped Sita. The mighty Bhim had to serve as a cook. The renowned Emperor Nala had to leave his dear wife Damyanti in a forest and serve as a charioteer to King Rituparn. Emperor Harish Chandra had to serve as a menial in a cremation ground. Draupadi had to serve as a maid. Even mighty Arjun took up the guise of a eunuch to teach dancing to Emperor Viratraj's daughter. None can escape the fruit of their deeds.

Why is it that one cannot escape the fruit of deeds? Deeds can be good and virtuous. They can also be bad or sinful. It is believed that there are ten kinds of sins. Of these, violence (murder), stealing and adultery are deeds by the physical self. Telling lies, speaking harshly and speaking ill of another are sins committed by speech. Thoughts of tormenting, oppressing or hurting others, finding faults with the virtuous and having ill feelings for innocent are sins committed by the mind. By indulging in these one creates problems for others and for oneself. They mean unhappiness for everyone.

In the **Skandpuran**, Kedar, 1, it is said:

अष्टादशपुराणेषु व्यासस्य वचनद्वयम् ।
परोपकारः पुण्याय पापाय परपीडनम् ॥

In the 18 Puranas by Vedavyas, two things are significant – thoughtfulness of others is a virtue and to hurt others is a sin. One must act keeping in view that one is vulnerable to both.

The same truth has been confirmed by Tulsidas in simpler words:

परहित सरिस धर्म नहिं भाई । पर पीड़ा सम नहिं अधमाई ॥

In the **Markandeypuran**, Karmphal, 14/25, it is explained that a thorn causes pain at one point only. However, the fruit that emerges from sin keeps pricking both the body and mind constantly.

In the **Parasharsmriti**, it is said that if one commits a sin it should not be concealed. By concealing it, suffering increases. The effect may continue through seven births by making a person a leper, impotent or unhappy. Irrespective whether a sin is small or big, it must be confessed through a religious ceremony. Thereby the sin is eliminated just as disease is cured through medical treatment.

91

In the **Mahabharata**, Vanparv, 207/51, it is said that one who honestly repents having committed a sin is absolved of it. A person who wholeheartedly resolves by saying, "I will not do it again," is protected from committing a sin in the future.

In the **Shivpuran**, 1/3/5, it is said that repentance is the ideal remedy to counter sin. Scholars confirm that through repentance one can be absolved of all sins. When repentance does not work, the only solution is to observe penance.

Those who do not atone for their sins are said to go to hell. Besides, these sins are carried forth to future births and emerge as physical deficiencies. Atonement of sins is necessary for future happiness.

Once a crowd of people were waiting at the gates of heaven to seek admission. Dharmraj was eager to shortlist people to ensure only the deserving entered heaven. To test them he handed two sheets of paper to each. He asked them to list their virtuous deeds on one sheet, and sinful actions on the other. Most exaggerated their virtues and concealed sins. There were a few who confessed sins honestly, and sought forgiveness for them. Dharmraj assessed the deeds of these people, and impressed by their desire to atone for sins, granted them admission into heaven.

Activities that help the progress of society and individuals are virtuous deeds. In all religious texts, thoughtfulness for others has been accepted as a commendable religious act.

Sant Tulsidas has said:

परहित सरिस धर्म नहिं भाई ।

There is no religion better than thoughtfulness for others.

Once Draupadi was bathing in the river Yamuna. She noticed that there was a saint who was also taking bath nearby in the river. A gush of wind came and unfortunately the loincloth of the saint lying on the bank fell into the river and was washed away with the current. The saint did not know what to do. How could he get back to his hermitage without the loincloth? He slipped out of the river and hid in some shrubs near the bank of the river. Draupadi noticed the predicament of the saint. She went near the shrubs, tore a part of her sari and gave it to him to use as a loincloth. The saint was extremely grateful for this act of thoughtfulness. He blessed her in his thoughts.

When Draupadi was brought to Duryodhana's assembly to be publicly insulted by pulling off her clothes, she called out to God for protection. God immediately thought of Draupadi's thoughtfulness when the saint was in a similar situation. God immediately converted the little piece of her sari into an endless sari that protected Draupadi. In this way, God protected her modesty.

What is the influence of heaven and hell on the Hindu way of life?

The mention of heaven and hell has a significant effect on the lives of Hindus. Other religions too give importance to the existence of heaven and hell. This means that people pass either through heaven or hell in between their death and rebirth. The description of heaven is such that everyone would like to go there. Hell is a place everyone shuns.

In the **Garudapuran**, it is said that in Yamlok (abode of the God of Death), the god Chitragupta maintains a record of the good and bad deeds of every individual. On the basis of this record one is sent to heaven if the good deeds predominate or to hell if it is the other way round.

Heaven is the abode of gods. Everyone finds happiness there. Lord Indra is the master of heaven. The happiness in heaven is not like the pleasures one experiences through the senses. The happiness is deep-seated within an individual. It is the happiness experienced when one is in complete control of the mind, feelings and the ego. It is far superior to pleasures derived from the senses.

The religious texts assert that those who are compassionate towards all living beings, are charitable and soft-spoken, who look at women as a mother, sister or daughter, are not attracted to ill-gotten wealth, do not steal, are content with what they possess, are truthful and free of jealousy, do not hurt anyone and look kindly towards everyone qualify for the happiness of heaven.

Wise people say that when one is endowed with positive qualities, there is heaven on earth for them.

Once God announced that for one week the admission to heaven would not be restricted to the assessment of good and bad deeds. It would be open to all without reservation. As people heard this, they rushed to heaven and there was a long queue awaiting admission at the gates.

As God was returning home soon after the announcement, he noticed a man carrying a load of firewood on his head walking towards his home. He hummed a tune as he walked home unmindful of the attractive announcement. Surprised, God stopped him and asked, "Have you not heard the announcement about unrestricted entry to heaven?"

The man, happy and content as he was, responded with a smile, "Sir, I have heard about the generous offer made by God. But to be honest, I experience the happiness of heaven in the laughing faces of my children, in the loving nature of my faithful wife, in the spirit of support and care from my brothers and the friendly gestures of my neighbours. When I have this heaven, why do I need to seek another heaven that I have not seen?"

93

Hell is a place where a person is confronted with sorrow. Those who go to hell experience constant hurt and pain. It is believed there are seven hells close to Yamlok. Hell has been described as a horrible and frightening place. The religious texts say that those who are lustful, hypocritical, ungrateful, adulterous, unscrupulous, and uncaring of orphans, the weak, the sick and the aged face the sorrows of hell.

In the **Bhagavad Gita** it is said that there are three gateways to hell – lust, anger and greed.

Gods and persons of virtue, although entitled to heaven on earth, often accept hell so that they can comfort others in distress.

Yudhistra qualified for one day in hell and 100 years in heaven. When asked where he would like to go first, he opted for hell. When he went to hell, the people there found great comfort from the fragrance that emanated from his virtuous body. With his virtues Yudhistra made a heaven out of hell for those people. That is the influence of good over bad.

Think it over...

A good man is influenced by God himself, and has a kind of divinity within him; so it is open to question whether he goes to heaven, or heaven comes to him.

–Lucius Seneca, Roman Stoic philosopher (4 BC?–AD 65)

What four stages of life does every Hindu pass through?

An important belief of Hindus is that there are four stages, or *ashrams*, of life every individual passes through. These stages are clearly defined. When one understands the four stages and how to respond to the changing circumstances in life, one can comprehend life in greater depth and achieve much more.

The first stage of life is termed **Brahmacharya ashram**. This extends from birth until the 25th year and is the period of celibacy. The religious texts direct that this period be utilised to prepare one to be a good person. Through prescribed sanskars good habits must be inculcated and the period dedicated to educational effort. One must study under the guidance of a guru.

Over millennia, circumstances have changed. The original Gurukul has given way to schools, colleges and universities. However, the needs have remained the same. Now there are several teachers and professors who play the guru's role. The purpose of education too has remained the same. One needs to prepare for a career to earn one's livelihood to support oneself and the family.

The second stage of the life is termed the **Grihasth ashram**. This extends from the 25th year until the 50th year. In this stage young men and women marry and raise a family. This is the householder's life and perhaps the most difficult stage when a person needs to interact with a variety of people and situations. Raising a good happy family is in itself a challenging task. On one hand, a person needs to build a lifelong relationship with the spouse who may hail from an altogether different background. On the other, there is the problem of raising

95

a new generation of children with rising needs and expectations. The professional life is no less challenging. One has to cope with both seniors and subordinates and also develop relationships in society. These relationships eventually influence the position and respect one enjoys in life.

The third stage is termed the **Vanprasth ashram**. This extends from the 50th year until the 75th year. At this stage it is expected that children born from wedlock have grown up and found a place in society. Daughters would be married and sons will have entered into a career and be well on their way to the *Grihasth ashram.*

At this stage, while children are gradually detaching themselves from parents, it is expected that parents too will slowly detach themselves from the householder's responsibilities and spend time in preparing for a new life. It is believed God grants the human form to a person as a reward for past good deeds. It is in this form that an individual can strive to freedom from the shackles of rebirths. This begins with gradual detachment from the family and worldly possessions. To attain this one requires understanding, faith and devotion for the Supreme Spirit that controls the universe.

The fourth stage of life is termed the **Sanyas ashram**. This stage extends from the 75th year until the final emancipation. If the third stage aims at detachment from worldly life, this stage aims at renunciation, asceticism, and abandonment of worldly ties or mundane interests. At this stage, if one is at peace with oneself, he/she makes the final effort to find ultimate freedom from rebirth.

Although Hindu traditions describe the four stages, each stage is not independent of the other. Nor does one stage follow the other automatically. One needs to strive to achieve the objectives of each stage. Only when one stage has been lived well can one strive to achieve similar success in the next stage. Since life is necessarily an interaction between many people and situations, if a person fails to achieve complete success in one stage one can continue to make up for shortcomings and ensure they are not repeated.

If the Hindu way of life has prescribed certain objectives for each stage, it has also given directions on how these can be achieved. Hindu religious texts have solutions to a large variety of needs.

In the chapters that follow many directions given by religious texts are discussed. For easier understanding, rather than discuss the first stage of life, the second stage is discussed first. Marriage is a major event in the life of a young man and woman. From marriage come children, and therefore the upbringing of children (the first stage) is discussed next. The making of a good person is largely the responsibility of parents and teachers, besides the individual. Therefore, the revised order. Finally, there is *Vanprasth* and *Sanyas ashram.*

Why is a Hindu marriage considered an eternal bond?

For Hindus marriage is not just a union between a man and woman with the intention of living as man and wife or simply a physical relationship where a man and a woman live together, bear children and raise a family. It is a much deeper bond. The physical relationship is an essential part of it. Equally important is a deep emotional bond that takes the couple towards spiritual bonding.

It is believed that marriage occurs through destiny and is the building of a relationship between two families, where not only the couple, but the other members of the two families also contribute to make it a wholesome relationship.

According to the **Vedas**, a marriage is a union between two bodies, two minds, two hearts, and two spirits or souls that lovingly resolve to live together just like Shiva and Parvati.

As per Hindu tradition, a marriage is an irrevocable, pure and religious relationship. Through marriage, two individuals sacrifice their independent identities to form a united family where both benefit each other through their abilities and emotional support, just as two wheels carry a vehicle forward with ease. Marriage is a union of two souls. The purpose is not restricted to sensual pleasures that marriage offers but extends to creating the foundation of a home, of having children and raising a family.

In Vedic literature, Rishi Shwetketu has clarified that it was the need for maintaining dignity and propriety of conduct between a man and woman that led to the evolution of the institution of marriage. Since then, it has withstood the test of time.

A Hindu marriage solemnised by chanting popular mantras is referred to as *Brahm vivah* – a union devoted to the eternal spirit. Manu notes the religious importance of such a marriage.

In **Manusmriti**, 3/37, it is said:

दश पूर्वान् परान्वंश्यान् आत्मन् चैक विंशकम् ।
ब्राह्मीपुत्रः सुकृतकृन् मोचये देनसः पितृन् ॥

A son born from a Brahm vivah absolves the sins of 21 generations. This includes 10 generations of the past and 10 generations of the future, and the current generation.

In the **Bhavishyapuran**, it is written that whoever motivates the daughter to marry according to *Brahm vivah* rites, protects seven generations of predecessors and seven generations of successors from hell.

In this context, the **Ashvalayan** said:

तस्यां जातो द्वादशावरान् द्वादश पूर्वान् पुनाति ।

A son born from a couple married according to Brahm vivah rites shall purify 12 generations of predecessors and 12 generations of successors.

According to Hindu literature, there are several ways of getting married. In **Manusmriti**, 3/21, it is written that there are eight kinds of marriages – Brahm (related to the Eternal Spirit), Dev (related to the gods), Aarsh (related to sages), Prajapatya (related to kings), Asur (related to demons), Gandharv (related to the Gandharv community – a love marriage), Rakshas (related to demons and evil spirits) and Paisach (related to Satan). Of these eight, Manu approves the first four and considers others inferior.

Amongst the many benefits of marriage, friendship, companionship, development of emotional maturity, sexual satisfaction, having children, physical and emotional health and long life are the most significant. Besides, the ability to face problems together and the deep sense of attachment that emerges in marriage helps promote happiness. Marriage is indeed the backbone of an orderly life and of society.

Your questions answered...

What is the difference between human love and divine love?

When a person loves another without any expectations in return, it is divine love. All other kinds of love can be described as human love.

Why do Hindus attach special importance to the selection of partners?

Amongst Hindus it is a firm belief that marriage partners should not be from the same family. To ensure that the man and woman are not from the same *gotra* (lineage or ancestry), it is customary to check the *gotra* before marriage. Religious texts say marriages within the family are irreligious, condemnable and sinful.

It is suggested that five generations from the maternal side and seven from the paternal side must be avoided in marriage. Only marriages beyond these are considered proper. When the partners are closely related, children born thereof do not develop normally. It is due to inbreeding that animals and birds have not developed substantially.

Genetics confirms this belief. When parents are closely related, recessive genes that control undesirable characteristics dominate in the children, causing improper development. In contrast, when the man and the woman hail from different families and lineages, the children are strong, healthy and normal.

In the **Manusmriti**, 3/5, it is said:

असपिण्डा च या मातुरसगोत्रा च या पितुः ।
सा प्रशस्ता द्विजातीनां दारकर्मणि मैथुने ॥

When the man and woman do not belong to six generations from the maternal side and also do not come from the father's lineage, marriage between the two is good.

Scientists have confirmed that children born of closely related parents are prone to deformities as well as health and emotional problems. The incidence of these problems is greater in such couples than in those who hail from different ancestries. Incidents of abortions, pregnancy-related problems, stillborn children, heart problems and those related to sight are also higher. By ensuring that men and women from the same ancestry do not marry, the incidence of twin births can also be reduced, which is much greater in rural areas than in urban ones.

Your questions answered...

What is the basis of lasting marital happiness?

Marital happiness is an attitude of the mind. When a person is committed to the relationship and seeks harmony to build a family, one finds happiness. When one thinks otherwise, there is unhappiness. This way the happiness is dependent upon individual thoughts, reactions and attitudes. When the couple is committed to the relationship, emotional bonds grow, and one finds lasting marital happiness.

Does comparing horoscopes help find compatible partners?

Since Hindus believe that a child's destiny depends upon the configuration of the nine planets at the time and place of birth, it is commonplace to have a horoscope made soon after birth. The effect of the planets on the marital life of the individual is also indicated in the horoscope. Therefore, many families compare the horoscopes of the prospective bride and groom.

In astrology, marital compatibility is based on eight parameters:

1. *Varna* refers to ego development. It carries one mark.
2. *Vashya* refers to the intensity of mutual attraction and affection. It carries two marks.
3. *Tara/Din* refers to the health and well-being of the couple. It carries three marks.
4. *Yoni* refers to biological compatibility and satisfaction. It carries four marks.
5. *Graha Maitri* refers to outlook, objective, intellectual level and spiritual plane of existence. It carries five marks.
6. *Gana* refers to temperamental characteristics. It carries six marks.
7. *Bhakut* refers to family welfare. It carries seven marks.
8. *Nadi* refers to outside appearance and health. It carries eight marks.

The eight parameters together carry 36 marks, or *gunas* as they are called in astrology. The parameters balance each other. When the two horoscopes are compared, a minimum of 18 gunas is necessary for a match to be declared compatible. The more the gunas scored, the better the outlook. Sometimes the horoscopes may predict total incompatibility.

With computerisation in every field of life, the matching of horoscopes can now also be done on the computer if the software is available. In most cases, the matching is satisfactory. However, when in doubt, particularly if one of the persons has a malefic Mangal, it is advisable to consult one who specialises in Astrology.

What is the importance of the Roka and Sagai ceremonies?

When two families agree that the young man should marry the young lady, the very next step is to perform the *roka* or *rokna* ceremony. The literal translation of the word *rok* is to *stop* or *halt*, and the word *rokna* means to *ban, prohibit, prevent* or *hinder*. In order to publicly ban a further search for a suitable match by either family, the *roka* ceremony is performed.

It is a simple ceremony where the girl's family may present a token gift in cash or kind, along with some sweets to the young man. Similarly, his family reciprocates this gesture. In some families, the two may exchange rings. The ceremony may be conducted between the two families, and announced amongst relatives and friends.

As for *sagai*, the literal translation is *betrothal ceremony*. It is a formal contract between the two families and more elaborate than the earlier ceremony. A Brahmin priest may conduct the ceremony. He first directs a prayer to Lord Ganesh followed by a prayer to the *Navgrah*, or nine planets. The prayer to Lord Ganesh seeks blessings so that there may be no obstacles. The prayer to the *Navgrah* seeks their blessings and benevolence. The young lady's brother then applies *tilak* on the young man's forehead and gives him sweets and gifts. Initially, jaggery (brown unrefined sugar) was given at the ceremony. With time, jaggery has been replaced by sweets. Gifts are given to the young man and relatives.

The young man's family presents clothes to the young lady. In some families, jewellery is also presented. The relatives of the young man may present gifts in cash or kind to the young lady. The ceremony completed, refreshments are served to all those present. A date for the wedding may be announced.

What ceremonies are performed at a Hindu wedding?

The marriage ceremony may vary in detail between different Hindu communities. However, despite regional variations and differences in languages, food and habits, the basic essentials of a Hindu wedding are common.

On the day of the wedding there is the ceremony of *Mangal Snan* for both the young man and lady. The word *Mangal* mean *auspicious* and *snan* denotes *bath.* It is customary to apply turmeric and sandalwood paste on their face and body. Turmeric has medicinal qualities and sandalwood is cooling. This is symbolic of preparing the two to look attractive to each other. Although a beauty parlour now does the needful, most Hindu communities follow the ceremony in detail.

Most girls like to adorn their hands and feet with *mehndi*, or henna paste. In many families, all ladies in the family apply henna. The ceremony is light and informal, with more singing than any serious rituals.

In some Hindu communities, the maternal uncle adorns the bride with a set of bangles on the day of the wedding. Earlier, these bangles were made of ivory, but plastic has now replaced ivory. The bangles are symbolic of the blessings from the maternal family. The bride may continue to wear these for several months after the wedding. The old bangles that the bride takes off are distributed to her unmarried friends. It is believed that by wearing these bangles they will get married soon.

At this ceremony, it is also customary for the maternal uncle and maternal grandfather to give gifts to the bride, the parents and other family members. In many communities it is called the *Bhath* ceremony. This was initially provided for so that women could derive some benefit from the wealth of their parents. In ancient times, girls were married young and were dependent upon support from the husband or his family. But the sons inherited wealth from parents. To balance the situation, support was ensured to girls through gifts from the maternal family.

With time, laws have been enacted to ensure equal rights to both sons and daughters. However, most religious ceremonies continue as per tradition.

Why is a wedding procession taken to the bride's place?

It is customary for the bridegroom to go to the bride's place in a procession. A band leads the procession and the groom is dressed in the finest clothes and rides a well-decorated horse. An attendant carries an umbrella over his head, as relatives and friends dance all the way. Despite changing times and the availability of cars, young people continue to be fascinated with this traditional ritual. This custom perhaps fulfils the young lady's dream of a prince charming on a white horse coming to take her away.

Prior to this, there is a short ceremony where the young man wears a turban, crown and *sehra* (nuptial headwear) with the blessings of all elders and relatives. The *sehra* may be made of flowers or decorative thread-work and serves two purposes. First, it covers the face of the groom like a veil and protects him from the evil eye. Second, it is humorously stated that the *sehra* reminds him that his search for a life partner is over and a veil across his face indicates he should not look at any other lady!

It is also customary to recite a poetic blessing for the groom, preparing him for the new life he is about to enter. This recitation is also known as *sehra*.

On arrival at the bride's place, the bride's brothers and relatives formally welcome the groom. Finally the bride and groom welcome each other by exchanging garlands. It is customary for the groom's parents to first offer a meal to the groom and the bride before everyone begins to eat. The formal marriage ceremony is conducted at the appointed hour declared auspicious by the priest.

Why is tying of the knot an important part of the Hindu wedding?

A knot literally means fastening together two ends of a string, rope or something similar. In the same way, when Hindus talk of *gathbandhan* in marriage, it means bringing together two individuals by symbolically tying the loose ends of their scarf and veil, or other clothing. From two individuals – two bodies and two minds – they become a single entity through marriage.

Tying of the knot also symbolises that the two are tied for a common purpose. It is desired that they shall remember this throughout life. It is also expected that in pursuing the common cause each shall supplement the efforts of the other. Therefore, tying the knot symbolises an irrevocable relationship.

Before tying of the knot, the parents of the bride formally hand her over in marriage to the groom. This is known as *Kanya Daan*. The word *kanya* means a *girl* or *daughter*, and *daan* denotes *charity*. Together the words mean *giving away the daughter in charity*. Amongst Hindus this is considered a noble form of charity. The parents feel proud of this action, which is an important responsibility for every householder. Those who are not blessed with a daughter often help people during the marriages of their daughter so that they can benefit from the deed of marrying a daughter.

Just as it is virtuous to give away a daughter in marriage, Hindus believe that the one who takes the girl in charity incurs a debt by accepting her. To repay this debt it is customary for the groom's parents to give charity for a good cause through the groom. Tying of the knot follows this.

When tying the knot it is customary to tie a coin, flower, turmeric, durva grass and rice within the knot. Each of these has a particular significance.

A coin is symbolic of money. Tying it in the knot signifies that neither shall be independent in controlling the family finances. It will be a joint responsibility and both shall have equal control over money.

A flower symbolises goodwill, contentment, joy, happiness and companionship. One must complement the other.

Turmeric has medicinal qualities. It is symbolic of a teacher. It also symbolises the need for the physical and emotional health of each partner. One should not let down or hurt the other.

Durva grass is evergreen and symbolic of everlasting love and care. Durva grass never dries up. Even when it looks dried, a little water turns it green. In the same way, there must be great love and intimacy between the couple.

Rice is symbolic of Annapurna, a form of Durga. She is worshipped for her power of giving food. Rice also symbolises that both will consume the food that is earned and brought home, after it is shared equally. It also reminds one of the responsibilities towards the community where one lives. Rice motivates one to follow a common path of mutual welfare.

Even after the wedding, whenever the couple sit together in a religious ceremony, it is customary that a knot is tied between them. This is symbolic of the couple being a single entity, not two separate individuals.

Your questions answered...

In a Hindu marriage, is the husband more important than the wife?

In a Hindu marriage, both the husband and the wife are equally important. Both fulfil different kinds of responsibilities. If you understand the vows that are a part of the Hindu wedding, it would be wrong to label either partner as more important. If some erroneously claim the husband to be more important, that is only because the wife takes on the name of the husband after marriage.

What ceremony fulfils the religious part of a Hindu wedding?

Taking the *pheras* simply means going around the fire. Amongst Hindus it is customary for the couple getting married to go around the fire seven times in a slow formal walk. Sikhs walk around the Guru Granth Sahib. According to the religious texts, it is customary to circumambulate the fire four times. However, many priests now have it done seven times, confusing this with *saptpadi*, which is a separate rite. This ceremony fulfils religious aspects of the marriage and is symbolic of the irrevocable faith a couple must have in each other.

During the ceremony the couple walk around the fire slowly amidst chants of wedding mantras. The two promise that in the presence of Agnidev (the god of fire), parents, relatives and friends they are getting religiously bound in a mutual relationship. They assert that they are morally bound and shall fulfil their promise to the best of their abilities. This ceremony is performed before the fire since it symbolises energy or Surya, the sun. Surya is the soul of the living world and a form of Vishnu. Therefore, when one walks around the fire, it is symbolic of going around with God as witness. Fire has the potential of destroying one's sins through burning. Therefore, marriage is conducted before the fire.

The couple walks clockwise. In the first four rounds, the bride leads and the groom follows. In the final three, the groom leads and the bride follows. The priest reads mantras during each round. At the end of each round the couple halt, repeat the Gayatri mantra, and offer prayers to the fire. During this ceremony the bride leads four times and the groom thrice. It indicates that in all household matters she shall lead, since she is more experienced in this sphere. In professional or vocational fields, the man shall lead because he is more experienced. When both consult each other in matters pertaining to the home and outside and work in unison, they establish a successful family together.

Why is Saptpadi an essential part of the Hindu wedding ceremony?

After going around the fire seven times, the next ceremony is *saptpadi*, literally *the seven steps*. In Hindu law, a marriage is not complete without *saptpadi*. Here, the bride and groom move step by step in unison taking seven steps, with the priest chanting mantras at each step, while the couple take vows and make commitments with the gods, parents and others as witnesses to ensure a lifetime of marital bliss.

The ceremony has a definite purpose. When two people meet they get to know each other. When they walk together they inquire about each other and make firm commitments. The seven steps are symbolic of walking together by a couple. The walk around the fire is equated with walking together. Since *saptpadi* is a requirement of Hindu law for a marriage to be valid, it is symbolised by making seven lines or mounds of rice grains or of turmeric powder. Each line represents a step. With each step the couple dismantles one line with their feet. A particular aspect of life is covered with each step.

With the completion of this ceremony, the groom tells the bride that since her father and mother have now married her before relatives and friends, she should sit on his left side as directed in Hindu religious texts. He further tells her that if she still has any doubts she is welcome to speak out. In response she gets seven points clarified. When both agree, a new step is taken by rubbing off a line.

Step 1: This step refers to the availability of ample food in the home and eating and living together. Food is related to health and welfare. It is important that both must eat wholesome food together.

Step 2: This relates to physical work around the house. Physical effort and co-operation in keeping the family happy is important. Mutual agreement and consultation promote physical and emotional well-being and confidence.

Step 3: It relates to mutual respect and prosperity. Both must co-operate with each other to provide the family needs. This ensures there is enough for all.

Step 4: The fourth step relates to happiness. Both must understand each other, be caring, pray together and enjoy each other's company.

Step 5: The fifth relates to personal duties and responsibilities. This includes the welfare of family members, dependents, animals and pets. These needs must be met throughout life. This can be difficult sometimes. Yet there is the need for happiness and contentment for all.

Step 6: The sixth step relates to mutual respect for each other's families. Personal misunderstanding must be overcome and families accepted as they are. The couple must find marital happiness together through an open mind.

Step 7: The seventh relates to mutual friendship between the couple. This includes kindness, obedience and affectionate behaviour towards each other. It also includes the need for forgiving wrong actions to ensure a happy and peaceful relationship between the couple. They must live together to raise a family and gain a standing in society.

With the *saptpadi* ceremony completed, the groom and bride change seats, the bride moving from the right to the left of the groom.

Think it over...

The husband must ensure that the wife is happy and the wife must ensure that the husband is happy. When both make each other happy, there will be auspiciousness and welfare for all in that house.

—**Dharm Shastra**

What marital vows do the husband and wife take in a Hindu marriage?

After the marriage ceremony is concluded the bride and groom are told about their duties and responsibilities in married life. To affirm their faith in building a lasting marital bond, both partners make separate vows. These vows direct the couple to a positive path of action. They help in promoting marital happiness for a lifetime. The priest reads the vows one by one and the individual accepts them by saying, "I agree to do so", after each vow.

Vows by the Husband

1. I will consider my wife to be the better half. I will look after her just as I look after myself.

2. Accepting her as in-charge of the home, I shall plan things in consultation with her.

3. I will never express dissatisfaction about any shortcomings in my wife. If there are any, I will explain them to her lovingly. I will support her in overcoming them.

4. I will always have faith in my wife. I will never look at another woman with wrong intent, nor have an illicit relationship.

5. I will be affectionate and treat my wife like a friend.

6. I will bring home all my income to my wife. The household expenses will be incurred with her consent. I will always make an effort to ensure her comfort and happiness.

7. I will not find fault or criticise my wife before others. We will sort out our differences and mistakes in privacy by ourselves.

8. I will have a courteous and tolerant attitude towards my wife. I will always follow a compromising policy.

110

9. If my wife is unwell, or is unable to fulfil some responsibility, or through some misunderstanding behaves wrongly, I will not withdraw support or refuse to fulfil my responsibilities towards her.

10. I will always do my best to encourage my wife to find self-fulfilment. I will always behave in a kind and loving manner towards her.

Vows by the Wife

1. I will merge my personality with that of my husband, and truly become the better half. We will begin a new life together.

2. I will always treat my husband's relatives with courtesy, respect and generosity, and spare no efforts to keep them happy and content.

3. I will work hard to perform the household work and support my husband. I will never be lazy.

4. With complete faith in my husband, I will live just as he desires. I will always be faithful to him.

5. I will always speak pleasantly, be service-minded, and have an attitude of contentment. I will never sulk, grumble or be jealous.

6. I will be frugal in running my home, and will avoid wastefulness.

7. I will never be indifferent towards my husband and will treat him like God. I will never insult or abandon him.

8. If there are any differences with my husband, I will resolve them peacefully and never present them in a derogatory manner.

9. I will always keep my husband content with humility and service.

10. Even if my husband is indifferent towards me, without any consideration I will faithfully fulfil my responsibilities.

Your questions answered...

In the many rituals laid down for marriage, why is there no provision for divorce?

According to the Hindu way of life, marriage is a sacred union between a man and woman. Before marriage both the man and woman are incomplete. Only after marriage do they become complete. Both are assigned responsibilities to make marriage succeed. When one of the partners fails to fulfil the responsibilities, the marriage vows stand broken. Each partner is incomplete again. As punishment, suffering follows. The purpose of rituals is to promote happiness, not suffering. Divorce too is a suffering. Therefore, there is no provision for divorce.

What is the purpose of changing seats on getting married?

When a man and woman get married, the first thing they do is change seats so that the wife sits on the left of the husband.

According to the **Mahabharata**, Shanti Parv, 235/18, a wife is part of the husband's body. For this reason she is often referred to as the better half. This also symbolises that only after marriage a man becomes a complete person.

In the **Taittriya Brahman**, 33/3/5, it is said:

'अथो अर्धो वा एव अन्यतः यत् पत्नी'

A man's body is not complete until a woman fills it to make it whole.

According to Hindu religious texts, Brahma created man from the right shoulder and woman from his left shoulder. A woman is referred to as *Vamangi*, or one who is on the left side. Throughout the marriage ceremony the bride sits on the right side of the groom. That is the place for strangers and acquaintances. Only after the *saptpadi*, when the bride and groom have exchanged marital vows, is the wife seated on the left side of the man. The left side is considered close and intimate. After marriage the wife becomes the prime manager of the household, and with transfer of responsibilities she also changes place from the right to the left. Hindus refer to this as 'change of seats'.

In the **Sanskarganpati**, 156, it is said:

वामे सिन्दूरदाने च वामे चैव द्विरागमने ।
वामे शयनैकस्यायां भवेज्जाया प्रियार्थिनी ॥

On the occasion of the bride's going to her husband's home after a post-marriage interval, when eating and sleeping, the wife must be on the left side of the husband. Besides these occasions, the wife must be on the left side when making offerings to God, when seeking blessings and when washing the feet of a Brahmin on welcoming him.

It must be noted that whenever the ritual or ceremony is male-dominated, as in marriage, *kanyadaan* (giving away of the bride), yagya and rituals for newborns like *jaatkarm*, *naamkarn*, *annprashan* and others, the wife sits on the right side. When the ritual or ceremony is female-dominated, the wife sits on the left side.

It is interesting to note that whereas the *mauli* (red protective thread) is tied on the right wrist of men, it is tied on the left wrist of women. In the same way, while palmists read the right hand of men, they read the left hand of women. Ayurvedacharyas see the pulse of the right wrist in men and of the left wrist in women. From this one can appreciate why the wife is made to sit on the left side of the husband.

Manu said that in the beginning God divided matter into two portions. One became man and the other woman.

In the **Devi Bhagwat** it is said:

स्वेच्छामयः स्वेच्छयायं द्विधारूपो बभूव ह ।
स्त्री रूपो वामभागांशो दक्षिणांशः पुमान् स्म तः ॥

Of his own will God divided into two portions. From the portion on the left woman emerged, from the portion on the right man emerged.

Your questions answered...

Why do Hindus say that after marriage, the man and the woman become complete?

A man is symbolic of knowledge. He has more opportunities to move out of the home. Through the many experiences, he gathers knowledge and wisdom. A woman is symbolic of devotion. With her commitment, she builds a home and ushers in harmony. Together the two create an ideal combination. They can achieve more together than what either can individually.

What is the significance of the husband applying *sindoor* in the wife's hair?

When the formal marriage ceremony is completed, the bride and groom change seats. Initially, the bride sits on the right side of the groom. Once married, the priest asks them to change seats. According to Hindu custom, the wife always sits on the left side of the husband. Even during religious ceremonies, the wife always sits on the left.

After the change of seats the priest asks the groom to put *sindoor* (vermilion) in the wife's hair parting. This ceremony is called *sumangali kriya*, meaning *an auspicious ceremony*. The wife then prays for the long life of her husband. She puts vermilion in her hair parting throughout life. This is symbolic of her being a married woman. Hindu religious texts have equated a husband with God, and women take pride in being married.

Vermilion in the hair parting enhances a woman's charm. It is also considered auspicious. It is symbolic of Brahma being lustrous and also of the flame being red.

In the **Devi Bhagwat**, Bhagwati has said, "Brahma and I (Shakti) are one. We create mankind." Shakti's favourite colour is red. Widows are prohibited from using vermilion.

The tradition of using vermilion in the hair parting by married women finds approval of Hindu religious writers because this point is just above the suture in the scalp and a little above the point where the soul resides. This point is more delicate in women than in men. The application of vermilion helps avoid wrinkles and skin problems and also protects one from evil influences. It also deters the spread of lice.

According to the **Samudrik-shastra**, women who have a hair parting or eyebrows inflicted by a snakelike line that is inauspicious should use vermilion to overcome the problem.

Why do married women wear a *mangalsutra* around the neck?

Mangal refers to the planet Mars. *Mangal* also means auspicious. *Sutra* denotes thread. Therefore, *Mangalsutra* literally means an *auspicious thread*. According to Hindu custom, married women wear a *mangalsutra* around the neck since it is symbolic of a woman being married. With time the thread is now a string of black beads interspersed with golden beads. Depending upon individual pockets, the *mangalsutra* comes in a wide variety of styles. However, the black beads prevail in all designs.

Irrespective of the jewellery a woman may wear, the *mangalsutra* has special significance. It is the symbol of good luck. Wearing it brings good fortune. It also symbolises the love between the couple. No woman wants to part with it for any kind of jewellery. A woman parts with it only after her husband's demise.

It is customary that after the marriage ceremony the husband gifts the wife a *mangalsutra*. Amongst many Hindu communities a marriage ceremony is not complete until the husband makes the wife wear a *mangalsutra* around the neck.

The use of black beads and figures like those of a peacock or a pendant are considered important components of a *mangalsutra*. There is a belief that a *mangalsutra* worn by a wife protects the husband from inauspicious and unfortunate happenings. A peacock is a symbol of a woman's love for her husband. Black beads ward off evil. They also help conserve one's energy. A *mangalsutra* may be made in gold or silver. Both are in popular use. It is believed that one made in gold is superior, since gold helps increase energy levels in the body and is a symbol of prosperity.

It is a religious belief that once worn the *mangalsutra* must not be taken off. If the *mangalsutra* is broken or lost, many women consider it inauspicious and unfortunate. However, amongst modern educated women, a *mangalsutra* is worn according to personal convenience and taken off at night when sleeping.

Think it over...

A householder's life is mainly one of action and those in that stage of life ought to do their best to keep their actions pure.

—**Swami Tapovan**

What is the purpose of *Shiksha* in a Hindu wedding?

Shiksha literally means *to teach or give instruction.* Just when the marriage ceremony is complete and the newly wedded couple ready to leave, it is customary to impart *shiksha* to the young bride who will soon assume the responsibilities of a wife. *Shiksha* is invariably in the form of a poem that includes the names of the couple, parents, relatives and friends. The poem includes both, blessings and instructions for a new life in a new home.

It is emotionally worded and when recited evokes an outburst of emotions with the bride and the family weeping at the parting. Some do not approve of it because of emotional outbreaks, but the crying reminds everyone of the changing relationships. It also arouses in the mind of the bride the need to adapt and adjust to new surroundings and relationships.

Although *shiksha* is directed at the bride, the emotional outpouring creates a deep influence on the groom, making him aware how his wife is leaving behind old relationships. It also creates awareness for the need of his becoming more understanding and tolerant towards her.

Leaving the parents' home after having lived there for over two decades is invariably a difficult situation. But it is a way of life. Every girl must one day leave the parental home for her husband's house to raise a family. As the couple leaves, the bride carries puffed rice in her hands and throws it over her head. Her parental family walking behind her catches the rice in their outstretched clothes.

117

This ceremony symbolises the fact that although rice (paddy) is planted in one place, it is uprooted and replanted in a new place where it grows rapidly and bears fruit. A bride too is like the rice plant. She spends her childhood and adolescence in one home, but finds personal fulfilment in her husband's house.

This ceremony also symbolises the fact that, although every individual brings good luck and fortune to a family, when the bride leaves her maternal home, the throwing of rice over her head is a prayer that prosperity continues in the home she is leaving behind.

Your questions answered...

Is a Hindu marriage free of the problems we witness in everyday life?

A marriage is a relationship between two people. Since there can be no relationship without some differences of opinion, complete harmony comes only after long periods of mutual adjustments. Problems are a part of everyday life. They offer an opportunity to learn and grow. To face them, one must draw on virtues like patience, tolerance and fortitude. A committed couple knows that no problem is that big as not to be resolved.

What is the concluding ceremony in a Hindu wedding?

*D*oli is the ceremony when the groom and his family take the bride away to their home after marriage. The word *doli* means a *palanquin,* which was used in earlier times by women as a mode of travel. After the marriage, it was customary for a groom to take a bride home in a *doli.* With changing times, cars have replaced the *doli* or palanquin. Earlier, it was customary for the bride's brothers and relatives to carry the *doli* for a short distance. Now the custom is to push the car for a few steps before it is driven off.

This custom is symbolic of the bride's family expressing their happiness in sending off the bride to make a home and raise a family. It is also symbolic of the good wishes the relatives extend on the occasion.

On arrival in the new home, it is customary for the mother-in-law or a senior lady to formally receive the bride. As she enters the home, she tips over a vessel filled with rice with her right foot so that the rice falls inwards. This symbolises that she brings along good luck and fortune. In some families it is customary for her to walk through milk-water in which vermilion is dissolved. The red footmarks she leaves on the floor are symbolic of good fortune.

Hindus believe that it is the wife who attracts prosperity. She is an embodiment of Goddess Lakshmi. The footmarks are symbolic of the entry of Goddess Lakshmi. It is also customary for all relatives to give the bride gifts on meeting her.

Think it over...

In those houses where women are honoured and respected, the gods dwell there. Where women are not respected and honoured, whatever one does is futile.

–**Hindu Shastra**

What are Hindu views on conception and childbirth?

Marriage brings a man and woman together and they start a new life where one complements the other. Hindus believe that neither the man nor the woman is complete. Together they project the complete picture. This is the first step in establishing a new family.

An important purpose of marriage is to have children. Every couple looks forward to having capable, healthy, intelligent children who learn good moral values and bring home honour and happiness. It is natural that when a man and woman are physically intimate, at an appropriate time the woman will conceive and eventually bear a child. But not all children possess the qualities parents desire. There is a belief that if the man and woman desire a capable child it must be well planned.

Planning does not only imply the time when the couple are ready to have the child, but also the physical and emotional harmony between the couple. Both must look forward to starting a happy family. This emotional harmony passes on to the child. It is for this reason that Hindus call a son *atmaj* and a daughter *atmaja*, both words being derived from the word *atma* – the soul or self. Both the son and daughter pertain to the self.

In the **Smriti Sangrah** there is reference to conception as follows:

निषेकाद् बैजिकं चैनो गार्भिकं चापमृज्यते ।
क्षेत्रसंस्कारसिद्धिश्च गर्भाधानफलं स्मृतम् ॥

120

A well-planned union in the couple ensures a suitable conception that results in a capable child. The negative qualities in the semen and the ovum become ineffective. A good conception is the fruit of understanding and mutual planning.

Medical research has confirmed that the mental state of the man and woman at the time of physical intimacy affects the characteristics conveyed through the semen and the ovum. A child is a good reflection of the emotional bonding of the mother and father.

In the **Sushrat Samhita**, Sharir, 2/46/50, it is said:

आहाराचारचेष्टाभिर्यादृशोभिः समन्वितौ ।
स्त्रीपुंसो समुपेयातां तयोः पुत्रेऽपि तादृशः ॥

Depending upon the diet, temperament and behaviour of the man and woman at the time of physical intimacy, the son born of such a union will also have a similar temperament.

Lord Dhanvantri has said that depending upon the kind of man a woman desires when she has physical intimacy midway between the menstrual cycles, she will be blessed with a son.

When a woman desires that her son should be capable like her husband, or should be brave and courageous like Abhimanyu, she should think of them. If she desires that he should be devoted like Dhruva, or possesses the knowledge of a soul like Janak or may be charitable like Karan, she should look at pictures of these great men. With pure thoughts she should think of them and have sexual intimacy at the appropriate time. It is believed the best time to conceive is between 12 midnight and 3.00 AM. A child that is conceived at this time would be religious and devoted to Vishnu.

Contrary to what many believe, in the Hindu way of life, sexual intimacy between couples is considered a sacred responsibility. It is believed that a couple should think of their favourite gods and goddesses and seek their blessings. Thereby, one is blessed with good children.

In the **Brihadaranyak**, 6/4/21, it is suggested that before physical intimacy with the aim of conception, Brahmins, Kshatriyas and Vaishyas must chant this mantra:

गर्भ धेहि सिनीवालि गर्भ धेहि प्रथुष्टुके ।
गर्भ ते अश्विनी देवावाधत्तां पुष्करस्रजौ ॥

O Goddess Siniwali! O broad-bottomed Goddess Prathustuka! Please bless this woman to conceive. Let the conception be confirmed by the two Ashvani Kumars adorned with garlands of the lotus flower.

To be blessed with good children certain restrictions have also been imposed for physical relations between couples. For instance, one should not have a relationship when one is not clean or during the menstrual cycle. It is also said that a relationship in the morning or in the evening is not good. It is also suggested that one should not conceive when worried, afraid, angry and mentally tense or unstable. A child conceived in the day is said to be mean and of bad habits.

The demon Hiranyakashipu, son of Kashyap and his wife Diti, was born a demon because he was conceived in the evening. Physical relations are also prohibited during *shraddh* days, when religious ceremonies are conducted or during the early part of night.

Good sexual relations have been given great importance in the Hindu way of life. In the **Bhagavad Gita**, 7/11, it is said:

धर्माविरुद्धो भूतेषु कामोऽस्मि ।

I am the sexual desire not conflicting with virtue or religious restrictions.

Your questions answered...

In ancient times were physical relations between husband and wife only a means of procreation?

That's not true. However, great responsibility was placed upon both partners to have a positive attitude towards physical relations. *Kamasutra* (the oldest sex manual) has covered a variety of situations. One can appreciate the Hindu attitude about this vital aspect from a study of this book.

What is the purpose of *Punsavan* ceremony?

In the Hindu way of life where children are symbolic of the flowing of the river of life, every step of conception, rearing the child within the womb, childbirth and other aspects are given special importance. Soon after the pregnancy is confirmed, formal ceremonies begin.

The *punsavan* ceremony is conducted during the third month of conception. At this time the foetus begins to grow physically. The body and the brain begin to take shape. The physical and emotional harmony of a couple has a great effect when the child is conceived. However, since the child is within the mother's womb, her feelings and emotions continue to affect him throughout the pregnancy. The *punsavan* ceremony is conducted to prepare the mother for her responsibility towards the unborn baby.

The religious texts give two reasons for the *punsavan* ceremony. The first is to have a son. The second is that the child must be healthy, good-looking and capable.

With reference to the first objective, the **Smriti Sangrah** states:

गर्भाद् भवेच्च पुंसूते पुंस्त्वस्यप्रतिपादनम् ।

May the conceived child be a son. The punsavan *ceremony is conducted with this desire.*

In the **Manusmriti**, 9/138, there is reference to the *punsavan* ceremony:

पुन्नाम्नो नरकाद्यस्मात् त्रायते पितरं सुतः ।

Pumo, who saves one from going to hell, is really a son.

It is to protect oneself from going to hell that one desires a son.

Manu further says:

गर्भाद् भवेच्च पुंसूते पुंस्त्वस्य प्रतिपादनम् ।

The desired fruit of the punsavan *ceremony is that the conceived child may develop into a boy and not a girl.*

The provision for the *punsavan* ceremony in the religious texts has been made principally to prepare the mother with emotional strength. Those who conduct the *punsavan* ceremony with devotion and chanting of mantras offered to the Supreme Spirit greatly influence the mental attitude of the mother. She begins to desire a son. It is suggested that after three months of pregnancy the following mantra (along with the meaning) should be repeated in the morning and at night before sleeping. This should be done along with the resolve that a son is born. It is believed that a son will then be born.

123

The religious texts say:

पुमानग्निः पुमानिन्द्रः पुमान् देवो बृहस्पतिः ।
पुमांसं पुत्रं विन्दस्व तं पुमान्नु जायताम् ॥

Agnidev is a male. Lord Indra is also a male. Guru Brihaspati is also a male. You too should grow a male.

The study of religious texts makes the belief clear that the sex of the child is subject to change with the *punsavan* ceremony. However, modern science disagrees with this aspect of the *punsavan* ceremony and confirms that the sex of the baby is decided at the time of conception. Whereas the ovum of the mother carries chromosomes that are all marked X, sperms from the husband carry chromosomes that are both X and Y. At the time of conception, if a sperm carrying the X chromosome, meets the ovum it is fertilised to produce a girl. If the sperm carries a Y chromosome a boy is born. Therefore, the deciding factor is the male sperm, which fertilises the female ovum and the sex is determined immediately on conception.

Three months later when the *punsavan* ceremony is conducted it is now possible to determine whether the unborn child is a boy or a girl, but it is not possible to change the sex at this stage. Therefore, religious texts and modern science are not in harmony on the point of sex change. However, the second objective of the *punsavan* ceremony holds well. It definitely prepares the mother to bear a healthy, good-looking and capable child and also prepares her to be a good and understanding mother.

Your questions answered...

What are the marks of a person born with divine gifts?

A person born with divine gifts is pure of mind, observes control over the senses, worships God and other deities and holds parents, teachers and elders in respect. The discharge of responsibilities and obligations is important even though they cause hardship and suffering. Such persons are truthful, speak gently, do not give in to anger and are not easily provoked. They are serene and do not indulge in gossip. They are kind and thoughtful towards everyone. They avoid frivolous pursuits.

What is the purpose of the *Simantonayan* ceremony?

The *Simantonayan* ceremony, or *simant-sanskar*, is performed in the fourth, sixth or eight month of pregnancy. The purpose is to ensure a happy, healthy child, and to motivate the mother to have good, positive thoughts.

From the fourth month, the child begins to develop various parts of the body, including the heart and brain. The child also develops awareness, which is manifested as desires in the mother's mind. The child becomes capable of learning. Intelligence begins to generate in the child's mind. At this stage, if good, positive thoughts are fed to the unborn child through the mother, these have a profound effect upon the thinking of the child after birth.

There is no doubt that at this stage the unborn child is very sensitive. It is said that Sati Madalsa could foretell the abilities, actions and temperament of her children. She would adapt her thinking, activities, lifestyle, food habits and behaviour so that the child was modelled after the activities she desired.

Bhakta Prahlad's mother Kyadhu would hear Narad narrate sermons pertaining to devotion to Bhagwat. Bhakta Prahlad heard and benefited from them when still in his mother's womb. Sukhdev, son of Vyas, gained wisdom when still unborn. When Arjun spoke to his wife Subhadra about *chakravyuh*, unborn Abhimanyu heard and learnt about it. In the *Mahabharata*, it was with this knowledge that the 14-year-old Abhimanyu entered the *chakravyuh* and fought single-handed against eight individuals.

The texts describe how the gular tree and other vegetation heard the husband chanting the following mantra to his pregnant wife:

ॐ भूर्विनयामि, ॐ भुवर्विनयामि, ॐ स्वर्विनयामि

It is also suggested that during the ceremony the following mantra must be chanted:

येनादिते सीमानं नयति प्रजापतिर्महते सौभगाय ।
तेनाहमस्यै सीमानं नयामि प्रजामस्यै जरदृष्टिं कृणोमि ॥

Just as Prajapati had performed the Simantonayan *ceremony for his wife Vedmata Aditi, I am performing it for my pregnant wife so that the son may be capable and long-lived.*

At the end of the ceremony, it is customary for elderly Brahmin women to bless the pregnant lady.

As part of the *Simantonayan* ceremony it is customary to feed the pregnant woman *khichdi* (a dish made of rice and pulses) that contains an appropriate amount of ghee.

There is reference to this custom in the **Gobhil Grahsutra**, 2/7/9-12, as:

किं पश्यस्सीत्युक्त्वा प्रजामिति वाचयेत् तं सा स्वयम् ।
भुञ्जीत वीरसूर्जीवपत्नीति ब्राह्मण्यो मंगलाभिर्वाग्भि पासीरन् ॥

When asked what you are looking for the woman said that she was looking for a progeny. She should eat khichdi. *The ladies present at the ceremony should bless her that she may give birth to a live child. She should live a fortunate life for a long time.*

Think it over...

The future destiny of the child is always the work of the mother.

—Napoleon Bonaparte

126

Why is the *Namkaran* ceremony important?

After childbirth the *namkaran* ceremony or giving a name to the child is an important one where relatives get together to bless the newborn child.

In the **Smriti Sangrah** it is said:

आयुर्वर्चोऽभिवृद्धिश्च सिद्धिर्व्यवहतेस्तथा ।
नामकर्मफलं त्वेतत् समुद्दिष्टं मनीषिभिः ॥

With the namkaran *ceremony the personality and the age of the child grows. The name plays a significant part in moulding the worldly behaviour of the individual. Through it one builds an identity.*

Hindus believe that in the event of a birth or death in the family there is defilement and, therefore, no auspicious activity should be done. The *namkaran* ceremony is possible only after the 10-day period of defilement passes away.

In the **Parashar Grihasutra**, it is said:

दशम्यामुत्थाप्य पिता नाम करोति ।

The namkaran *ceremony can be done on the tenth day after a purification yagya.*

Some people have the custom of performing the ceremony after 100 days. Some do it after the child is one year old.

In the **Gobhil Grihasutrakar**, it is said:

जननाद्दशरात्रे व्युष्टे शतरात्रे संवत्सरे वा नामधेयकरणम् ।

127

The child is made to lick honey, then gently talked to and made to see the Sun, seeking blessings that the child may be brilliant and glorious like it. The child is then made to touch the ground to devotedly surrender it to Hindu culture. The name of the child is then announced and all the relatives and friends present bless the child with good health, happiness and a long life.

Earlier it was customary to name the child after certain important people or some special abilities. It was believed that the name should constantly motivate the person to do what the name implies. Psychologists believe that by whatever name you call a person, s/he responds with abilities in harmony with it. When a child is given a crude name, he responds accordingly. Therefore, a child must be so named that it may be pleasing to the ears and motivate him/her to noble things in life.

A child is named on the basis of three criteria. The first is the planetary configuration at the time of birth. The child should be identified with it. Therefore, the first letter of the name should be such as can be identified with the planetary configuration and the influences thereof. This is the scientific basis for naming an individual. The second criterion is that the name should be able to motivate the person towards the object of life. The third criterion is that one should be able to identify family details from the name.

It is customary to identify Brahmins by using the last name Sharma; Kshatriyas by using the last name Varma, Vaishyas by using the last name Gupta and for others the last name is Das.

Think it over…

A good name, in man or woman, is the immediate jewel of their souls.

−**William Shakespeare**

Why do many Hindus perform the *Chhochak* ceremony?

It is customary that when a woman is blessed with a son, the child's maternal uncle (*mama*) and maternal grandfather (*nana*) present clothes, ornaments and other things to the baby, parents and relatives. This custom is known as *chhochak* ceremony. It is usually performed along with the *namkaran*. In many families, this ceremony is performed even when a daughter is born.

When the daughter is getting married the maternal uncle (*mama*) and maternal grandfather (*nana*) perform a similar ceremony. Clothes, ornaments and gifts are given to the daughter, the parents and other relatives. A similar ceremony is also performed for the son. These ceremonies are meant to help a daughter at the time of the wedding of her children. In this way the daughter benefits from her father's wealth.

Hindu religious texts have often been wrongly interpreted to mean that only son/s have a right over the father's wealth. Daughters are married young and the responsibility of their living is upon their husbands. It has therefore been customary to offer gifts on these occasions.

In the **Manusmriti**, 9/130, it is said:

यथैवात्मा तथा पुत्रः पुत्रेण दुहिता समा ।

Just as the soul and a son are alike, so are a son and daughter equal.

Manu had devised that daughters be given a share just like sons from the father's estate.

129

In the **Manusmriti**, 9/118, it is said:

स्वे स्वेभ्योऽशेभ्यस्तु कन्याभ्यः प्रदद्युर्भ्रातरः पृथक् ।
स्वात्स्वादंशाच्चतुर्भागं पतिताः स्युरदित्सवः ॥

Sons must give a part of their share to unmarried sister(s). The brother who does not give one-fourth of his wealth to the sister is depraved.

Besides, Manu provided that daughters of the sister are also entitled to help and support.

In the **Manusmriti**, 9/193, it is said:

यास्तासां स्युर्दुहितरस्तासामपि यथार्हतः ।
मातामह्या धनात्किंचित्प्रदेयं प्रीतिपूर्वकम् ॥

The unmarried daughter(s) of a sister must get what they desire from their maternal grandmother's wealth.

In ancient times girls were married very young. At that time the father's wealth would not be divided. The brothers too were not in a position to give. Therefore it was devised that the support must come from the maternal grandmother.

There have been many changes in society. Laws have been enacted that give equality to all. People have fewer children now. Both boys and girls receive good education. People are more understanding and supportive. Since not all people act in a fair manner, these customs continue so that a woman should not feel ignored or deprived.

Your questions answered…

Why is it that the modern generation has lost much because of lack of moral values?

Lack of moral values is significant in the *Kaliyug*. With the lack of moral values, we hear much, but see no positive actions. There is more of frustration, suspicion and fear rather than peace and security. Promises are broken everyday. Those who possess merit and work hard remain poor; the crafty become rich. Wealth is in the hands of a few. Malnutrition, physical and mental sickness is rampant. Only self control and discipline can help regain the lost moral values.

What is the purpose of the *Nishkraman* ceremony?

*N*ishkraman literally means *going forth*, or *going out*. This ceremony is performed the first time a child goes out of the home. The religious texts say:

निष्क्रमणादायुषो वृद्धिरप्युद्दिष्टा मनीषिभिः ।

The nishkraman *ceremony aims at wishing the child a long healthy life.*

The *nishkraman* ceremony is done in the fourth month after birth, by which time the newborn child is accustomed to the sun, breeze and noise in the environment. It is customary to make formal offerings to Surya and Chandrama and also expose the child to the sun and the moon. Since the body of the child is made up of the five elements it is customary for the father to formally seek blessings of gods controlling these elements.

In the **Atharva-Veda**, 8/2/14, it is said:

शिवे ते स्तां द्यावापृथिवी असंतापे अभिश्रियौ । शं ते सूर्य
आ तपतु शं वातो वातु ते हृदे । शिवा अभि क्षरन्तु त्वापो दिव्याः पयस्वतीः ।।

O child! At the nishkraman *ceremony may the earth and the world shower welfare and benevolence upon you. May the Sun shine brightly upon you. May your chest be filled with fresh life-giving air. May the divine waters of Ganga and Yamuna quench your thirst.*

> ## Your questions answered...
> ### What is the purpose of so many rituals recommended for Hindus?
> The basic purpose is to live a life that is meaningful. This is possible only through self-discipline. This includes the purification of the mind, positive actions and thoughtfulness for others. The rituals help us achieve this purpose.

What is the purpose of the *Annprashan* ceremony?

In our religious texts it is said:

अन्नाशनान्मातृगर्भे मलाशाद्यपि शुद्ध्यति ।

The food reaching the child through the mother may not be as good as it should be. The child should be introduced to good food.

To wean the child away from the food reaching him through the mother, the ceremony of offering food to him for the first time is called *annprashan*. There is great emphasis on this ceremony and the texts suggest that the food reaching the child through the mother may not be ideal. When the baby is in the mother's womb, nature provides nutritional requirements through the mother. However, the mother's diet may not be proper, or it may be deficient. Even after birth, when the mother breastfeeds the baby, whatever the mother eats influences the child. This ceremony is conducted when the child is six to seven months old and is first introduced to solids. A family yagya and prayer is organised and the child is given the first morsel of solid food. The purpose of this ceremony is to begin teaching the child to eat the right kinds of food.

In the **Chhandogya Upanishad**, 7/26/2, it is said:

आहारशुद्धौ सत्त्वशुद्धिः ।

With pure food the best abilities are generated within the body.

By the time a child is six to seven months old, teething begins. The child's digestive system is ready to accept solids. Whatever food is introduced to the child, the body adapts to it. The body and the mind begin to take shape in harmony with the kind of food the child eats. Indeed, every person is what he eats. A person's thought, feelings, desires and the inner self are governed by the kind of food he eats.

Cereals constitute the basic food. One obtains nutritional requirements from food. Blood, bones, muscles and every part of the body are formed through the food one eats. Therefore, one must accept it as a gift from God.

In the religious texts it is explained that the ceremony is conducted by offering food items to the gods. At an auspicious time, a yagya and prayers are performed. Seeking the blessings of the gods, the mother and father feed the child *kheer* (rice porridge) with a silver spoon and chant the following mantra from the **Atharva-Veda**, 8/2/18:

शिवौ ते स्तां ब्रीहियवावबलासावदोमधौ ।
एतौ यक्ष्मं वि बाधेते एतौ मुंचतो अंहसः ॥

O child! May barley and rice give you strength and nourishment. Both destroy serious diseases. Being divine both destroy sin.

There is an interesting story about the effect of food in the *Mahabharata*.

The Pandavas went along with Draupadi to meet Bhisma Pitamah as he lay on the bed of arrows. During the visit as Bhisma spoke to them, Draupadi suddenly laughed, unable to control herself. Bhisma Pitamah was surprised at this lack of control by Draupadi. He asked her why she had laughed.

"Pitamah," she said courteously, "the essence of religion is camouflaged in what you are telling us. You are guiding us so well with the noble things you speak. As I heard you, I was reminded of the assembly of Kauravas when they attempted to undress me. I was shrieking and begging for justice and help. You were there but preferred to keep quiet. You did not object or stop their immoral behaviour. Pitamah, why did you remain silent? Why did you not stop Duryodhan? This is what made me laugh as I heard you today."

Bhisma Pitamah responded seriously, "Daughter, at that time I was eating food that was provided by Duryodhan. My blood was formed of that food. Just as Duryodhan was contemptible, eating the food provided by him, my behaviour, mind and wisdom were similarly affected. But now the blood formed of sinful food has bled away with Arjun's arrows. I have once again regained my pure feelings. I am presently saying whatever is moral and right."

Your questions answered...

Doctors say that mother's milk is best for a child. What should we believe when some religious texts say it may not be good for the child?

Like all other things the food one eats also possesses the three attributes of Satogun, Rajogun and Tamogun. Many mothers are not conscious that the food they eat is not being converted to just milk that is fed to the child. The milk possesses the attributes of the food the mother is eating. Rajogun food cannot produce Satogun milk. Therefore, it may really not be best for the child.

How can one be certain of feeding the child the best food?

By being conscious that food possesses the three different attributes, and by training the child to be conscious of this fact. Tasty food need not necessarily be the best.

What is the purpose of the *Mundan* ceremony?

The *mundan* or *chudakarm* ceremony is the time when a child's head is shaved. It is customary to perform this ceremony before a child is a year old, or after the completion of two years, that is, in the beginning of the third year. Some prefer to wait until the fifth or seventh year.

It is believed that since the hair on the child's head was formed in the womb of the mother, it could be affected by bad influences that are not good for the child's development. Removal of the first hair on the child's head aims at development of the mind, mental capabilities, good health, charm and a long life.

Most have a quiet ceremony at home. However, many people travel to places of pilgrimage and perform the ceremony there. The hair is shaved off and offered to a holy river or stream. After shaving the hair, *Aum* is written on the child's head and family elders bless him and give gifts. This symbolises that the old malefic influences have been rid of and the child will now start a new life with good deeds and influences.

In the **Ashvalayan Grahsutra**, 1/17/12, it is said:

तेन ते आयुषे वपामि सुश्लोकाय स्वस्तये ।

With chudakarm *the child is blessed with a long life. The child develops charm and becomes inclined towards useful occupations.*

135

In the **Yajur-Veda**, 3/63, it is said:

निवर्त्तयाम्यायुशेऽन्नाद्याय प्रजननाय
रायस्पोषाय सुप्रजास्त्वाय सुवीर्याय ॥

O child! I perform the chudakarm sanskar *so that you may be blessed with long life. That you may be able to digest the food you eat. That you may be productive in what you do. That your glory and fame may grow. That you may be blessed with a happy family and children. That you may be acclaimed wherever you go.*

The *chudakarm*'s simple aim is to put the mind to best use. Whoever has a good mind will have good thoughts, which will encourage one to do good deeds that benefit everyone. There could be no better start to a child's life.

Your questions answered...

Is it necessary to have the *mundan* done at a place of pilgrimage?

It is perfectly in order to perform the *mundan* ceremony at home. The hair can be offered to a holy river later, as per convenience. Some prefer to go to a holy site since they feel it gives the ceremony sanctity and added importance.

What is the purpose of a *choti*?

It is a common practice for Hindus to keep a *choti* or *shikha* – a braid of long hair on top of the head. The end of the hair is tied in a simple knot. Although modern youth avoid this, traditionalists still insist upon it since it is an ancient practice.

The *choti* is symbolic of the restraint one places upon oneself, intended to remind us of our ideals and principles. It is supposed to help generate noble thoughts within the mind.

The head houses the brain and pituitary gland that control not only the whole body, but also our thoughts, feelings and emotions that guide us through life. It is believed that the roots of the hair forming the *choti* go down to the control centres in the brain. This is the seat of wisdom and thoughtfulness. Externally this place is marked with a *choti*.

In the **Katyayansmriti**, 1/4, it is said:

सदोपवीतिना भाव्यं सदा बद्धशिखेन च ।
विशिखो व्युपवीतश्च यत्करोति न तत्कृतम् ।।

Without a choti *yagya, charity, penance, fast and other auspicious acts are redundant.*

Maharishi Vedavyas has said:

विना यच्छिखया कर्म विना यज्ञोपवीतकम् ।
राक्षसं तद्धि विज्ञेयं समस्ता निष्फला क्रियाः ।।

Without a choti *even virtuous actions become demonical.*

137

In the **Manusmriti** it is said:

स्नाने दाने जपे होमे सन्ध्यायां देवतार्चने ।
शिखाग्रन्थिं सदा कुर्यादित्येततन्मनुरब्रवीत् ।।

When bathing, giving charity, meditating, offering oblations to fire and praying to the gods the end of the choti *must be tied in a knot.*

It is believed that when a knot is tied at the time of prayers the energy generated within the mind is not lost. With no loss of energy there is better growth of mental faculties, wisdom and good thoughts. This keeps desires and passion within control, boosts self-confidence and increases physical strength and stamina. It also protects one from harmful influences, prevents laziness, improves eyesight and generally helps in attaining success.

Your questions answered...

Doubts assail me. Why can't I understand the true meaning of life?

Doubts are a stepping-stone to wisdom. Do not be lured by the pleasures of the world. Seek the company of good people. Your doubts will vanish.

What is the purpose of the *Karnvedh* ceremony?

Karnvedh literally means *piercing or boring ears.* This ceremony is performed when the child is six to 16 months old. It could also be done later in odd years like the third or fifth year. In some families there are other times indicated for this ceremony. It is said that piercing the ears helps femininity grow in girls and masculinity in boys. It is also believed that the rays of light pass through pierced ear lobes, increasing the intelligence of both boys and girls. Piercing of ears in girls helps them in wearing ornaments. Piercing of ears has also been equated with acupuncture techniques that are in vogue for preventing sickness.

Religious texts say that a man who does not have pierced ears is not entitled to do the *shraddh* of his forefathers. It is also suggested that the ears of Brahmins and Vaishyas should be pierced with a silver wire. The ears of Kshatriyas and well-to-do individuals should be pierced with a gold wire. The ears of Shudras should be pierced with a steel needle. In actual practice, most people get ears pierced with a silver wire.

In the **Yajur-Veda**, 25/21, it is recommended that at an appropriate time and place one should pray to the gods, and exposing the child's ears to the rays of the sun, chant the following mantra:

भद्रं कर्णेभिः शृणुयाम देवा भद्रं पश्येमाक्षभिर्यजत्राः ।
स्थिरैरंगैस्तुष्टुवां सस्तनूभिर्व्यशेमहि देवहितं यदायुः ॥

In boys the right ear should be pierced first, followed by the left. Since the child's ear lobe is tender, the wire should be rounded to make earrings. In girls, the left ear is pierced first, followed by the right. In some families it is customary for the girls to have the left side of the nose pierced for wearing ornaments.

It is believed that the working of both sides of the mind is enhanced with gold in the ears and nose. The wearing of jewellery in the nose protects it from nasal problems and provides relief in coughs and colds. It is believed that wearing of gold earrings by women helps regulate menstrual periods and also provides relief in problems like hysteria.

Your questions answered...

Why is there great emphasis on devotion to God?

Devotion links us to the god of our choice – Ram, Krishna, Shiva or Durga. Once the link is established, one receives inspiration and positive vibrations. That speeds up spiritual evolution in a person.

What is the purpose of the *Vidyarambh* ceremony?

The word *vidya* means *knowledge* and *arambh* denotes *beginning*. Together *vidyarambh* means *the beginning of gaining knowledge* or *the first day in school*. Education of the child is a very important aspect of life and deserves all the importance it can be given.

This ceremony was held when a child was considered old enough to learn the mysteries of life through study of the Vedas and the Upanishads and the child's mind was receptive to serious learning. In modern times, the learning curriculum has changed, but the purpose is the same. Normally a child is fit to go to school at the age of five.

The purpose of this ceremony is to invoke the blessings of Sri Ganesh, who ensures there are no obstacles and that of Ma Saraswati, the Goddess of Knowledge. With their blessings a child becomes knowledgeable. It is also customary for the child to offer reverence to the teacher with devotion, since it is the teacher who encourages and guides the child to become an important citizen in the years to come.

Before going in for a serious study of the Vedas, the religious texts mention an additional *medhajanan* ceremony. The name *medhajanan* literally means *arousing the intellect*. It is believed that with this ceremony the child's intellect, brilliance, knowledge and devotion are greatly enhanced. It not only helps in the study of the Vedas, but also ensures there are no obstacles.

In the **Jyotirnibandh** it is said:

विद्यया लुप्यते पापं विद्ययाऽयुः प्रवर्धते ।
विद्यया सर्वसिद्धिः स्यादिद्विद्ययामृतमश्नुते ।।

141

With the study of the Vedas all sins are eliminated. One lives longer. One succeeds in everything. The nectar of learning comes just like normal food and water.

The religious texts explain that one who is not knowledgeable is deprived of wonderful fruits like morality, wealth, love and salvation. Therefore knowledge is indispensable.

In the **Subhashit Bhandagar**, 31/14, it is said:

मातेव रक्षति पितेव हिते नियुक्ते,
कान्तेव चापि रमयत्यपनीय खेदम् ।
लक्ष्मीं तनोति वितनोति च दिक्षु कीर्तिं,
किं किं न साधयति कल्पलतेव विद्या ।।

Knowledge is protective like a mother. Like a father it involves one in useful pursuits. Like a wife it helps one overcome problems and attain contentment. It helps make one prosperous. It helps bring recognition from all directions. Like the Kalptala (a mythological creeper that grants all wishes), it gives you everything.

Think it over...

The important thing is to know that there are gradations of duty and morality and that the duty of one state of life, in one set of circumstances, will not and cannot be that of another.

—**Swami Vivekananda**

What is the purpose of the *Yagyopavit* ceremony?

A *yagyopavit* is a sacred thread traditionally worn by Hindus. The *yagyopavit sanskar* is the ceremony when a young boy is given the thread to wear for the first time. It is one of the 16 sanskars recommended for all Hindus.

In the **Manusmriti**, 2/169, Manu has said:

मातुरग्रेऽधिजननं द्वितीयं मौञ्जिबन्धने ।

A child's first birth is from the womb of the mother. The second birth is when the yagyopavit *is worn for the first time.*

The fruits of good and bad deeds of many births threaten the birth from the mother's womb. The purpose of the *yagyopavit* is to isolate the fruits of previous deeds and begin with a new account of good deeds. The new account is symbolic of the second birth. Brahmins, Kshatriyas and Vaishyas are all said to have a second birth because of the new life they adopt after the *yagyopavit*.

In the **Manusmriti**, 2/171, it is said:

न ह्यस्मिन्युज्यते कर्म किंचिदामौञ्जीबन्धनात् ।

Without having gone through the yagyopavit sanskar *nobody is entitled to perform any other sanskar.*

It is only after the *yagyopavit sanskar* that a boy is entitled to other religious rights. It opens the door to all kinds of yagyas. The wearing of the *yagyopavit* means accepting of moral laws and directions and responsibilities towards mankind in daily life. When one is constantly reminded of this one attains God.

There are many references to the *yagyopavit* in Hindu religious texts. In **Padampuran**, Kaushal Kand, it is written that the ill effects of sins committed knowingly and unknowingly are absolved by wearing the *yagyopavit*. In the **Paraskar Grahsutra**, 2/2/7, it is written that just as Brihaspati gave the *yagyopavit* to Lord Indra, one should wear it to attain long life, strength, wisdom and wealth.

The *yagyopavit* motivates one to have good character and be able to undertake difficult responsibilities. It is a definite step from mankind to divinity.

In the **Brahmupanishad**, it is written that the *yagyopavit* is a symbol of purity and has been devised by the Supreme God. It enhances long life and dynamism. It helps break the shackles of bonds and gives purity, strength and charm.

In the **Narad Samhita**, it is written that those who do not hold the *yagyopavit* for sons qualify to go to hell along with their family priest. It is also said that when one who does not adorn a *yagyopavit* offers nectar, it is like liquor. The tulsi leaves are like grass. Even *pind daan* to the forefathers is no more than the droppings of a crow.

In the **Vedanta Ramayana**, it is written that when one who does not wear a *yagyopavit* chants mantras and meditates, the efforts go waste.

A *yagyopavit* has three strands symbolic of three kinds of religious duties. In the **Taittriya Samhita**, 6/3/10/5, there is mention of three debts one needs to repay – to the teacher, to the gods and to forefathers.

The three strands are also symbolic of Brahma, Vishnu and Mahesh. They are pleased with the offerings of one who wears a *yagyopavit*. The three strands symbolise three qualities – strength, fertility and splendour and the three Vedas – Rig-Veda, Yajur-Veda and Sama-Veda. They symbolise the three gunas, or qualities of Satogun (purity and goodness), Rajogun (love of sensual enjoyment) and Tamogun (illusion). They are also symbolic of the three worlds and remind one of surrender, devotion and duty towards the mother, father and teacher.

In the **Samvediya Chhandogyasutra** it is said that drawing one strand from each Veda, Brahma made a composite string of three strands. Vishnu multiplied it by three with knowledge, action and worship. Chanting the Gayatri mantra, Shiva tied an eternal knot. In this way, the *yagyopavit* comprises nine threads. Each thread represents a god. Together the nine threads represent nine gods. The first Onkar – Brahma, the second Agni – brilliance, the third Anant – patience, the fourth Chandrama – cool illumination, the fifth forefathers – love, the sixth Prajapati – duty towards society, the seventh Vayu or air – cleanliness, the eighth Surya – splendour and ninth all the gods – impartiality. Thus the nine threads are symbolic of the nine gods and the qualities they inspire in us. The *yagyopavit* is a reminder for one to be virtuous with the nine godly qualities.

The nine threads in the *yagyopavit* are also symbolic of the nine desirable good qualities in a person. A heart full of love, a voice that is gentle, simple behaviour, noble attitude towards women, the expression of art and beauty in work, large-heartedness and service towards to all, courtesy and discipline, study and good company, cleanliness and freedom from laziness. One should constantly make efforts to imbibe these qualities.

Adorning the *yagyopavit* on the basis of instructions in the Vedas and the Gayatri, and chanting the Gayatri mantra expresses the reason for the 96 handbreadths in the *yagyopavit*. There are 24 words in the Gayatri mantra and four Vedas. When we multiply the two, the resultant figure is 96. Therefore, there are 96 handbreadths in the *yagyopavit*.

Another explanation in the **Samdevi Chhandogyasutra** says that there are 15 dates, seven days of the week, 27 planets, 25 elements, four Vedas, three *gunas* (qualities), three periods and 12 months. Together they make a total of 96. Thus the *yagyopavit*, through the 96 handbreadths, is symbolic of the 96 important things in life. One who adorns a *yagyopavit* must remember this.

In everyday speech a *yagyopavit* is referred to as *janeu*. It is customary that when one passes urine or visits the toilet, the *janeu* is tied on the ear. In the **Shankhyayan** it is stated that Aditya, Vasu, Rudra, Vayu and the Fire God reside in the right ear of Brahmins. In **Parashar**, there is mention of Ganga and other rivers and pilgrim sites that reside in the right ear.

In the **Kurmpuran**, 13/34, it is said:

निधाय दक्षिणे कर्णे ब्रह्मसूत्रमुदङ्मुखः ।
अग्नि कुर्याच्छकृन्मूत्रं रात्रै चेद् दक्षिणामुखः ॥

When one evacuates urine or faecal matter the janeu *must be raised to the right ear and in day one must face the north, and at night the south.*

From the practical point, since the *janeu* hangs from the neck it is natural to raise it when visiting the toilet so that it is not soiled even unintentionally. In all likelihood the custom of raising it to the ear began from this simple necessity. When the *janeu* is raised to the ear it also reminds one of the need to cleanse the hands after visiting the toilet.

In the **Ahinkkarika** it is said:

मूत्रे तु दक्षिणे कर्णे पुरीषे वामकर्णके ।
उपवीतं सदाधार्य मैथुनेतूपवीतिवत् ॥

When passing urine the janeu *must be raised on the right ear and when passing stools it should be raised on the left ear. At the time of sexual union it must be left as it is.*

In the **Manusmriti**, 1/92, it is said:

145

ऊर्ध्व नाभेर्मेध्यतरः पुरुषः परिकीर्तितः ।
तस्मान्मेध्यतमं त्वस्य मुखमुक्तं स्वयम्भुवा ॥

A man is pure above the navel. He is impure below the navel. The lower portion has the bladder and intestines that contain urine and faecal matter. It becomes impure when they are evacuated. Therefore, purity of the janeu is maintained by raising it to the head level, tied to the ear.

In the **Gobhilgrah Sangrah**, 2/90, it is said:

मरुतः सोम इन्द्राग्नी मित्रावरुणौ तथैव च ।
एते सर्वे च विप्रस्य श्रोत्रे तिष्ठन्ति दक्षिणे ॥

Vayu, Chandrama, Indra, Agni, Mitra and Varun reside in the ear of the Brahmin.

Dr S R Saxena working at Queen Elizabeth Children's Hospital in London is of the opinion that tying of the *janeu* on the ear by Hindus when visiting the toilet has a scientific explanation. According to him, tying the *janeu* on the ear enhances spasmodic movement of the intestines enabling easy and complete evacuation of faecal matter. At the same time, the bladder evacuates the urine completely without hindrance.

With better clearing of the intestines and bladder and tying of the *janeu* on the ear, which presses certain nerves, blood pressure is kept under control. It is also believed that with the strings of the *janeu* tied around the ear the pressure on the nerves strengthens the activity of the heart.

In Ayurveda, there are references indicating that the nerves around the right ear are linked with muscles controlling evacuation of the bladder and those on the left are linked with the anus. Therefore, tying the *janeu* on the right side when passing urine and on the left side when passing stools is said to keep one free of diseases like excessive urination, diabetes, piles, fistula and other ailments pertaining to passing urine and stools. Some are of the opinion that the *janeu* must be tied on both ears when one passes stools.

Your questions answered...

Why don't many Hindus perform the *yagyopavit* ceremony or wear the *yagyopavit*?

Brahmins aware of the need for the *yagyopavit* perform the ceremony and also adorn a *yagyopavit*. Others miss out due to ignorance and lack of guidance. Since marriage is a *sanskar*, and it is prescribed that one must undergo the *yagyopavit sanskar* before the *vivah sanskar*, many priests insist upon it before marriage. Likewise, *shraddh* is not valid unless the performer has undergone the *yagyopavit sanskar*. Even when a person does not wear a *yagyopavit* regularly, priests insist upon it during specific periods. Thereby the shortcoming is overcome.

Why do Hindus emphasise a good student-teacher relationship?

Amongst traditional Hindus the teacher has always been accorded an important position. Even amongst kings and emperors, the role of the teacher was not diluted. The teacher was responsible for not only teaching the three Rs, but also etiquette and manners that differentiated royalty from the common man. Many teachers became lifetime guides. In importance, the teacher was second only to parents.

Since ancient times a teacher has been accepted as the guru – a mentor, preceptor and spiritual guide. It is widely admitted that without a guru there can be no understanding or knowledge. One needs a teacher not only to teach the basics in life, but also to show direction in life, and bring about spiritual initiation. A good teacher is always remembered. In many cases even worshipped, as it is he who sets the student on the path to success and fulfilment.

In the **Gurugita**, 43, it is said:

गुरुर्ब्रह्मा गुरुर्विष्णुः गुरुर्देवो महेश्वरः ।
गुरु साक्षात् परब्रह्म तस्मै श्रीगुरुवे नमः ॥

A guru is an embodiment of Brahma, Vishnu and Mahesh. The guru is the Supreme Spirit. Salute such a guru repeatedly.

In the **Ramcharitmanas**, Uttarkand, 92/3, Sant Tulsidas has said:

गुरु बिनु भवनिधि तरइ न कोई ।
जो बिरंचि संकर सम होई ॥

Without guidance no one can swim across the vast ocean-like life. One may be a creator like Brahma or a destroyer like Shiva, yet to understand one's mind and feelings, and to rise above one's beliefs, one definitely needs a guru to direct one to the right path.

147

In the **Aapastambgrah Sutra** it is said:

स हि विद्यातः तं जनयति तदस्य श्रेष्ठं जन्म ।
मातापितरौ तु शरीरमेव जनयतः ॥

The mother and father give birth to the physical self. It is the teacher who gives true birth. Wise people call it a special birth.

Explaining the importance of the guru, Shiva tells Parwati:

गुरु-भक्ति-विहीनस्य तपो विद्या व्रतं कुलम् ।
निष्फलं हि महेशनि ! केवलं लोक रंजनम् ॥
गुरु भक्तारंव्य दहनं दग्ध दुर्गतिकल्मषः ।
श्वपचोऽपि परेः पूज्यो न विद्वानपि नास्तिकः ॥
धर्मार्थ कामैः किल्वस्य मोक्षस्तस्य करे स्थितिः ।
सर्वार्येश्री गुरौ देवि ! यस्य भक्तिः स्थिरा सदा ॥

Devi! A person may be an ascetic, very knowledgeable, an aristocrat or a mixture of all, yet if he does not have a guru or is not devoted to his guru, his wisdom is meaningless. His knowledge, aristocracy and penance may win him popularity. But it will bear no fruit. A depraved person becomes respectable when he offers his wood-like sins to the fire-like devotion of the guru. However, when an unbelieving knowledgeable person does not accept the divinity in the guru, such a person cannot be revered.

In the **Ramayana**, Ayodhyakand, 30/36, Valmiki has said:

स्वर्गो धनं वा धान्यं वा विद्या पुत्राः सुखानि च ।
गुरुवृत्त्यनुरोधेन न किंचिदपि दुर्लभम् ॥

Whoever serves teachers finds it easy to attain knowledge, prosperity, happiness, sons and heaven.

In the **Mahabharata**, Vanparv, 326/22, it is said:

न विना गुरुसम्बन्ध ज्ञानस्याधिगमः स्मृतः ।

Without serving the guru one cannot attain knowledge.

In the **Bhagavad Gita**, 17/14, it is said:

देवद्विजगुरुप्राज्ञपूजनं शौचमार्जवम् ।
ब्रह्मचर्यमहिंसा च शारीरं तप उच्यते ॥

The worship of gods, Brahmins, elders and the wise, purity, celibacy, straightforwardness and non violence – this is penance through the physical self.

One who imparts knowledge and takes one towards spirituality is a guru. A good guru has wisdom and also evidence to prove what he says. The religious texts commend *Gurupurnim* to offer salutations to the gurus. Amongst the new generation, Dr Sarvepalli Radhakrishnan birthday is celebrated as Teacher's Day.

What is the importance of *Diksha*?

The attainment of wisdom begins with *diksha*, meaning *initiation*. The guru's favour and the student's devotion together initiate the learning process. The guru agrees to share his wisdom and experience and the student surrenders himself to follow the path directed by the teacher. This is the beginning of a foundation that will support a lifetime of knowledge and experience.

In the **Gurugita**, 2/131, it is said:

गुरुमंत्रो मुखे यस्य तस्य सिद्धयन्ति नान्यथा ।
दीक्षया सर्वकर्माणि सिद्धयन्ति गुरुपुत्रके ॥

Whoever has the Guru mantra is always successful; others are not. With proper initiation, one is always successful.

The process of *diksha*, initiation, is a fine spiritual experience where like a little bud or branch, the student is grafted on to a guru, an embodiment of an established plant. To grow and flower, the bud or branch derives nourishment from the main plant. To serve the guru the student needs to give his time, effort and learning ability along with money for the upkeep. Because of his devotion and resolve the student remains united with the teacher to learn.

On the other hand, the guru responds to the efforts of the student by imparting his knowledge and experience gained through sacrifice and effort. Thus the two build a unique student-teacher relationship. It is important that there is a regular flow of inputs from both sides. Otherwise the relationship becomes futile.

149

Diksha can be in several forms. When the guru gives a verbal mantra to the student, it is known as *mantric diksha*. When the *diksha* is given through a signal or gesture, it is called *shambhvi diksha* and when it is given by touching a certain part of the body to arouse the kundalini, it is known as *sparsh diksha*.

By chanting the guru mantra the student awakens his hidden potential and powers. The intellect grows. In a short time the student achieves greater understanding of life. Success follows.

Dhruva was Narad's student. When he repeatedly chanted the mantra *Om namo Vasudevaya nama*, God appeared before him. In the same way Narad gave the dacoit Ratnakar the mantra *mara-mara*. When he repeatedly chanted it, it became *Ram-Ram*. The guru's purpose was achieved.

Through a proper initiation ceremony a special bond is built between the student and teacher. Both are psychologically prepared to give and receive knowledge. When the student-teacher relationship is good one learns quickly, the path of learning is free of obstacles, and one attains success. Without a good relationship nothing is achieved.

Think it over...

A relationship is like a diamond, which has to be cut and polished to enhance its lustre and beauty.

—**Rabindranath Tagore**

What is the importance of *Dakshina* to the teacher?

When a student receives invaluable knowledge from a teacher, it is only appropriate that he makes token payment for it in the form of *dakshina* or an honorarium. By giving the honorarium the student affirms his faith and devotion to the teacher. The honorarium is also important because anything free is never given the same attention as that which is paid for.

In modern times, school and college fees take care of the honorarium. But since seeking the blessings of a spiritual guru is not like studying in a college, one does need to give an honorarium. Without the honorarium, teaching is incomplete. There are accounts that even Ram and Krishna who were incarnations of Lord Vishnu gave honorariums to their gurus. Religious texts have many examples where an honorarium to the guru is mentioned.

Once a young Bhil lad Eklavya went to Guru Dronacharya to learn the art of archery. However, Guru Dronacharya refused. Not discouraged by the refusal Eklavya made a statue of Guru Dronacharya with clay, and drawing inspiration from the statue of the guru, Eklavya practised regularly and became an expert archer.

One day when Guru Dronacharya went to the forest along with the Pandavas, a dog accompanied them. In excitement, the dog ran ahead. When he saw Eklavya, he began barking. It was time for the evening prayer, and not to be disturbed by the barking of the dog, Eklavya shot arrows in such a manner that the dog was not hurt, but he could not bark with a closed mouth. Frightened, the dog rushed

151

back to Guru Dronacharya and the Pandavas. Surprised at what they saw, they rushed to meet Eklavya.

"Son," Dronacharya inquired, "where did you learn such archery?"

"I have learnt it through your favours, Gurudev," Eklavya responded.

Guru Dronacharya was shocked to hear how Eklavya had become an expert. He had already committed to Arjun that he would be the finest archer of all time. This lad was already ahead of him. Guru Dronacharya was lost in thought. What should he do? Then he had an idea. Eklavya had said that he had learnt it through his favour. If so, then Eklavya owed him *guru dakshina* – the honorarium.

When Guru Dronacharya asked him for the honorarium, Eklavya asked him what he desired. Remembering his promise to Arjun, he asked him for the thumb of his right hand. Without a thought, Eklavya cut the right thumb of his hand and placed it near the feet of the guru.

Guru Dronacharya was more than pleased. He could now keep his promise to Arjun. He blessed Eklavya and said, "Son! As I had promised, Arjun may become the greatest archer ever, but as long as there is the sun, the moon and the stars, you shall forever be remembered for your faith in the guru. You shall forever be remembered for your devotion to the guru and be honoured for it."

There is no doubt that by giving a unique honorarium to the guru, Eklavya showed great courage, sacrifice and surrender that shall be remembered for all times to come.

Your questions answered...

How does one move towards spirituality?

When one lives in harmony with the inner self and values, one moves towards spirituality. This spirituality gives happiness based upon a simple life free of desires. It is the desires that hinder lasting happiness.

How can one attain the true purpose of life?

The real purpose of life is to make it meaningful. When this body is attained after unlimited births and deaths, it must be put to the best use. When it is the medium to carry us forward towards God, we must take care of it. Care must be both physical and mental. We must gradually move towards our goal.

Religious texts state that one must begin the day by looking at the hands palms upwards when still in bed. Simultaneously one must chant the following mantra:

कराग्रे वसते लक्ष्मीः करमध्ये सरस्वती ।
करमूले तु गोविन्दः प्रभाते करदर्शनम् ॥

In the front portion of the palms Goddess Lakshmi resides. In the mid-portion there is the Goddess of Knowledge Saraswati and in the rear portion Lord Govind resides. In the morning I see all the three with reverence in my palms.

The purpose of this *shloka* is to simultaneously remember and offer prayers to Goddess Lakshmi and Saraswati and to Lord Vishnu. It ensures prosperity, knowledge and the blessings of Lord Vishnu, who sustains the whole universe.

The purpose of seeing one's palms every morning is that one may concentrate on them rather than view any other object or light that may affect the sight. This helps improve concentration and also offers an opportunity to quickly remember the three gods.

Vedavyas has described hands as an important medium of success. It is through the hands that we do all important tasks. Besides, when we look for the gods in our own palms it adds to our confidence. We know where to find immediate relief when faced by a problem. This also encourages us to do good deeds that benefit mankind. With the gods in our palms we are also motivated to work ethically in our vocations. When we know that the gods residing in our palms are witness to what we do, we refrain from using the hands for bad deeds.

Think it over...

Happiness and work are really wedded together, for there can be no true happiness without the feeling that one is doing something worthwhile.

–Jawaharlal Nehru

Why should one rise early in the morning?

It is believed that between 12.00 midnight and 4.00 AM the influence of demons and evil people is powerful. From 4.00 AM onwards, divine powers take over. This period is known as *Brahm Mahurat*. The literal translation of these two words is *Brahm* for Brahma and *Mahurat* denotes an auspicious moment to begin or do something. However, the religious texts indicate that the word *Brahm* refers to Brahmi or Saraswati, the Goddess of Knowledge. For this reason, since ancient times young students were taught the Vedas early in the morning. Devotees and the learned, particularly many elderly people, rise early, and finish the morning routine when others are still sleeping.

Ayurveda has specified the time from 4.00 to 5.30 AM as the *Brahm Mahurat*. It is believed the cool morning air has rays of the moon penetrating, which is good for health and like celestial nectar. This air is particularly rich in oxygen and promotes peace, happiness and contentment. With the sun rising, the level of pollution increases.

The period of *Brahm Mahurat* is particularly good for mental activities like offering prayers, meditation, yoga, studying, thinking and planning. In the serene morning atmosphere it is easier to concentrate on tasks. Most creative work in almost all fields is completed at this time of the day.

In the **Rig-Veda**, 1/125/1, it is said:

प्राता रत्नं प्रातरित्वा दधाति तं चिकित्वान्प्रतिगृह्या निधत्ते ।
तेन प्रजां वर्धयमान आयू रायस्पोषेण सचते सुवीरः ॥

Those who get up before sunrise are endowed with good health. The wise never let this time go waste. Those who rise early are robust, healthy, strong, brave and long-lived.

In the **Sam-Veda**, Purvarchic, 11/1/5, it is said:

यद सूर उदितेऽनागा मित्रो अर्यमा । सुवाति सविता भगः ॥

A person must get up before sunrise. After visiting the toilet and bathing, one must offer prayers to God. The cool breeze that flows before sunrise promotes good health and perfection.

In the **Mahabharata**, Shantiparv, it is said:

न च सूर्योदये स्वपेत् ।

One should not sleep after sunrise.

In the **Atharva-Veda**, 7/14/2, it is said:

उद्यन्त्सूर्य इव सुप्तानां द्विषतां वर्च आ ददे ।

Those who do not wake up at sunrise lose their glow and splendour.

In the **Vadhool Smriti**, 4-5, it is said:

ब्रह्मे मुहूर्ते सम्प्राप्ते त्यक्तनिद्रः प्रसन्नधीः ।
प्रक्षाल्य पादावाचम्य हरिसंकीर्तनं चरेत् ॥
ब्रह्मे मुहूर्ते निद्रां च कुरुते सर्वदा तु यः ।
अशुचिं तं विजानीयादनहः सर्वकर्मसु ॥

One should give up sleep and rise from bed in the Brahm Mahurat *to find contentment. After personal cleansing one must chant auspicious mantras and offer prayers. One must sing devotional songs. This promotes personal happiness and welfare.*

Think it over...

"Only sacred thoughts can lead to sacred speech. The tongue has been given to man to speak the truth, to be sweet to others, to praise the Divine and enjoy the bliss derived from such sacred speech."

—Gautam Buddha

Why is the earth like the mother?

For many Hindus it is customary to touch the ground with reverence on stepping out of bed. To all Hindus the earth is a mother. It provides all the needs of mankind just as a mother provides the needs of a child. The practice of touching the earth gives us an opportunity to convey our gratitude to Mother Earth and to God, who made it.

Our body is constituted of minerals that come from within the earth and the environment that surrounds it. Even the food we eat comes from the earth. The water we drink and the medicines we consume also come from the earth. Each of us is indebted to Mother Earth for her bounty. It is our helplessness that we cannot help placing our feet on the mother who gives so much. Our apologies and gratitude are the only solution to this predicament.

In the **Vishwamitra Smriti**, 1/44-45, the following prayer is suggested:

समुद्रवसने देवि! पर्वतस्तनमण्डिते ।
विष्णुपत्नि नमस्तुभ्यं पादस्पर्श क्षमस्व मे ॥

One who is covered with the great oceans as clothes, one who cares for all living beings in the universe, one who gives life through the streams of milk that flow in the form of rivers, one whose breasts are in the form of the great mountains, O Mother Earth, wife of Vishnu, forgive me for placing my feet upon you.

When we revere Mother Earth we also revere our motherland where we are born, brought up and live.

157

When we sleep on a bed covered with a sheet or blanket, the temperature of our covered feet rises. Under such circumstances one should not place one's feet on the ground. The feet are particularly sensitive to varying temperature and transmit it immediately to the body. To avoid sudden change in temperature that can affect health, it is appropriate that one should uncover the body, permit the temperature to stabilise, and rise gradually after offering prayers to Mother Earth.

Your questions answered...

I am eager to learn. My teacher knows his subject, but I do not like him. What should I do?

The relationship with your teacher is that of a student, not a friend. Your problem is that you are not concentrating on what you need to learn, but upon the person who is providing the information. As a student, look up to your teacher; don't look down upon him. For a teacher all students are equal. When learning even princes need to conform to the teaching environment. To be useful knowledge must be accepted with gratitude.

Why is *pranayam* an ideal way to begin the day?

The word *pranayam* is made up of two words, *pran* and *ayama*. The word *pran* means the *vital breath* or *vital air*. The word *ayama* denotes *regulation* or *control*. So, *pranayam* means *regulated or controlled breathing*. The purpose of *pranayam* is to take full advantage of the vital breath. *Pranayam* is an important part of Asthangyoga.

Maharishi Patanjali has said:

तस्मिन् सति श्वास-प्रश्वासयोर्गतिच्छेदः प्राणायामः ।

The process of inhaling and exhaling step by step, first inhaling air deeply into the lungs, holding it there for some time and then exhaling, is known as pranayam.

In the **Manusmriti**, *pranayam* is praised as:

दह्यन्ते ध्यायमानानां धातूनां हि यथा मलाः ।
तथेन्द्रियाणां दह्यन्ते दोषाः प्राणस्य निग्रहात् ॥

Just as fire removes the impurities of gold, silver and other metals when they are heated to high temperatures, in the same way pranayam *removes waste matters not only enhancing effectiveness of the senses, but also cleansing the body and the mind and removing disorders. It helps bring the body and senses in control.*

In the **Yogdarshan**, 2/52, it is said:

ततः क्षीयते प्रकाशावरणम् ।

159

Pranayam *removes the film of ignorance covering wisdom in an individual.*

In the **Yogchudamani** it is said that *pranayam* burns sins. It is a bridge to cross the ocean of life.

Pranayam is simply control of the breathing process constituted of deep inhaling, holding the breath and then gradually exhaling. While breathing, one may repeat the name of a deity or chant a mantra. One may also practise inhaling through one nostril and, after holding the breath for some time, exhaling through the other nostril.

The basic purpose of *pranayam* is to widen the path of spiritual attainment. It is equally important for physical and emotional well-being. Through *pranayam* one generates additional inner strength and energy and promotes mental peace. By clearing the mind of waste matters, it improves memory and mental faculties.

With regulated breathing lung capacity and efficiency improves. The blood takes in more oxygen. Waste matters are cleansed. Good health and longevity is assured. The digestive ability of the body is aroused; fickleness of the mind is brought under control. The senses function better. There is a glow on the face. Obesity, hunger and thirst are brought under control. It is possible to increase one's lifespan through *pranayam*. Some are known to have achieved death at will through *pranayam*.

From the scientific point of view, controlled breathing through *pranayam* improves the flow of blood to various parts of the body. This improves the functioning of these parts promoting good health. Controlled breathing helps pump more blood through the body than is possible through any other exercise.

Pranayam is essential for good health and longevity. Besides physical well-being it helps build self-confidence. For this reason Hindu saints and sages have always recommended *pranayam* with evening prayers.

Think it over...

Health is the greatest acquisition, contentment the greatest wealth, confidence the best of relationships and nirvana the highest happiness.

—**Gautam Buddha**

160

Why is care of parents the best service?

Amongst Hindus, service to parents is described as the best service. Religious texts equate parents with gods. Amongst parents, the mother has been accorded a higher position than the father. The mother who gives birth and the motherland that sustains an individual are described as more outstanding than heaven.

In reality a child is born of its father and mother. Since they are instrumental in giving the body to a child they are the first gods to the child. Since the mother rears the child in her womb for nine months, bearing the pains of carrying it, and giving the child good thoughts through this period, parents are worthy of reverence.

Amongst Hindus, rendering services to parents has been described as *Pitra-rin* – a loan from the parents. It is the duty of every child to repay this loan or debt in adult life. Therefore, a son cannot refuse to get married. Sanyas or renunciation is also prohibited unless the son has settled this loan or debt.

A teacher has a significant role in imparting knowledge to a child. However, the mother has been specially commended as the first teacher of the child.

In the **Manusmriti**, 2/145, the situation has been described as:

उपाध्यायान्दशाचार्य आचार्याणां शतं पिता ।
सहस्रं तु पितृन्माता गौरवेणातिरिच्यते ॥

A religious teacher is 10 times more important than a teacher. A father is 100 times more important than the religious teacher. A mother is 1000 times worthier than the father.

In the **Manusmriti**, 2/227, it is further clarified:

यं मातापितरौ क्लेशं सहेते संभवे नृणाम् ।
न तस्य निष्कृतिः शक्या कर्तुं वर्षशतैरपि ॥

Parents who give birth and rear children face agony that cannot be got over in a hundred years. Therefore the father, mother and teacher must always be kept happy and content through care and service. This is important to attain truth and success in life.

In the **Manusmriti**, 2/233, it is further written:

इमं लोकं मातृभक्तया पितृभक्तया तु मध्यमम् ।
गुरुशुश्रूषया त्वेवं ब्रह्मलोकं समश्नुते ॥

One attains happiness in the community through reverence to the mother. One attains happiness in the world through reverence to the father. One attains happiness of Brahmlok (the abode of Brahma) through reverence to the teacher. Those who have the blessings of all three find happiness that all the religions can give. Without the blessing of the three no religion can give honour or respect. None of their deeds bear beneficial fruit. As long as parents and teachers are alive, they must be served. No rituals or customs are necessary. Serving them is a duty. It is the best religion.

In the **Shivpuran**, the importance of parents is described thus:

पित्रोश्च पूजनं कृत्वा प्रकान्तिं च करोति च ।
तस्य वै पृथिवीजन्यफलं भवति निश्चितम् ॥
अपहाय गृहे यो वै पितरोतीर्थमाव्रजेत् ।
तस्य पापं तथा प्रोक्तं हनने च तयोर्यथा ॥
पुत्रस्य च महत्तीर्थं पित्रोश्चरणपंकजम् ।
अन्यतीर्थं तु दूरे वै गत्वा सम्प्राप्यते पुनः ॥
इदं सन्निहितं तीर्थं सुलभं धर्मसाधनम् ।
पुत्रस्य च स्त्रियाश्चैव तीर्थं गेहे सुशोभनम् ॥

That son who reveres his father and mother wholeheartedly attains the fruit of having gone around the world. Whoever leaves them home and travels alone even though on pilgrimage sins as though he has killed his parents. For a son the feet of the parents are like a pilgrimage. To visit other pilgrimages one needs to travel long distances. This pilgrimage is close at hand. For the man the love and respect of his parents and for a woman the love and respect of her husband are the best pilgrimages available within the home.

In the religious texts, the best example of love and respect for parents one comes across is that of Shravan Kumar, who achieved immortality through his devotion. Lord Ram became an ideal son by honouring his father's commitment and went in exile into the forests for 14

162

years. Motivated by the lives of great men and women one must always revere and look after parents to repay the debt of their having brought one into this world.

Your questions answered...

Is it not unfair to bind people to many responsibilities like those to teachers, parents, and forefathers? Why can't one decide what one wants to do or not?

At no stage have any responsibilities been thrust upon anyone. The responsibilities suggested in the religious texts have been known to give happiness to many. You are free to choose what you would like to do, or not do. If you think these responsibilities invade your freedom, are you really free? Your own likes and dislikes already bind you. Greed, anger, jealousy and selfishness bind you. You are free to live with them. You are free to suffer the consequences of these attributes. When responsibilities are assigned to individuals, the purpose is not to benefit one at the expense of another. The purpose is to break the chain of weakness in human beings. This lifts them to higher levels of spiritual attainment.

What is the purpose of conveying respect through *Charan Sparsh*?

The word *charan* means *feet* and *sparsh* denotes *to touch*. Together they mean *to touch one's feet*. It has been a Hindu tradition since Satyug, Tretayug and Dwaparyug to touch the feet of one's father and mother, teachers and elders. The custom has continued in Kalyug.

In the **Atharva-Veda**, great importance has been given to the way a person greets others when meeting. Through *charan sparsh* an individual exhibits the respect one holds for the elderly, the wise, and those with ideals and outstanding contribution to society. It is a way of accepting their superiority. This promotes humility in an individual and also makes the other person feel important. Thereby a person learns to be humble, courteous and respectful. The physical effort involved provides useful exercise and promotes vigour, enthusiasm and concern for others. It rids one of tension. It is motivating.

It is believed that in the *Mahabharata*, the Pandavas were victorious over the Kauravas as they had sought the blessings of Pitamah, the elders and teachers before the battle began.

In life one of the most difficult things is to repay the debt owed to parents. In the **Manusmriti** 2/228, it is said that the problems faced by parents during childbirth and upbringing cannot be repaid even in a hundred years. It is also explained that the father is like Prajapati and the mother like earth. Serving them has been described as penance. One who serves parents in real earnest can be said to have respect for all religions in the world. Whoever fails to serve them eventually ends a failure.

In the **Manusmriti**, 2/232, it is said that those householders who serve their parents regularly attain the three worlds. They achieve success everywhere. These people are blessed through glory and honour and find great contentment.

In the **Manusmriti**, 2/121, it is said that whoever respectfully greets elders and teachers is blessed with strength, knowledge, honour and long life.

The procedure for *charan sparsh* is explained in the **Manusmriti**:

ब्रह्मारम्भेऽवसाने व पादौ ग्राह्यौ गुरोः सदा ।
संहत्य हस्तावध्येयं स हि ब्रह्मांजलिः स्मृतः ॥
व्यत्यस्त पाणिना कार्यमुप संग्रहण गुरोः ।
सव्येन सव्यः स्प्रष्टव्यो दक्षिणेन व दक्षिणः ॥

Before beginning to learn the Vedas, and after the learning is complete, the student must regularly greet and touch the feet of teachers. This is Brahmanjali – an ideal offering to them. Drawing close to the teacher one must touch the right foot with the right hand and the left foot with the left hand.

It is also directed that one should never greet with a single hand only:

जन्मप्रभृति यत्किंचित् सुकृतं समुपार्जितम् ।
तत्सर्वं निष्फलं याति एकहस्ताभिवादनात् ॥

One should never greet with one hand only. This way all virtues earned over a lifetime are wasted. It is important that greetings must be conveyed with both hands and with humility and devotion.

There is a scientific basis to *charan sparsh*. Since the human body is releasing vibrations and also receiving them from people who come close, touching the feet encourages flow of energy. And when elders touch the head of the person in blessing, energy is again exchanged between them. This exchange of energy gives one vigour, self-confidence and contentment. One experiences an inner glow. The blessings received after *charan sparsh* are like invisible armour. They motivate and give strength.

In the **Mahabharata**, Vanparv, there is a narration.

Once the Yaksh asked Yudhistra, "How can a person become great and powerful?"

Yudhistra responded, "By devotedly touching the feet of the mother and father, teachers and elders and by serving them until they are content to give blessings that make a person great and powerful."

Think it over…

When Ram refused to return to Ayodhya until he completed his exile, Bharat brought his *padukas* (sandals). He gave them the reverence he had for his brother. Whenever he required guidance he would talk to them, and received answers to his problems. When *padukas* can be so effective, how benevolent would be the feet of God?

What is the purpose of the *Samavartan* ceremony?

Just as we have convocations, and a convocation address to mark the completion of education, in the same way at the end of the first stage of life when one steps from *Brahmacharya ashram* to *Grihast ashram* in the Hindu way of life we have *Samavartan sanskar*. This marks the completion of the initial educational phase and entry into a vocation and settling down through marriage and setting a home. *Samavartan sanskar* aims at providing the final instructions on control of the senses, on charity and welfare of mankind.

In the **Rig-Veda**, 3/8/4, it is said:

युवा सुवासाः परिवीत आगात् स उ श्रेयान् भवति जायमानः ।
तं धीरासः कवय उन्नयन्ति स्वाध्यो३ मनसा देवयन्तः ॥

When a young man gives up his school and college uniform and adorns good clothes to enter into the Grihast ashram, *he is greeted with auspicious praise and acclaim. With patience, intelligence, wisdom and best wishes he is accorded an important position to utilise the education he has received.*

In the **Atharva-Veda**, 11/5/7-26, it is explained that a Brahmachari (celibate student utilising all his abilities goes through the vast ocean of knowledge to seriously pick up knowledge that would help him in his livelihood. As one who has graduated he receives honour through modesty, ability and measured application of the knowledge in his work.

There is a popular story about the *Samavartan sanskar.*

At one time the gods, humans and demons together went as students to Brahma to acquire knowledge. When the course was completed they requested Brahma to end it with the *Samavartan sanskar*.

The gods were the first to go to Brahma for the *Samavartan sanskar*. "O Master!" the gods said. "Please give us your final instruction and advice."

In response Brahma just said: "D."

On hearing this the gods said, "We have understood what you have advised. As those living in heaven our attention is always towards personal pleasure and enjoyment. With time this causes degeneration and fall from a good life to a lesser life. By saying 'D' you have drawn our attention to *daman*, meaning control over us. You have rightly noted that we must maintain control over our senses."

"Yes," said Brahma, "you have correctly understood the meaning of this instruction."

When humans asked Brahma for the *Samavartan sanskar*, once again he said: "D."

"O Master! We have understood what you have advised us through the letter 'D'," the humans said. "By 'D' you have meant *daan* or charity. You want us to give charity in life."

"Yes," said Brahma, "you have correctly understood the meaning of this instruction."

When the demons asked Brahma for the *Samavartan sanskar*, once again he said: "D."

The demons thought about it for a while. By temperament they were violent. Anger and violence were part of their daily life. In response they said, "O Master! We have understood what you have told us through the letter 'D'. You want us to display *daya* or mercy and be merciful. By being merciful we can overcome our sinful activities and become virtuous. You have rightly asked us to adopt *daya* in our life."

"Yes," said Brahma, "you have correctly understood the meaning of this instruction."

Thereby, each of the three groups interpreted the same thing in different ways, simply because of their varying temperaments. In their own way, each group was right. Education does teach us to have control over ourselves, and to be charitable and merciful.

Why do Hindus use the swastika on auspicious occasions?

The swastika 卐 is a benedictory or auspicious mark in the form of a cross, the four arms of which are bent at right angles. Besides Hindus, other communities and religions also consider this mark auspicious. It is therefore customary to make this mark before any auspicious ceremony or function.

In the **Ganeshpuran** it is said that the swastika is a form of Lord Ganesh. It is necessary that this be made before beginning any auspicious work. It has the power to remove all obstacles. Those who ignore it may fail. It is therefore customary to make all beginnings with the swastika.

In the **Yajur-Veda**, 25/19, it is said:

स्वस्ति न इन्द्रो वृद्धश्रवाः स्वस्ति नः पूषा विश्ववेदाः ।
स्वस्ति नस्ताक्ष्यों अरिष्टनेमिः स्वस्ति नो बृहस्पतिर्दधातु ॥

One who is renowned and glorious, Lord Indra, bless us with well-being. One who is the embodiment of knowledge of the world, Dev Pusa, bless us with well-being. One who has the weapons to destroy misfortune, Garuda Dev, please protect us. Bhagwan Brihaspati, please establish well-being in our home.

In the **Atharva-Veda**, 1/31/4, it is said that may our mother be blessed; may our father be blessed; may our cattle bring good fortune. Let it be auspicious for all the people in the world. May this world be blessed with the best of wealth and knowledge. May Surya bless us everyday indefinitely. May we be blessed with long life.

The swastika is also known as 'Satiya', which is symbolic of the Sudarshan Chakra. People also consider it as a symbol denoting plus (+). That makes it a symbol of prosperity. The four dots around the swastika are symbolic of the four directions around us.

Religious texts explain that the eight arms of the swastika are symbolic of the earth, fire, water, air, sky, mind, emotions and feelings. The four main arms point in four directions. They represent the four eras – Satyug, Tretayug, Dwaparyug and Kalyug. They also represent the four castes – Brahmins, Kshatriyas, Vaishyas and Shudras. They represent the four ashrams of life too – Brahmacharya, Grihast, Vanprasth and Sanyas. The four arms are also symbolic of the four basic aims of human pursuit – *dharm* (righteousness), *arth* (prosperity), *kaam* (passion) and *moksha* (salvation). They are also symbolic of the four faces and four hands of Brahma and of the four Vedas – *Rig-Veda, Yajur-Veda, Sam-Veda* and *Atharva-Veda.* They are also symbolic of the four constellations – Pushya (8th), Chitra (14th), Shravan (22nd) and Revti (27th).

In one of the hymns in the **Rig-Veda** it is said that the swastika is symbolic of Surya. In the **Amarkosh**, it is referred to as a pure and auspicious blessing. In the **Acharya Yask**, the swastika has been described as indestructible Brahma. It is also believed to be a symbol of Lakshmi, the Goddess of Prosperity. In this way, the swastika is really symbolic of all the directions and of gods and auspicious circumstances. One must appreciate its importance and adopt it as a part of everyday life.

Think it over…

Who has faith has all, and he who lacks faith lacks all. It is faith in the name of the Lord that works wonders, for faith is life and doubt is death.

–**Sri Ramakrishna**

Why should all guests be respected?

To Hindus a guest is like a god. Serving a guest is like serving God. It is believed that one can offer no greater welcome than to offer hospitality to a guest. The welcome of a guest at the doorstep is not only a responsibility but has been equated with a religious duty.

Religious texts describe the welcome of a guest as *atithi yagya*. *Atithi* means *guest*, and *yagya* denotes *sacrifice or offering*. Therefore offering hospitality to a guest is a personal sacrifice or offering. Hospitality to guests is included amongst the responsibilities of a householder. *Atithi yagya* is one of the five principal yagyas recommended to Hindus. A guest must be entertained and honoured irrespective of caste, status or ability. This kind of hospitality is unique and unknown in other religions.

Maharishi Shatatap has explained that a guest who comes home without a cause, without an invitation, at any time, from anywhere must be considered a god. Whoever is known and comes with an appointment is not a guest.

In the **Mahabharata**, Udyogparv, 38/2, Mahatma Vidur tells Dhritrashtra:

पीठं दत्त्वा साधवेऽभ्यागताय आनीयापः परिनिर्णिज्य पादौ ।
सुखं पृष्ट्वा प्रतिवेद्यात्मसंस्थां ततो दद्यादन्नमवेक्ष्य धीरः ॥

O King! When a person comes as a guest to one's home a patient man must first offer a seat and then wash his feet with water. Then he must ask about the welfare of the guest and reciprocate according to the situation. Thereafter, depending upon circumstances, a meal must be offered to the guest.

170

In the **Atharva-Veda**, 9/6/1, it is said:

जग्धपाप्मा यस्यान्नमश्नन्ति ।

The sins of a person who offers hospitality to a guest are absolved.

In the **Atharva-Veda**, 9/6/3, it is said:

यद् वा अतिथिपतिरतिथीन् प्रतिपश्यति देवयजनं पेक्षते ।

To welcome a guest at the doorstep is like making offerings to gods.

In the **Mahabharata**, Vanparv, 200/23-24, it is explained that whoever offers water to a guest to wash the feet, oil to massage the legs, a lamp to have light, food to eat and a place to stay shall never go to Yamlok.

Learned writers say offering a seat to a guest pleases Brahma. The washing of the guest's hands pleases Shiva. When the feet are washed it pleases Indra. Offering food to a guest pleases Vishnu. Thus the hospitality offered to guests pleases the gods. Guests should always be welcomed.

In the **Manusmriti**, 3/106, it is said that whatever food householders eat must be offered to the guest. Hospitality offered to a guest ensures good fortune, honour, a long life and happiness.

In the **Mahabharata**, there are several instances of outstanding hospitality. Mordhwaj did not hesitate to offer his son. Kunti offered her son Bhim to the demon as a meal to protect Brahman Kumar. A Brahmin family offered food to a poor destitute even during famine. King Shiv offered his own flesh as food to protect a pigeon. There are several other instances that speak of exceptional hospitality offered to guests.

The **Taittriya Upanishad** has equated hospitality to a guest to fasting. The spirit of sacrifice in a fast is present in the hospitality offered to a guest. In the *Ramayana*, Lord Ram mentions the pigeon that offered hospitality to Vyaghra by feeding him with its flesh.

In the **Mahabharata**, Shantiparv, 191/12, the outcome of refusing hospitality to guests is explained:

अतिथिर्यस्य भग्नाशो गृहात् प्रतिनिवर्तते ।
स दत्त्वा दुष्कृतं तस्मै पुण्यमादाय गच्छति ॥

When a guest returns from a householder's home without food, water or care, the home faces ruin. The householder is overwhelmed with sorrow. The unhappy guest exchanges his disappointment with the virtues of the householder. It is essential that one must fulfil the responsibility towards a guest.

In the **Atharva-Veda**, 9/8/1, 7, it is said:

इष्टं च वा एष पूर्तं च गृहाणामश्नाति यः पूर्वोऽतिथेरश्नाति ।
एष वा अतिथिर्यच्छ्रोत्रियस्तस्मात् पूर्वो नाश्नीयात् ॥

He who eats before the guest destroys the happiness of the family. He destroys goodwill. A guest is like the knowledge of the Vedas. One must not eat before the guest.

171

Why do Hindus consider charity as a responsibility towards society?

It is the responsibility of everyone to give charity. One should give charity as a duty towards society and expect nothing in return. It is very noble to feed a hungry person. However, imparting knowledge is even better. Feeding a person is momentary support. Imparting knowledge is permanent support.

In the **Rig-Veda**, it is said that of all charities imparting knowledge is best. It cannot be stolen or destroyed. With time it grows and continues giving happiness to many people.

Hindu religious texts suggest that charity in different forms must be given on festivals and special occasions. This charity must be given happily with love and devotion. One should leave the fruit thereof to God. He responds with great happiness and contentment.

In the **Bhavishyapuran**, 151/18, it is said that three kinds of charity are particularly meritorious – the giving of a cow, the giving of land and the giving of knowledge. It is believed that the benefits continue for seven generations.

In the **Manusmriti**, 4/229-234, some interesting benefits of giving charity are explained. It is said that whoever feeds a hungry person finds great satisfaction. One who gives sesame seeds in charity is blessed with cherished progeny. One who gives a lamp or some form of light in charity is blessed with good eyesight. One who donates land receives land in return. Whoever donates gold is blessed with long life. Those who donate silver are blessed with beauty and charm. Of all charities, the best is teaching of the Vedas.

When a donor gives charity with love and devotion, and the benefactor receives it with the same sentiments, both the donor and benefactor go to heaven. When there is disrespect in giving or receiving, both go to hell. With whatever sentiments one gives charity, it returns in the same way.

In the **Skandpuran**, Maheshwarkhand, it is said:

न्यायोपार्जित वित्तस्य दशमांशेन धीमतः ।
कर्त्तव्यो विनियोगश्च ईश्वरप्रीत्यर्थमेव च ॥

No virtue accrues from charity that is given out of ill-gotten wealth. In giving charity out of duty it is important that one must adhere to morality and ethics.

"What is the best charity?" the Yaksh asked Yudhistra.

"That which is given to a deserving person," Yudhistra said. "Charity must be given to a person who can put it to the best use. Only then is it virtuous."

Hindu texts tell us that Karan gave his skin in charity, Shivi gave his flesh, and Ddhichi gave his ashes. Of all donors, Karan shall forever be remembered for his charitable disposition.

When the gods could not kill the powerful Vritrasur, who was creating havoc everywhere, they were frightened. In desperation, the gods went to Brahma seeking a solution. They were told that only a weapon made from the ashes of an ascetic could kill Vritrasur. Ddhichi was the best known amongst the ascetics. When the gods led by Indra went to him and explained their predicament, he agreed to give up his body for the welfare of the gods. With ashes obtained through cremation of the body the weapon was made and ultimately Vritrasur was killed.

Think it over...

Consecrate your life to the realisation of something higher and broader than yourself and you will never feel the weight of the passing years.

–**The Mother**

What is the purpose of fasts for Hindus?

The purpose of fasting is not to starve oneself. A fast is symbolic of self-control. Since food is the most common weakness in mankind, control over eating is considered difficult. There are ample examples in the Puranas that saints and sages learnt to control their physical and mental self through fasts. Thus they purified their mind and soul and developed divine powers.

In the **Yajur-Veda**, 19/30, it is said:

व्रतेन दीक्षामाप्नोति दीक्षयाप्नोति दक्षिणाम् ।
दक्षिणा श्रद्धामाप्नोति श्रद्धया सत्यमाप्यते ॥

Mankind develops the ability for progressive living through fasts that serve as diksha *(initiation). From* diksha *one moves tc* dakshina, *that is, whatever one does one finds success. From this, faith and devotion grow, and from them, one attains truth or one's aim in life. This is the basic conclusion.*

One should not compromise with moral responsibilities and character in difficult situations. The fulfilment of these responsibilities devotedly is the purpose of making a resolve, or observing a fast. Living by resolutions and beliefs and adopting actions that lead us to our aims is important.

To overcome imperfections and tensions that are a part of modern life, the best solution is self-purification through fasting. The use of cereals in the diet produces toxins, which make one lazy and inefficient. These also neutralise spiritual energy generated through prayers and devotion to God. Through fasting, toxins are removed and the mind and body feel better. Self-confidence grows. One develops greater harmony. These, in turn, develop other abilities and powers within a person. Through patience, energy is conserved. Thus fasting helps protect a person and makes him more efficient.

In the **Bhagavad Gita**, it is said that the best way to control your senses and the mind is to fast.

Science too commends control over diet. By fasting once a week, one is able to rest organs within the body. This promotes good health and long life. Through fasting one also benefits emotionally and spiritually.

The purpose of the fast is not to ignore the body, but rather a means to achieve a particular aim in life. It is the firm resolution and the steps taken to achieve it that benefits the person.

Lord Buddha resolved that whatever happened, he would not leave his asana until he had attained nirvana. He was unmindful that the muscles and fat in his body would waste away. The bones would get porous. He would shrivel without food and drink. But he did not move from the asana. With this firm resolution he attained nirvana.

174

There are seven days in the week. A different god governs each day. Depending upon the purpose of the fast, one fasts accordingly. A common reason for fasting is to get over the malefic effect of a particular planet or god, or to achieve something through a blessing of the god. For each day there is a different procedure, different ways to pray to God, and also a different *katha* to read or *arti* to sing. However one resolves to fast, one must understand the details of different fasts.

A fast on **Sunday** is devoted to Surya – the sun. Eye problems or those pertaining to heat and skin may affect one. Blessings from Surya enable one to receive honour and fame and achieve success over enemies. Food is eaten once in the day before sunset. Food must not be eaten after sunset. It must be free of salt and oil. It must not be *tamsik*. One must offer prayers to Surya and read or listen to the prescribed *katha*. Only then one must eat. To appease Surya one should wear ruby. When inclined to give charity one must give wheat, red pulses, jaggery, or metals like gold and copper or ruby amongst gems. The best time to give charity is at sunset.

A fast on **Monday** is devoted to Chandrama – the moon. Prayers are offered to Lord Shiva and Goddess Parvati. Since they had a long, happy married life, fasting on Mondays helps one find a suitable marital partner. There are three kinds of fasts observed on Mondays. The routine fast observed on a Monday is the *saumya pradosh* – the fast to seek pardon for a fault, and a fast for 16 Mondays. The procedure to be followed is similar, but in each case the *katha* to be read or heard is different. Food is eaten once in the day. Cereals are permitted. After prayers to Shiva and Parvati one must read or hear the appropriate *katha*. To appease Chandrama one must wear pearls and silver. When inclined to give charity, one must give white things like rice, white clothes, conch shells, silver or pearls.

A fast on **Tuesday** is devoted to Mangal – the planet Mars. It is believed that fasting for 12 Tuesdays helps overcome the malefic effects of this planet. All kinds of obstacles are overcome. It also brings fame and honour. Prayers must be offered to Hanuman. Use of red clothes and red flowers is auspicious. Food prepared of wheat and jaggery must be eaten once in the day. After prayers to Hanuman one must read the *katha*.

A fast on **Wednesday** is devoted to Budh – the planet Mercury. One must preferably eat green things once in the day. One must pray to Lord Shiva and follow it by reading or hearing the *katha*. To appease Budh one must wear emerald in gold. When inclined to give charity one must give moong (green gram – *Phaseolus mungo*), kasturi (musk), blue clothes, gold, copper and five gems.

A fast on **Thursday** is devoted to Brihaspati – the planet Jupiter. It promotes greater learning and prosperity. Prayers must be offered to Brihespeshwar Mahadev, followed by reading or hearing the *katha*. One must preferably wear yellow clothes and use yellow sandalwood. Food must be eaten once. One must include yellow pulses in the meal. To appease Brihaspati one should wear topaz in gold. When inclined to give charity one should give yellow things like turmeric, salt, yellow clothes, rice, yellow pulses, gold and topaz.

A fast on **Friday** is devoted to Shukra – the planet Venus. The procedure for this fast is similar to that of Monday. It is preferable that food is eaten once a day. It must include white preparations like *kheer* (rice porridge) or *rabri* (milk preparation). To appease Shukra one must wear *mani* (a gem) in silver. Those inclined to charity must give rice, white clothes, a cow, ghee, diamonds and gold.

A fast on Friday is also devoted to Santoshi Maa. She is the daughter of Sri Ganesh and blesses one with happiness and contentment. Prayers are offered to her followed by *katha* and *arti*. Food must be eaten once. This is a strict fast and nothing sour or acidic must be eaten or offered to anyone else. It is customary to fast for 16 Fridays. On the final day, young boys are fed.

A fast on **Saturday** is devoted to Shani – the planet Saturn. The effect of Shani is harsh and lasts for a long time. Therefore this fast is observed. Shani is fond of all kinds of black things like black clothes, black peas, black sesame, iron and oil. Prayers are offered to Shani followed by the *katha* and *arti*. To appease Shani one must use sapphire and iron. When inclined to give charity one should give black things like an iron vessel with oil, an umbrella, a black shoe, black clothes, black sesame and black peas.

Fasts by Hindus are not restricted to just the seven gods that represent each day of the week. For instance, twice a year there are **Navratris** or the nine nights in the months of Chaitra and Ashvin when special worship of Goddess Durga is performed. These nine nights or ten days are very important to Hindus. Special prayers are performed in almost all homes. Even when prayers are not performed at home, group prayers are conducted. Many people observe fasts on all the days. Some observe them on particular days. No cereals are eaten. Only vegetables and fruits are eaten. In Chaitra on the ninth day the birth of Lord Ram is observed. In Ashvin on the tenth day, Lord Ram killed Ravana and Dashera is celebrated. The Navratris are very special occasions for Hindus, celebrated with great gaiety and religious fervour. Prayers are performed on all days. At the culmination of the celebrations, many Hindus offer food and gifts to young girls, symbolising Goddess Durga.

Many Hindus fast once a month on the full moon day, when prayers are offered to Lord Satyanarayan. The *katha* is read followed by *arti*. Food is eaten once in the day. Other special days include Mahashivratri and Krishna Janmashtmi. While one is dedicated to Lord Shiva, the other is dedicated to Lord Krishna.

There are several fasts observed by women, the most important being Karvachauth. This fast is observed to seek a long life for the husband and also happiness in marriage. This is one of the strictest fasts where women wake up early, eat before sunrise and then do not eat or drink anything for the whole day. They eat only at night after they have seen the moon.

There are several other fasts observed amongst Hindus, but they are not as popular as the ones described. What is significant about a fast is not missing out on food because there are ignorant people who eat twice as much the next day! The important aspect of a fast is the faith and devotion to the cause for which the fast is observed. When one is devoted and observes discipline the resolution becomes effective and bears the desired fruit.

What benefits accrue from *Maun-vrat*?

*M*aun-vrat literally means *a vow to keep silent*. For spiritual growth it is essential that one's speech must be pure. To acquire purity of speech the practice of silence is important. Hindu religious texts commend *maun-vrat* for this purpose. In Bhadon, the sixth month of the Hindu calendar, 16 days of *maun-vrat* are said to be useful. It is believed that through silence one is able to achieve one's desires. One attains the abode of Lord Shiva. Along with *maun-vrat* it is essential that some time must be spent in offering prayers.

In the **Bhagavad Gita**, 17/16, it is said:

मनः प्रसादः सौम्यत्वं मौनमात्मविनिग्रहः ।
भावसंशुद्धिरित्येतत्तपो मानसमुच्यते ॥

Contentment of the mind, amiable temperament, silence, religious meditation and good though reflect austerity of the mind.

Silence is placed mid-way between other qualities. It begins with control of the mind. On the mind is controlled, one becomes friendly. One begins to look kindly towards others. O cuts down on useless speech and thinks more of God. One begins to generate good though

In the **Chanakya Niti**, 11/9, it is said:

ये तु संवत्सरं पूर्णं नित्यं मौनेन भुंजते ।
युगकोटिसहस्रैस्तु स्वर्गलोके महीयते ॥

178

Whoever can remain silent everyday for a full year becomes worthy of thousands of years of praise in heaven.

Silence can change the personality of an individual. Through silence a person controls anger and speech. One grows stronger through greater determination and self-confidence. One is more at peace and free of tension. There is conservation of energy and a person experiences greater inner strength. *Maun-vrat* definitely helps one develop into a better person.

In the *Mahabharata*, there is a story pertaining to silence. After Maharishi Vedavyas had dictated the last *shloka* and Lord Ganesh had noted it down on the *bhojpatra*, Maharishi Vedavyas said, "Viganeshwar! Blessed is your writing! The Supreme Spirit has created the *Mahabharata* and you have written it. What is most amazing is your silence. During dictation I must have spoken almost twenty hundred thousand words, but all along I did not hear a single word from you."

Lord Ganesh thoughtfully responded, "Bdryan! Some lamps have a lot of oil; others have only a little. No lamp has a continuous supply of oil. In the same way, gods, mankind and demons have a limited life. Only those who have self-control and use their powers with patience and understanding can fully benefit from their life. The first step to self-control is to control one's speech. Whoever cannot control his speech loses energy unnecessarily. Through control of speech one avoids such a loss. I have always believed in the power of silence."

Your questions answered...

Why is there an emphasis on silence?
We all know that if speech is silvern, silence is golden. Silence helps to conserve energy, to concentrate and introspect. It helps one in the search of divinity. By observing silence one gains goals easily.

Why is the Hindu calendar full of a variety of festivals?

Any culture that goes back thousands of years and is interspersed with lives of great men and women is bound to have many occasions to celebrate each year. The Hindu way of life is no different. Outstanding people have not only given us opportunities to celebrate and remember them on these special occasions, but have continued to inspire us through their dedication and sacrifices so that we could live a better life.

Once a devotee asked Maharishi Kanad, "Gurudev! Our everyday life is full of occasions to fast, and to celebrate anniversaries and special occasions. Hardly does a day go by without them. Why is it so?"

"My dear child," Maharishi responded, "a fast is observed so that a person can learn to observe greater control over oneself. They promote purity of self. The anniversaries of great people are celebrated so that we can draw inspiration from their great lives. It gives one an opportunity to think of their love, dedication and sacrifices for mankind. We can respond by observing fasts, through silence and introspection and by learning more about them. We can resolve to give up some bad habit, or strengthen a good one. It is not possible to observe too many fasts, but if one wants to observe a fast once a month, the full moon day is best. Those who wish to fast twice a month can observe them on Ekadashi. If a weekly fast is desired, Sunday or Thursday are most suitable."

180

Festivals are occasions to convey our gratitude to the Supreme Spirit, to share what we have with our family and others. The celebrations help break the monotony of everyday life and usher in change. They bring people closer and take people closer to nature and God. They inspire us to live a virtuous life.

India is a vast country. There are climatic variations. There are differences of language, food and habits. There are regional variations. Some festivals are celebrated with greater zest in certain areas. Many festivals are celebrated simultaneously all over the country. There is something going on around the year.

The conventional New Year begins with **Lori** on 13 January. This is the coldest time of the year, particularly in the northern regions. A bonfire is built. Prayers are offered to Agni. Sweets and dry fruits are served. Special greetings are offered to those who are newly married, or have been blessed with a baby.

The next day is **Makar Sankranti** when the sun changes course. On this day people bathe in the Ganga and other holy rivers and give food items in charity.

In the last week of January, or the beginning of February, **Basant Panchmi** is celebrated. This festival is symbolic of oncoming spring. The fields look beautiful with wheat and mustard in full flower. To be in harmony with the yellow of the flowers people wear cream or yellow clothes. Kite flying is particularly common in the northern region. This day is dedicated to Ma Saraswati. Teachers, writers, musicians and others offer prayers to her. Sweets are distributed. The evening is marked by organising musical concerts.

In mid-February we have **Mahashivratri**. This is the day when Shiva manifests Himself. Devotees observe a strict fast until midnight. The mantra *Om Nama Shivaya* is chanted. A very large number of people carry Ganga water for the Shivaling in their village or town. The festival is symbolic of rising from ignorance to knowledge.

In March, we have **Holi**, a festival unique in its observance. People start making preparations for it many days in advance when they begin collecting firewood in important public places. This is intended to symbolically burn Holika, and celebrate Holi the next day by throwing dry and wet colours on each other in a festive mood. In the religious texts there are accounts of Krishna and the gopis playing Holi. This is a festival of friendship, an occasion to forgive and forget. The festival is marked with eating, drinking, fun and laughter.

Soon thereafter there is **Navratri** – the nine nights devoted to Goddess Durga. Special prayers are offered. Fasts are observed. The birth anniversary of Ram falls on the ninth day and is celebrated as **Ramnaumi**. Prayers are offered in temples and homes. Offering of food to young girls symbolic of the Goddess on the 8th or 9th day is customary amongst families and concludes Navratri.

Then, 13 April is celebrated as **Baisakhi**. It coincides with the harvest of wheat and other winter crops, and is symbolic of thanksgiving. People bathe in Ganga and other holy rivers. They wear new clothes and celebrate by singing and dancing.

Mahavir Jayanti and **Buddha Purnima** fall in May and are appropriately celebrated.

In the beginning of June, **Ganga Dashera** and **Nirjala Ekadashi** are celebrated by bathing in the Ganga and other holy rivers. It is common to offer thirst-quenching drinks to people to ward off heat.

All devotees of Shiva look forward to the *amavasya* (dark night) falling in the end of July. Hundreds of thousands of devotees collect Ganga water at Hardwar and carry it in decorated *kavads* walking long distances to their destinations to offer it on *amavasya* day. The collection of the Ganga water begins a fortnight earlier on the full moon day. Perhaps no other religious activity matches this 15-day effort by hundreds of thousands of devotees who converge at Hardwar to collect the water and carry it to temples near their homes.

The full moon day is celebrated as **Guru Purnima** when all devotees offer thanksgiving prayers and gifts to gurus.

The birth of Krishna is celebrated as **Janamasthmi** that falls in August. Many devotees fast on the day and offer prayers. Tableaus depicting the birth of Krishna are made in many temples and homes. The fast continues till midnight.

On the full moon day in August, **Raksha Bandhan** is celebrated. This festival could be termed Brother's Day, when sisters tie a thread on the brother's wrist, apply tilak and offer sweets. They wish him long life. In reciprocation, brothers give gifts. This festival is symbolic of sisters wishing their brothers long life, and brothers offering sisters protection.

An important festival celebrated in Maharashtra, Tamil Nadu, Karnataka and Andhra Pradesh is **Ganesh Chaturthi**. People establish Ganesh temples in their homes and buildings for nine days, and invite relatives and friends for prayers and devotional singing. On the ninth or tenth day (some families do it before this), the idol is carried to the sea, river or inland body of water and immersed there.

Just before the second Navratris in early October, there are 15 days of **Shraddh** dedicated to remembering forefathers. During this period no auspicious work is done. Food is offered to Brahmins in memory of forefathers.

The second **Navratris** are celebrated with much singing and dancing in some parts of the country. Prayers are offered for eight or nine days as is customary amongst families. Many observe fasts on all days. Some observe them on select days. Temporary temples with huge idols of the Goddess are erected. Young girls are offered food at the conclusion of prayers. At the end of the celebrations, the idols are immersed in nearby rivers or the sea.

Dashera marks the victory of Lord Ram over Ravana and is celebrated on the tenth day. This festival is celebrated throughout India with much gaiety. It is symbolic of the victory of good over evil. It is customary to build huge effigies of Ravana, his brother Kumbhkaran and son Meghnath and consign them to flames accompanied with fireworks.

On the eighth day after Dashera most Hindu ladies observe the **Karvachauth** fast for the long life of their husbands. This is one of the strictest fasts observed by ladies.

On the 20th day after Dashera, Lord Ram returned to Ayodhya, and for this reason **Diwali** is celebrated. This festival is of great significance to businessmen. Gifts are exchanged amongst business colleagues and family members. Homes are decorated with lights. Bonus is offered to employees. People greet each other wishing happiness and prosperity.

The next day after Diwali is celebrated as **Gowardhan Puja**. Cows and bullocks are decorated, and offered special feed. It is a thanksgiving to them by the farming class for their support in their work. Many offer prayers to Vishvakarma on this day.

Two days after Diwali, **Bhaiya Duj** is celebrated. Again, this is a festival dedicated to brothers, where sisters apply tilak on the brother's forehead and wish them good health and long life. It was on this day that Ram was formally declared the king of Ayodhya.

The full moon that follows is celebrated as **Gurpurb**, Guru Nanak's birthday. It is the most important day of celebration for Sikhs and is marked with prayers and offering of food and charity.

Your questions answered...

How can one be happy at all times?

One who follows the will of God is always happy.

Why are prayers offered to Ma Lakshmi on Diwali?

On Diwali evening every Hindu offers prayers to Lakshmi for wealth and prosperity. It is believed that on Diwali Lakshmi visits all homes. As a symbolic gesture many people paint the feet of Lakshmi entering from the threshold. Prayers are offered to Lakshmi on several occasions around the year, but prayers on Diwali are most popular. Businessmen offer prayers to Lakshmi, and open new account books. Since it is customary to first offer prayers to Lord Ganesh, it is popular to first establish a temporary temple within the home with idols of Lord Ganesh and Goddess Lakshmi and then offer prayers.

Lakshmi is said to be unsteady and transient and does not stay at one place for long. Since everyone desires that she stay within the home permanently, prayers are offered to Lakshmi. It is believed that the art of attracting Lakshmi through devotion is secret and difficult to achieve. This is because of a strict direction by Vishvamitra, who directed that the procedures must be kept secret and taught to a capable successor only at the end of one's life.

In the **Ravana Samhita**, Ravana has said that devotion to Lakshmi is an outstanding devotion, and that he learnt it from Kuber, the God of Wealth. He said that with that knowledge he was able to make Lanka prosperous.

In the **Goraksh Samhita**, Guru Gorakhnath has also described devotion to Lakshmi as outstanding. Lord Krishna stressed that through devotion to Lakshmi great prosperity can be attained as he did in Dwarka.

It is believed that during the churning of the ocean by the gods and the asurs when Lakshmi appeared, Indra offered prayers that pleased her. In blessing, she told him that whoever receives the 12-letter mantra from him and repeats it devotedly during the three prayers everyday shall attain prosperity like Kuber. This was the beginning of prayers to Lakshmi.

In the **Mahabharata**, Udyogparv, 38/38, it is said:

धृतिः शमो दमः शौच कारुण्य वागनिष्ठुरा ।
मित्राणां चानभिद्रोहः सप्तैताः समिधः श्रियः ॥

Patience, self-control, control over the senses, compassion, gentle speech and holding no grudges against friends and others promote glory and prosperity.

In the **Hitopadesh**, 178, it is said:

उत्साहसम्पन्नमदीर्घसूत्रं क्रियाविधिज्ञं व्यसनेष्वसक्तम् ।
शूरं कृतज्ञं दृढ सौहृदंच लक्ष्मीः स्वयं याति निवास हेतो ॥

Whoever is enthusiastic, active, capable in his work, not addicted to vice, grateful and devotedly friendly shall find that Lakshmi voluntarily comes to reside in his home.

In the **Sharda Tilak**, 8/161, it is said that those who desire prosperity must be truthful, must eat facing the west, and must speak gently and laughingly.

Once with the welfare of mankind in mind, Pradyuman's mother Rukmani asked Lakshmi, "Devi, what kind of people and places please you to reside with them?"

Lakshmi responded, "I reside with people who speak moderately, are efficient, do not lose their temper, are devoted, grateful, have control over self and are generous. I always live with people who are virtuous, religious, those that respect the elderly, are pure at heart and are wise and forgiving. I live with women who serve their husbands, who are forgiving, truthful, balanced, simple and virtuous. They must respect the gods and Brahmins. I live with all those who are endowed with virtuous qualities. Wherever yagyas are performed, prayers are offered to gods, cows and Brahmins are cared for, I never leave those homes."

The religious texts also say that Lakshmi never resides where people wear dirty clothes, do not clean their teeth or fail to take a bath, eat excessively or use abusive language, or sleep after the sun has risen high. It is also said that Lakshmi forsakes those who wear others' clothes, or use others' vehicle or have relations with other women or live in others' homes.

Lakshmi never resides with people who are lazy, get angry quickly, are miserly, given to addiction, are immoral, egoistic, short-sighted and use crude or abusive language.

In the **Mahabharata**, Shantiparv, 225, it is explained that once when King Bali opposed the Brahmins after eating offensive food, Lakshmi immediately left his palace. She said, "I detest those who steal, are addicted, impure and restless. I am leaving Bali's palace even though he is devoted to me."

Do pilgrimages really benefit people?

In ancient times, when people thought they were ready to learn more about God, they set out on a pilgrimage. The journey was difficult, but it would be a unique experiment in interacting with people and situations. They went to a place that was specially blessed by nature. It could be near a river or lake, near the sea or deep in the hills, lush green and cool. There would be others like them in similar search of God, or to give life a new perspective. Since they were away from home there would be no interruptions to respond to everyday challenges of life. These were occasions to exchange knowledge and learn from each other.

With time, the places of pilgrimage have not lost their character. Only, they are now more crowded and commercialised. Larger numbers of pilgrims visit them every year, but not all are in search of God or to find a new meaning of life. Some travel for fun and to relax in new surroundings. If nothing else, they do so to shed some of their tensions and cares of life.

The religious texts say:

तारयितुं समर्थः इति तीर्थः ।

A pilgrimage is a place where one can learn to float or cross over the vast river of life.

One can learn to swim in this vast river of life through noble thoughts and deeds and in the company of good people. Pilgrimages are places where one finds strong magnetic vibrations emerging from gods and goddesses, from the beauty of natural surroundings, from hills and rivers that exert a special influence, from the presence of saints and ascetics who sing and preach the glory of the Supreme Spirit.

The religious texts are full of descriptions and benefits of going on pilgrimage. Large parts of the **Shivpuran**, **Padampuran** and **Skandpuran** are devoted to the benefits of pilgrimages. Even in the Vedas, Puranas and Upa Puranas and in the *Mahabharata* there are portions which say that by going on pilgrimage one gets rid of sins, accumulates virtues, finds favour with gods and goddesses, achieves inner peace, finds fulfilment in everyday life and steps towards heaven. These benefits inspire the common householder to go on a pilgrimage.

In the **Mahabharata**, Vanparv, it is said that through a pilgrimage one can conveniently attain the benefits that cannot be easily attained even through the special Agnistome yagya. However, those who travel for fun or sightseeing and are devoid of the devotion required for a pilgrimage cannot attain these benefits. A pilgrimage should have two objectives – the cleansing of the mind and welfare of the self. Those who travel with these objectives benefit from a pilgrimage.

In the **Mahabharata**, Vanparv, 85/92, it is said:

पुष्करे तु कुरुक्षेत्रे गंगायां मगधेषु च ।
स्नात्वा तारयते जन्तुः सप्त सप्तावरांस्तधा ॥

Whoever bathes in the holy pilgrimages at Pushkar, Kurukshetra, Ganga and Magadh benefits seven generations each of forefathers and successors.

In the **Devi Bhagwat**, it is said that just as the purpose of agriculture is to produce grain, the purpose of a pilgrimage is to become sinless. In the **Atharva-Veda**, 18/4/7, it is said that pilgrims get over sins and shortcomings through pilgrimages and advance towards a pure wholesome life. It is also said the benefits that accrue from a pilgrimage are in direct proportion to the devotion of the pilgrim.

In the **Bhavishyapuran**, Uttara, 122/7-8, it is said:

यस्य हस्तौ च पादौ च वाङ्मनस्तु सुसंयते ।
विद्या तपश्च कीर्तिश्च स तीर्थफलमश्नुते ॥
अश्रद्दधानः पापात्मा नास्तिकोऽच्छिसंशयः ।
हेतुनिष्ठाश्च पंचैते न तीर्थफलभागिनः ॥

When the hands, the legs, the mind and the speech are in balance, and the person is knowledgeable, reputed and devoted, one benefits from a pilgrimage. One who is not devoted, is a sinner, is suspicious, an unbeliever or a sophist – these five kinds of people never benefit from a pilgrimage.

In the **Naradpuran**, it is said:

कामं क्रोधं च लोभं च यो जित्वा तीर्थमाविशेत् ।
न तेन किंचिदप्राप्तं तीर्थाभिगमनाद् भवेत् ॥

Whoever controls passion, anger and greed when on a pilgrimage achieves everything from it.

In the **Skandpuran**, 2/6, it is said:

यस्य हस्तौ च पादौ च मनश्चैव सुसंयतम् ।
निर्विकाराः क्रियाः सर्वाः स तीर्थफलमश्नुते ॥

Whoever has control over his hands, legs and the mind and has all the faculties in good order benefits the most from a pilgrimage.

In the **Skandpuran**, it is also said that speaking the truth is a pilgrimage. Forgiveness is a pilgrimage that bears fruit. Control over the senses is as beneficial as a pilgrimage. Kindness to all people is as virtuous as a pilgrimage. A simple life too is like a pilgrimage. Amongst all pilgrimages the most outstanding one is the purification of the mind.

In the **Padampuran**, it is said that during pilgrimages one comes across saints and ascetics and those that are specially blessed by God. Meeting them can help destroy sins just as if one would burn them with fire.

Religious writers affirm that passion, anger, greed, attachment and pride are like dirt in the mind. To cleanse the mind of this dirt is the best pilgrimage.

At the end of the *Mahabharata*, Yudhistra decided to go on a pilgrimage. His four brothers – Bhim, Arjun, Nakul and Sahadev and Draupadi were to accompany him. Before leaving they called on Lord Krishna. Handing over his *kamandal* (wooden pot used by mendicants), Krishna said, "During the pilgrimage wherever you get an opportunity to bathe in a river, a lake or the sea, do dip this *kamandal* in the water."

After many days when they returned from the pilgrimage they visited Lord Krishna and handing over the *kamandal* told him that it had been dipped in all holy bathing places. Lord Krishna took over the *kamandal* and smashed it against the floor. It broke into tiny pieces. He distributed the pieces to all present as *prasad*. Whoever put the *prasad* in the mouth found it bitter and spat it out. When Lord Krishna saw the faces of those who had tasted the *prasad*, he turned towards Yudhistra and asked, "This *kamandal* has visited all the pilgrimages and also bathed in all the holy places. Why does it still taste bitter?"

"What are you saying?" Yudhistra responded. "Can washing of the *kamandal* rid it of its bitterness?"

"If that be so," Lord Krishna said, "then by following the spiritual advice of bathing in holy places how can one cleanse the inner self just by washing or purifying the body or using ornaments?"

Yudhistra corrected himself and understood the need for cleansing of the inner self through a pilgrimage.

Your questions answered...

Does going to places of pilgrimage help get rid of sins?

Places of pilgrimage offer opportunities for personal growth because of the natural environment of the place, and also because many holy people live in such places. However, the benefit a person derives from visits to these places is directly proportional to one's faith and devotion. It also depends upon the effort the person makes to seek guidance and develop the personal self.

Why do Hindus aspire to go on the *Char Dham Yatra*?

*C*har means *four*. Dham denotes *the abode of a deity* and *yatra* refers to a *pilgrimage*. Therefore, *Char Dham Yatra* means *pilgrimage to offer obeisance to the four important abodes of Hindu gods*. It is noteworthy that the four dhams are situated at four different ends of the country. Jagannath Puri is alongside the sea on the east, Dwarka is on the seaside in the west, Badrinath is deep in the hills in the north and Rameswaram is on the seaside in the south.

It is the secret desire of every Hindu to visit all the four *dhams* in his lifetime. That would qualify him for a place in heaven. Earlier, with thousands of kilometres between one *dham* and another it was a very difficult task. Few had the time and wherewithal to do it. It is still not easy now either. But with many swift forms of travel and more conveniences, it is not as difficult. It is said that in the Hindu traditions just as there are four Vedas, four castes and four directions, there are four important places of pilgrimage.

Perhaps these four places of pilgrimage are recommended to Hindus to make them aware of the extent of influence of Hindu deities. Visiting these places is also a test of one's devotion. Travelling such long distances is not always easy. Therefore it is a challenge to all those who undertake to visit all the four *dhams*. Besides the spiritual influence of a visit to each of these four powerful deities, one cannot ignore the experience or gains through such long travel and interaction with people who look, eat and speak differently.

Jagannath Puri has been described as a heavenly pilgrimage. Lord Krishna spent some time here. *Jagannath* literally means *master of the universe*, that is, Lord Vishnu. The deity in the temple is that of Vishnu/Krishna. Alongside the main deity the idols of Balram and Subhadra are also present. The idols are made of sandalwood. It is believed that Brahma presented the eyes of the principal deity and Lord Vishnu conducted the *pran pratishtha* ceremony. It is believed that within the deity there is a casket containing a portion of Krishna's ashes. Every 12 years the casket is transferred into a new idol and the old one is replaced. Within Jagannath Puri there are five sacred places – Markandya, Chandan, Parvati Talab, Shwetganga and Inderghuman.

The *prasad* distributed at Jagannath Puri is renowned worldwide as extremely pure and wholesome. It can be consumed even when one is on fast. Interestingly, people of all religions sit together and eat. A visit to this site is particularly virtuous.

Dwarka has ancient, historic and religious importance. After leaving Mathura Lord Krishna, his brother Balram and the Yadavs moved to Dwarka to establish it as a capital city. Dwarkapeeth was established here in the 8th century by Adi Shankaracharya to promote Sanatan Dharm. Since then Hindus have accepted it as one of the four dhams. Vajranath, son of Anirudh, constructed the abode of the deity in Dwarkadheesh temple. Here an idol of Lord Krishna reigns supreme. Dwarkapeeth Math holds special significance for all Hindus. A temple dedicated to Rukmani, one of Krishna's queens, is famous for its unique architecture.

189

In the **Skandpuran**, Prabhaskhand, it is mentioned that the deity at Dwarka is very benevolent. Even those born as bacteria, insects, birds, animals and reptiles are absolved of their sins and attain salvation. Those who live there are specially blessed because they are always serving Lord Krishna. Even sages and ascetics cannot attain the righteousness achieved by them. It is believed that the very touch of the people who live there absolves others of their sins. It qualifies them for heaven. Even the dust of Dwarka is said to be special. All those who pray, meditate, offer sacrifices and penance in Dwarka offer it all to Lord Krishna who comes closer to them.

Rameswaram is well known because after his victory over Ravana in Lanka, Lord Ram came here and offered his gratitude to Shiva. The *Ramayana* says that it was here that Lord Ram bathed and offered his prayers to Shiva before he advanced to wage war against Ravana and his demon force. It was in Kotandarmar temple that Ravana's brother Vibhishan surrendered before Lord Ram and sought his protection. In Dhanushkodi temple there are idols of Lord Ram, Sita, Lakshman, Hanuman and Vibhishan. The corridors of the Ramnath Swami temple are larger than those of any other temple in India. The temple fulfils all the requirements of Vaastu.

Of the 12 famous Jyotirlinghas one is at Rameswaram. In the **Skandpuran**, Brahmkhand, it is said that Rameswaram is important because of the bridge constructed here by Lord Ram. By seeing the bridge one is blessed. The devotion for Lord Vishnu and Shiva increases and one becomes virtuous. A person succeeds in whatever he does through physical or mental effort or through speech. Just thinking about and visualising the Rameswaram *lingam* absolves one of all sins.

Badrinath is situated deep within the Himalayas between Nar and Narayan peaks alongside the Alaknanda River. The beauty of Badrinath has been described in the *Mahabharata, Skandpuran* and several other Hindu religious texts. The principal deity is Lord Vishnu. Made of shalgram stone, the idol is artistically carved. According to old descriptions, Adi Shankaracharya located the idol in a nearby pond in the 7th century. While the rapidly flowing water in the Alaknanda River is freezing cold, there are hot springs next to it. The devotees bathe in the Tapti kund before offering prayers in the temple. When the Pandavas visited Badrinath, Bhim placed a huge boulder in the river to help others cross it. This is known as the Bhim shila. I is said that in a nearby cave known as Vyas Gufa, Vyas wrote the Puranas. The rocks outside the cave resemble a book and are known as Pustika. The two hot water ponds are known a Narad kund and Surya kund.

In the *Mahabharata*, it is said that to benefit from pilgrimages to other holy places one mus perform religious ceremonies. However, a visit to the area in the viscinity of Badrinath templ is enough to attain salvation. Of all pilgrimages, a visit to Badrinath is most outstanding. Lor Vishnu resides here. A visit to Badrinath frees one from worry, greed and grief. By offerin prayers at the temple one attains heaven.

Situated deep within the Himalayas at a height of over 10,000 feet above sea level the templ is surrounded by snow for long periods. The temple is open for about six months every yea

When it is opened in the beginning of summer people from all over the country assemble to see the Akhand Jyoti that continues unattended through the winter months.

Your questions answered...

When hundreds of important temples and pilgrimage sites are spread all over the country why has special emphasis been given to the *Char Dham Yatra*?

The principal reason for the recommendation is that all the four places of pilgrimage are special. The deities are very powerful. However, an important reason for recommending them is that they are situated in four different corners of the country. Travelling to them is difficult. It arouses faith and devotion. Besides travelling to far-off places affords an opportunity to come across a variety of people and situations. The experience helps one grow spiritually.

Why are Kumbh Melas celebrated only at four places of pilgrimage?

A pilgrimage unique to India is the Kumbh Mela celebrated every 12 years. It is celebrated at four different places of pilgrimage at different times. Millions of people from within the country and abroad get together to bathe in the holy rivers, hear religious discourses, meet saints and sages and give charity. It is believed that those who participate in the Kumbh Mela attain salvation.

The four places where the Kumbh Mela is celebrated are Hardwar on the banks of the Ganga, at Allahabad (Prayag) where the rivers Ganga, Yamuna and Saraswati meet, at Ujjain alongside the river Shipra and at Nasik.

The beginning of the Kumbh Mela can be traced back to the time when the gods and the asurs churned the ocean to obtain valuable things. One of the things obtained was a *kalash* (pot) full of the celestial nectar, *amrit*. Both the gods and the asurs wanted it. When the gods ran off with it, the asurs followed in pursuit. The chase lasted 12 days. During the chase the *kalash* was rested at four places. Some even believe that Garuda flew away with the *kalash*, and during the chase a few drops of the nectar fell at these four places. At each of the four places the Kumbh Mela is held.

The twelve divine days of the chase are equivalent to 12 years of man. Therefore the Kumbh Mela is held every 12 years. Since the *kalash* was placed at different times in the four places, the Kumbh Mela is celebrated at different times in each place.

Kumbh means an *earthen pot or kalash.* The celestial nectar was inside. Therefore it is said that the human body that is also made of elements that come from the earth is like the Kumbh, and the soul within the body is like the celestial nectar. It has the divinity of God. The purpose of the Kumbh Melas is to provide an opportunity to millions of pilgrims to rise spiritually by identifying the divinity within them.

The Kumbh Melas at the four places of pilgrimage are unique festivals that have no parallel anywhere in the world. Elaborate arrangements are made. Saints and sages congregate from all over the country. Millions of people visit and benefit from these Melas.

Your questions answered...

• **How does God communicate? Why can't we understand Him?**

We converse with words. We expect God to respond the same way. God does not always speak. He communicates through thoughts, feelings and experiences. We fail to understand them because of our ignorance.

• **Does God communicate with a selected few, or with everyone?**

Why should God differentiate between people? They are His children. When people think that God differentiates between people, it is their imagination. However, God does take special care of those who are devoted to Him.

Are Hindus generally superstitious?

Hindus are overly conscious of auspicious or inauspicious situations and occasions. They are equally conscious of a day or time being auspicious or inauspicious for an activity or occasion. This consciousness has not emerged from nothing and the subject is discussed in the Vedas, Upanishads and other religious texts.

In the **Ramcharitmanas**, Balkand, 302/2-4, the situation when Lord Ram was ready to leave for the bride's home has been described as:

दाहिन काग सुखेत सुहावा । नकुल दरसु सब काहूं पावा ॥
सानुकूल बह त्रिविध बयारी । सघट सबाल आव बर नारी ॥
लोवा फिरि फिरि दरसु देखावा । सुरभी सनमुख सिसुहि पिआवा ॥
मृगमाला फिरि दाहिनि आई । मंगल गन जनु दीन्हि देखाई ॥
छेमकरी कह छेम बिसेषी । स्यामा बाम सुतरु पर देखी ॥
सनमुख आयउ दधि अरु मीना । कर पुस्तक दुइ विप्र प्रबीना ॥

The blue jay picked up food as though to announce good fortune. A cow and mongoose could be seen in the field on the right. The breeze was soft, cool and fragrant, blowing in a favourable direction. A blessed woman carrying a child in her arms and a pitcher on her head appeared to see the procession. A fox turned round and was visible again and again. A cow suckled its calf in front of the procession. Just then a herd of deer appeared on the right as though to announce good omens from all sides. A Brahman kite promised great blessings. A Syama bird was visible on an auspicious tree on the left. A man carrying curd and fish and two Brahmins carrying books came from the opposite direction.

In the **Vasantraj Shakun**, it is said:

शुभाशुभज्ञानविनिर्णयाय हेतुर्नृणां यः शकुनः ।

Signals that give indication of a situation being auspicious or inauspicious indicate it as an omen. When the signals reflect an auspicious occasion, it is a good omen. If the signal indicates inauspicious happenings, it is an ill omen.

It is believed that omens give an indication of what the future is going to be. In reality, it is the repetition of similar situations and associating them with our successes and failures that gives rise to such omens and beliefs. In astrology, it is commonplace to seek an appropriate date and time to commence new work, undertake a journey or celebrate a special occasion like a wedding.

Strange things and situations signal a good or bad omen. A variety of things and situations are considered a good omen. These include meeting a Brahmin, a little girl, a happily married woman or someone carrying cowdung or a quilt. It could also be a happy laughing child. Or a palanquin or a procession to the cremation ground. Animals too are symbols of good omens. Seeing a peacock, a white bullock, a cow, an elephant or a horse are considered fortunate. Things also signal good fortune. A full vessel, a conch shell, white clothes, sugarcane, ghee, curd, honey, rice and cooked cereals are considered good omens. Can sounds be auspicious? Yes, the sound of a conch shell, the sound of a religious discourse and sweet melodious music are good omens. A temple or religious place, gold jewellery, sandalwood in a bowl, sweets, a blue sky and a field full of grain are symbols of a good omen.

Things and situations that signal a bad omen include seeing a shooting star, seeing a woman in wet clothes, or somebody sneezing as you leave. A cat crossing the path, a crow cawing in the afternoon, wailing dogs and cats fighting are bad omens. Stumbling over something, the foot slipping, clothes getting entangled and meeting a one-eyed person are considered inauspicious. Amongst things, cotton, mud, leather, ash, a broken utensil, a bone, dried wood, oil, jaggery, soap and black peas are symbols of bad omens.

Excessive dependence upon good and bad omens makes a person superstitious. This means dependence more upon the supernatural than upon personal capabilities. This is not the right thing to do. One's success or failure depends upon the individual's thoughts, actions, habits and deeds.

To be successful in anything it is important that one must be eager, enthusiastic, patient and self-confident. When the level of these qualities comes down, one loses spontaneity, concentration and ability to work. The chances of success too take a downturn. This is the biggest problem when one is overly conscious of good and bad omens. These fill the mind with uncertainty, doubt and even terror. These are the seeds of failure, not success. One thinks of bad omens when one is confronted with failure. When one is successful the bad omens have no meaning. One must remember that success or failure depends upon our ability and preparedness.

Amongst Hindus even today twitching of the right eye in men and the left eye in women is considered auspicious. If it is the other way, it is considered inauspicious. The truth is that twitching is a physical aspect more to do with blood vessels and has nothing to do with a good or bad omen. When we know the facts why should we let it lower our self-confidence?

Sneezing is a normal body activity in certain situations. One sneezes when there is some irritation in the nasal passage. The act of sneezing removes it. Why make it a symbol of a bad omen? It could happen with anyone in a variety of situations.

Your questions answered...

Festivals provide a change from the monotony of everyday life. So does a vacation. Is there need for so many festivals and celebrations?

A vacation is a personal pursuit for relaxation and change. Very often it ends in exhaustion, both physical and financial. A festival involves many people from all strata of life. Friends, relatives and acquaintances are involved. Many aim at building goodwill and learning to develop control over oneself. It may involve fasting, charity and religious activity, which promote spiritual development. They do not end in exhaustion.

Does the 'evil eye' exist?

Everyone is afraid of the evil eye. This is something not restricted to Hindus. Even in other countries people are wary of the evil eye. The evil eye does not hurt only living beings. It can damage inanimate things too. The evil eye can befall anyone and anything. A beautiful statue can be damaged for no reason whatsoever. Without any indication a child can fall sick. A cow that gives milk regularly may stop giving milk. The evil eye can strike at any time.

What is the evil eye? It is difficult to find the exact cause. Yet when anyone stares at someone or something excessively with a negative intention, the negative vibrations get focussed with concentration on the person or thing and cause damage. A hungry man with an evil eye is believed to poison another's food with his wicked stare. That is the reason why people like to eat in privacy.

It has been observed that the evil eye mostly affects those who are tender, children, women and pets. Besides these, homes, industries, business, vehicles, shops and items like electrical appliances can also be affected. Amongst children, infants are most affected. An infant may be hale and hearty at one time and then suddenly become unwell. He may give up drinking milk and turn irritable. He may cry incessantly. The eyes may be swollen, the breath may be acidic and the digestion disturbed.

Women are invariably affected at the time of marriage or when they are going through a pregnancy. When a man is affected the common symptoms include mental tension, uneasiness, lack of balance, aches and pains, disturbed digestion and similar things.

The evil eye can be attributed to the use of negative human energy or vibrations for a damaging cause. In some individuals the negative vision is so overwhelming that an infant's positive energy is neutralised and with the disturbed vibrations the infant falls sick. It has been noted that a leopard can make a calf freeze with its vision. Similarly a wolf has an affinity for sheep and a cat has an affinity for pigeons. The victim loses the ability to flee.

To protect individuals from the evil eye, it is customary to use a black spot or a black thread. Black is a good conductor of electricity. Black colour neutralises the effect of negative vibrations. It has been observed that lightning falls on black objects. They may be individuals dressed in dark clothes, or black animals or objects. During winter darker clothes absorb and retain warmth.

To protect children from the evil eye, *kajal* (lamp black) is applied behind the ear or on the head, under the feet or on arms and in the eyes. It is also customary to tie a black cotton string around the waist, on the arm or around the neck. The practice of feeding an infant with the milk of a black goat or making it lick a black powder is to protect it from the evil eye. To protect children from the evil eye some tie a lion's nail on a black thread around the neck. Others use the feather of the blue jay.

Most adults use copper or silver charms, which may have a protective mantra written on them. Truck owners tie an old shoe to their truck to ward off the evil eye. Shopkeepers tie a lemon and green chillies on a thread at the entry to their store. Factory owners nail a used horseshoe at the entry of their premises. Householders hang an earthen bowl painted black in front of the house. These measures reduce the focus and concentration of the vibrations emitted by the evil eye.

Your questions answered...

Why are fun things always labelled wrong, immoral and illegal?

Fun things usually refer to the pleasures that one enjoys through the senses. These appear enjoyable to worldly people, but are a source of suffering. They are a cause of degeneration of mankind. They have a beginning and an end. They come and go. A wise person avoids them.

Do predetermined *Mahurats* ensure success and happiness?

Many people consult a Brahmin priest before starting anything new. It may be the laying of the foundation of a new house or shifting to a new house, starting of new work, a marriage in the family, a journey to a distant place or something similar. Some call it superstition. Others emphasise that in nature there are days and times when one is likely to succeed better.

In the **Brahmvarchas Panchang** it is said:

सदुद्देश्यकृते कार्ये विवाहे जातकर्मणि ।
विघ्नाऽशुभमुहूर्तानां प्रभावो नोपजायते ॥

Nothing inauspicious can affect a noble deed done with a noble objective.

How true! Whatever is good and noble will always succeed. Delaying it to search for an auspicious time would be wrong. One who is capable and confident will always succeed. If there are obstacles sometimes, they may be due to natural reasons and should be accepted as part of life. They should not be allowed to damage one's self-confidence.

In the **Brahmvarchas Panchang** it is also said:

यदानास्तं गतो भानुगोधूल्या पूरितं नभः ।
सर्वमंगलकार्येषु गोधूलिः शस्यते सदा ॥

The time when the sun is setting and the cows are returning home is auspicious for all good deeds.

199

It is also explained that Akshay Tritiya (the third day of the moonlit half of Baisakh), Akshay Naumi (the ninth day of the moonlit half of Kartik), Basant Panchmi (the fifth day of the moonlit half of Magh), Ganga Dashera (the tenth day of the moonlit half of Jaisth), Vijay Dasmi (the tenth day of the moonlit half of Ashwini), Mahashivratri (the fourteenth day of the dark fortnight of Phagun), Ramnaumi (the ninth day of the moonlit fortnight of Chaitra), and all the full moon days are auspicious for marriages and other new activities.

It is also believed that all activities conducted after religious rites or those conducted in places of pilgrimage need no special day or time. The purpose of the activity and circumstances are important. Success follows automatically.

Your questions answered...

What are the marks of persons born with demonic qualities?

Persons born with demonic qualities are given in to anger, greed, hypocrisy, pride and arrogance. Such persons do not understand when to act, and when not to. They do not believe in God, or His having created this universe. Such people have insatiable desires and through ignorance cherish false doctrines. They are devoted to the enjoyment of sensuous pleasures. To them that is the highest limit of joy. Given to lust and anger, they amass wealth by all kinds of means. They believe that they have supernatural powers and are mighty, and none could be like them. Even when they pray and give charity, it is only with ulterior motives.

Is prayer an important element in Hindu life?

For Hindus, praying to God is a part of everyday life. It may be a short thanksgiving to God or a request for some favour. Many are involved in a complete session with all its frills. Some pray individually. Others pray in a group. India is a land of gods. Everyone is free to choose one's God, or the mode of prayer. The Hindu way of life is liberal in this aspect.

Why is praying so important to Hindus? It is a way to express their faith and devotion to God. It is a way of looking up to a powerful force that has no equal. It not only gives one an ideal to strive for, but also an ability to transform oneself to become a better person. A little is achieved each day. It helps cushion problems of everyday life.

In the **Rig-Veda**, 1/113/11, it is said:

ईयुष्टे ये पूर्वतरामपश्यन्युच्छन्तीमुषसं मर्त्यासः ।
अस्माभिरू नु प्रतिचक्ष्याभूदो ते यन्ति ये अपरीषु पश्यान् ॥

Those people, who wake up before sunrise, bathe and pray to God are religious and wise. They are ethical. Their activities are directed towards God. Those men and women who speak softly, pray together and enjoy a good relationship are blessed with happiness.

Vedavyas explains the importance of daily prayer to God in the **Mahabharata**, Anushashan Parv, 149/5-6, as:

तमेव चार्चयन् नित्यं भक्त्या पुरुषमव्ययम् ।
ध्यायन् स्तुवन्नमस्यच यजमान स्तमेव च ॥
अनादि निधनं विष्णुं सर्वलोक महेश्वरम् ।
लोकाध्यक्षं स्तुवन् नित्यं सर्वदुःखातिगो भवेत् ॥

The person who devotedly bows, offers prayers and meditates to the Almighty shall forever become free from all problems through reverence and offerings to the omnipotent, omnipresent and omniscient God.

In the **Bhagavad Gita**, 9/26, Lord Krishna says:

पत्रं पुष्पं फलं तोयं यो मे भक्त्या प्रयच्छति ।

तदहं भक्त्युपहृतमश्नामि प्रयतात्मनः ॥

The devotee who lovingly offers me flowers, fruits, food and other items is unselfish and wise. I accept the offerings as a token of love and symbolically eat them.

In the **Padampuran**, 5/84, the details of 'flowers' desired by God are given. Non-violence is the first flower, control over the senses the second, compassion the third, forgiveness the fourth, peace the fifth, control of the mind the sixth, meditation the seventh and truth the eighth. Although God is pleased with roses and other flowers, it is inner peace within individuals that pleases Him the most.

By offering prayers to God one can repent for unintended sins and find mental peace. Devotion arises within the individual and self-confidence grows. One sees a new purpose in life, stays motivated to rise above the ego, surrender pride and keep away from sin. One also becomes free from worry and stress and finds contentment. However, this is possible only when one truthfully offers prayers with devotion. Just as one finds valuable gifts like water and minerals by digging deep within the earth, by looking deep within oneself one finds divinity.

The purpose of offering prayers is to make one's mind placid, gentle and calm like the water in a lake. One must be able to keep smiling like a flower, have steadfast faith and devotion. Good etiquette and manners must be conspicuous in the personality. One must show light to others even if one were to burn like a wick in the lamp, sharing its light at the cost of burning itself.

In the **Bhagavad Gita**, 18/46, Lord Krishna says:

स्वकर्मणा तमभ्यर्च्य सिद्धिं विन्दति मानवः ।

Through one's good deeds and prayers to God an individual finds divine contentment and salvation.

Swami Vivekananda has said, "To do one's duty is the best prayer to God."

Once a devotee asked Chaitanya Mahaprabhu, "Gurudev, why is it that God is not pleased with prayers offered by prosperous people? He is happy with the skimmed milk offered by the gopis. He is happy with the vegetables offered by the learned. It appears that the choice of offerings is not related to God's pleasure."

Chaitanya responded, "Son, you have understood it correctly. God has created all things. Whatever would He need? Prayer is just a medium to emotionally awaken the spirit of devotion within an individual. Whatever a person offers to God in prayers is symbolic of devotion. God accepts it accordingly."

Why should one face the east when praying?

When offering prayers it is suggested that a person must face the east. Even during auspicious ceremonies the person conducting the ceremony faces the east. There are specific reasons for this.

The sun rises in the east. The Vedas accord great significance to the rays of the rising sun. In the **Atharva-Veda**, 17/1/30, it is said:

उद्यन्त्सूर्यो नुदतां मृत्युपाशान् ।

The rising sun destroys all kinds of diseases. It protects one from all causes of death.

Again, in the **Atharva-Veda**, 5/30/15, it is said:

सूर्यस्त्वाधिपतिर्मृत्योरुदायच्छतु रश्मिभिः ।

To break the bondage of death stay connected with the light of the sun.

Again, the **Atharva-Veda**, 8/1/4, says:

मृत्योः पड्वीशं अवमुंचमानः । मा च्छित्था अस्माल्लोकादग्ने सूर्यस्य संदृशः ॥

To live in the light of the sun is like living in the land of immortality.

Hindus look up to the sun, which is God Surya. Since God Surya is symbolic of Lord Vishnu or Narayan, the sun is also called Surya Narayan. Surya also symbolises Brahma. Surya is the sight of the world, giving and sustaining life and looking after the welfare of mankind. By praying to Surya one is amply rewarded and finds personal fulfilment. The Vedas recommend praying to Surya for special powers. Surya is witness to the good and bad activities of mankind and nothing can be hidden from Surya.

According to the **Surya Upanishad**, sages, saints and gods reside in the rays of the sun. To obtain maximum benefit of the rays when performing noble deeds and auspicious ceremonies, the Vedas direct that one must sit facing the east.

The rays of the rising sun are rich in a variety of ways with the ability to destroy harmful diseases. Sunlight is constituted of seven colours – violet, indigo, blue, green, yellow, orange and red. On either side, ultraviolet and infrared rays flank these. Each of these colours contributes their energy to sunlight. This energy assists the successful completion of auspicious ceremonies.

When the rays of the rising sun fall on the face and body, one is assured of a disease-free life and is greatly benefited.

Your questions answered...

• Why is prayer important in life?

When we pray we immediately communicate with the Supreme Power. It helps us forget our ego, even if for a short time. When we convey gratitude in prayer, we acknowledge a higher power fulfilling our needs. When we seek favours through prayer we acknowledge that we are unable to attain those favours without the divine blessings. Regular prayer keeps one in touch with the Supreme Spirit. This provides both happiness and contentment and helps one advance spiritually.

• When God is benevolent, why does He create suffering in this world?

How can one who is benevolent cause suffering? It is not God who creates the suffering and sorrow. It is the people who create suffering and sorrow through their thoughts and actions. Sorrows come from the five vices – lust, anger, greed, attachment and ego. God protects people from suffering and sorrow. Hindus believe that when there is excess of suffering and sorrow, God comes to alleviate the suffering.

What is the importance of the *asana* we sit upon when praying?

Amongst Hindus it is customary to sit cross-legged on the floor during a prayer or ceremony. People use an *asana* to sit upon. An *asana* can be a small square piece of mat or carpet, or even the skin of a deer, leopard or tiger. *Kusha* grass is considered particularly sacred and an *asana* made of this grass is often used. Those living in huts, as in the vast rural areas, are advised to keep the place of prayer clean by coating it with wet cow dung.

The use of animal skins was permissible when seers and sages lived in forests, and these skins were available. In modern times, the possession and use of such animal skins is prohibited under the Wildlife Protection Act. With more people becoming aware of the need for prayer, but unable to sit on the ground, they use a variety of things to sit comfortably during prayer.

Religious texts say there is great significance in sitting on an appropriate *asana* when offering prayers or performing a religious ceremony. The **Brahmandpurana Tantrasaar** says that when performing religious rituals, sitting on the ground invites unhappiness, sitting on stone invites sickness, sitting on leaves promotes mental doubt, sitting on wood invites misfortune, sitting on grass invites unpopularity, sitting on cloth invites loss and sitting on bamboo invites laziness.

It is significant that without using an appropriate *asana* when performing a religious ceremony one does not achieve complete success. Religious texts emphasise this. It is believed that the use of black deerskin as an *asana* helps gain knowledge successfully. By sitting on an *asana* made of *kusha* grass one benefits from chanting a variety of mantras. By sitting on a seat coated with cowdung one achieves purity. By sitting on an *asana* made of the skin of a leopard or tiger one attains salvation. By sitting on an *asana* made of a red woollen carpet wishes are fulfilled.

The significance of the *asana* is in conserving energy generated through prayer and penance. Seers and sages who perform religious rituals regularly accumulate potent energy within them, which is reflected through a magnetic personality and the glow on their face. By using an appropriate *asana* they conserve energy created through religious activities. This energy could easily be lost by leakage into the ground where they are seated and the benefit of religious rituals and ceremonies is then lost. Understanding the purpose of an appropriate *asana*, one can sit comfortably ensuring one feels energised after the prayer.

Think it over...

If you are a *vidyarthi* (seeker of knowledge), you must give up the idea of comforts. If you are a seeker of comforts, then forget your search for knowledge.

–Anon

Why are flowers always offered during prayer?

Flowers are dear to everyone. For Hindus they carry special significance and are offered to gods and goddesses when praying, fasting and conducting rituals or ceremonies. No ritual or ceremony is complete without them. The fragrance of flowers is said to please gods and goddesses. The beauty of flowers inspires us. They are a symbol of happiness and contentment.

In the **Kularnvatantra**, there is a reference to flowers:

पुण्य संवर्धनाच्चापि पापौघपरिहारतः पुष्कलार्थप्रदानार्थ पुष्पमित्यभिधीयते ।

They are called flowers because they promote purity; they shun sin and bear special fruit.

In the **Sharda Tilak** it is said:

देवस्य मस्तकं कुर्यात्कुसुमोपहितं सदा ।

The forehead of a god must always be adorned with flowers.

In the **Vishnu Nardiye** and the **Dharamottarpurana** it is said:

पुष्पैर्देवां प्रसीदन्ति पुष्पैः देवाश्च संस्थिताः
न रत्लैर्न सुवर्णेन न वित्तेन च भूरिणा
तथा प्रसादमायाति यथा पुष्पैर्जनार्दन ।

Gods are never as satisfied with gold and gems, or with fasting or penance, as they are when flowers are offered to them.

207

In the **Kalikapurana**, it is mentioned that one should never offer flowers that are stale or have been picked up from the ground. Damaged flowers or those infested with disease or insects are also forbidden. Neither should flowers be borrowed or stolen.

In the **Lalitashahasranaam**, flowers stringed together on a thread to make a *mala* are praised thus:

मां शोभां लातीति माला ।

A mala is an ornament. Of all kinds of malas offered to God, those made of lotus and pundreek (white lotus) are considered most auspicious.

Like humans, even gods have preferences for certain flowers. It is good to know what flowers to offer different gods.

✦ **Sri Ganesh:** Except for *Tulsi*, the holy basil plant (*Ocimum sanctum*) Sri Ganesh likes all flowers, according to the **Aachar Bhushan**.

✦ **Lord Shankar:** It is customary to offer him flowers of *maulsari* (a perennially blooming tree – *Mimusops elengi*), *dhatura* (the thorn apple – *Datura stramonium*), *harsingar* (a sweet smelling flower), *naagkeshar* (the ironwood tree – *Mesua ferrea*), dried lotus, *kaner* (oleander), *jabakusum*, *aak* (*Calotropis gigantea*), and *kush* (*Doa cynosuroides*).

✦ **Bhagwati Gauri:** She is fond of all flowers offered to Lord Shankar. Besides, it is also customary to offer her flowers of *apamarg*, *bela* (a variety of jasmine), *madar* (a variety of *Calotropis gigantea*), white lotus, *palash* (the flame of the forest – *Butea frondosa*), *champa* (the temple tree – *Pulmaria acutifolia*) and *chameli* (Spanish jasmine – *Jasminum grandiflorum*).

✦ **Lord Vishnu:** He is particularly fond of the lotus and flowers of *maulsari* (*Mimusops elengi*), *juhi* (jasmine – *Jasminum auriculatum*), *kadamb* (*Nauclea cadamba*), *kewra* (the screw pine – *Pandanus tectorius*), *chameli* (*Jasminum grandiflorum*), *ashok* (*Saraca indica*), *malti* (a variety of *Jasminum grandiflorum*), *basanti* (a variety of jasmine – *Jasminum auriculatum*), *champa* (*Pulmaria acutifolia*) and *vajyanti* (the garland of Lord Vishnu).

✦ **Lakshmiji:** She is most pleased with the lotus.

✦ **Surya Narayan:** Flowers of *kutaj* (the ivory tree – *Wrightia tinctoria*) are offered to him in prayer. Besides these, flowers of *kaner* (oleander), lotus, *champa* (*Pulmaria acutifolia*), *maulsari* (*Mimusops elengi*), *palash* (*Butea frondosa*), *aak* (*Calotropis gigantea*), *ashok* (*Saraca indica*) and others are also offered. Flowers of *tagar* are never offered to him.

✦ **Lord Krishna:** In the *Mahabharata*, talking of flowers, Lord Krishna tells Yudhistra that he is particularly fond of *kumud* (the red lotus), *karvari*, *chanak* (*Cicer arietinum*), *malti* (*Jasminum grandiflorum*), *nandik* (from the mahogany family), *palash* (*Butea frondosa*) and *vanmala* (wreath of wild flowers).

It is significant that lotus and *kumud* stay fresh for as long as 15 days. *Agastiya* flowers are never considered stale. Besides the buds of *champa*, no other flower buds are offered to the gods. Flowers should not be picked in the evening. The flowers of *ketaki* are never offered in prayers.

With widespread urbanisation, it is not always possible to procure many flowers mentioned in religious texts. Even if available, they cannot be procured in the quantities required. India is a vast country and every region has its own varieties of flowers. When you offer flowers in prayer, you find eternal joy.

Think it over...
Flowers are God's thoughts of beauty, taking form to gladden mortal gaze.

–**Anon**

Why is the lotus flower most important to Hindus?

In Hindu spiritual contemplation the lotus has a special place. It is not only considered pure and beautiful, but also a symbol of goodwill, peace, prosperity and happiness. It helps get rid of unpleasant things and is referred to as the king of flowers.

According to the Puranas, it is said that a lotus emerged from the navel of Lord Vishnu Brahma was seated on the lotus. Thereafter, he proceeded to create mankind. Brahma Saraswati, Lakshmi and other gods and goddesses have used the lotus as a seat. When it wa important to them, could it be any less to others?

The symbol of Lakshmi and prosperity, it is customary to offer the lotus in prayer to sever gods. In many instances, the number of flowers to be offered is also mentioned as a conditio for conducting certain yagyas and ceremonies.

The lotus grows in mud and water. Yet it is untouched or affected by either mud or wate This quality motivates one to live a pure life and is symbolic of the fact that undesirab elements can be refined and converted into superior and useful items. The blossoming of th lotus is considered auspicious and blessed.

Temples are given the shape of a closed lotus bud. The shape of the earth too is simil to a closed lotus flower. To awaken the kundalini, yogis suggest the division of the eight dis into sections. Each division is referred to as a *kamal* (lotus). Only through this division c one attain knowledge of Brahman.

In the **Shatpat Brahman**, the forepart of the uterus in a woman has been equated w the lotus. Both are symbols of creation. In the **Lalit Vistar Granth**, Buddhists have equat the lotus to a combination of eight important things. It is indeed a unique flower and Hin religious texts have given it an extraordinary place for use as an offering to God.

What items do Hindus use at prayer time?

Offering prayers is not a simple everyday routine for Hindus. It is a ritual. India is a land of gods and goddesses. Everyone has the option to choose the god or goddess of one's choice. Many pray to several gods at the same time. Even when a temple is built for a special deity, there are smaller temples within the main temple, each devoted to a deity. Hindus find convenient to pray to several gods simultaneously.

Every home has a little place for prayer. The bigger homes may have a small room devoted clusively for this. The smaller homes may have a small corner. Even in a hut one finds a le space reserved for God. The larger homes may have an idol made of marble or silver. hers may have small idols or pictures of gods, which help one concentrate better.

Besides the idol or picture(s) of gods it is customary to have a small plate to place flowers d offerings like fruit and money. There may be a small throne or pedestal for the idol, a all oil lamp, a stand for incense sticks, a bell, a small bowl and spoon and similar items d exclusively for prayers.

Religious texts rate gold as the most valuable metal. Therefore, the ornaments that adorn ls in temples are either gold, or silver covered with gold. Even the little throne or pedestal he idol is golden. In many places the idols are made of gold, or made of silver coated h gold. When idols are made of marble they are dressed attractively and painted golden ropriately. Gold does not tarnish or rust and only requires some cleaning.

In Ayurveda too, gold is highly acclaimed. A pure, superior metal, it does not degenerate ose its qualities with time and enhances one's strength, virility and immunity.

Compared to gold, silver is a cold metal. With a cooling effect on the body, it calms down flow of bile. It is good for eyesight and promotes mental tranquillity. Utensils made of

211

silver are considered pure and easy to clean. In the more important temples, and even in some homes, silver utensils are used for rituals and ceremonies. Silver tends to tarnish because of oxidation. However, it shines when cleaned.

After gold and silver, the metal of choice in many temples and homes is copper. Most utensils used in temples are made of copper. It is much cheaper than gold and silver. Water left in a copper vessel overnight and consumed the next morning relieves constipation, aches and pains and improves immunity. Copper tends to tarnish. When regularly cleaned, copper utensils are considered pure and used extensively in temples for a variety of purposes.

Bronze and brass are two other metals also used for rituals. Bronze is an amalgam of copper and brass or copper and zinc, and brass looks like gold when polished and shined. Bronze is known to cool down bile and improve memory and mental faculties. Phlegm and mucous is controlled by food cooked in brass utensils. These metals do not permit development of bacteria. However, they react quickly with sour food that can then turn poisonous.

Iron and aluminium utensils are not recommended for use in prayers. When exposed to moisture and air, iron rusts. Aluminium tends to corrode. Both metals tend to degenerate and neither is used for making idols nor during prayers.

Some people opine that stainless steel too should not be used because it contains iron. Religious texts forbid iron because it rusts. This shortcoming has been overcome through stainless steel that holds a variety of foods without deterioration. Stainless steel is easy to clean and widely accepted because of its qualities. It is gradually replacing other metals.

Religious texts recommend cleaning utensils with wood ash. The **Manusmriti** says:

निर्लेप कांचनं भांडमद्भिरेव विशुद्ध्यति ।
अब्जमश्ममयञ्चैव राजतं चानुपस्कृतम् ॥

Gold, silver, stone and seashells can easily be cleaned with water. They must have a smooth surface. If there are lines or crevices, dirt can settle in them. Gold and silver items must be free of other metals.

In most urban homes wood ash is hard to find. Everyone uses gas as fuel. Therefore cleaning prayer items with wood ash is out of question. Wood ash is recommended for cleaning because it is pure, abrasive and cleans well. But every home now has detergents and scouring agents that are equally pure and effective. For more delicate cleaning, liquid detergents also available.

Your questions answered...

How can one inculcate discipline in one's life?

One easy way is to follow a simple reward system. For instance, if you resolve not to have your morning cup of tea unless you brush your teeth and have a bath, it can be a good beginning. You can also resolve not to have breakfast until you have prayed every morning. One disciplines the self slowly.

How do Hindus conduct their prayers?

It is customary to offer betel leaf, betelnut or arecanut (*Areca catechu*), a coin, rice, sandalwood paste, turmeric-lime powder mixture for tilak, an oil lamp, incense sticks, *dhoop* sticks, saffron, turmeric powder, sweets, fruits and other similar items during prayers. Each of these has specific significance.

Betel leaf, betelnut and a coin are as important as the coconut. Betel leaf and betelnut symbolise the unity between the north and south. In prayer they are as important as offering these to a guest as a symbol of welcome on arrival at home. Their use is symbolic of one's reverence for God and one's surrender to the divinity within a person. The plants of both the betel leaf and betelnut are considered divine, and all gods appreciate them.

One begins by saying *shnanam samarpiyum,* offering water with a spoon. This is akin to saying, "I offer myself to serve physically, mentally, financially and emotionally." These are the four states through which one serves society. Water symbolises washing away the ills of society. With these thoughts, four spoons of water are offered at the feet of God.

Next, offering a few grains of rice, one says, a*kshant samarpiyum.* This symbolises acceptance that whatever food, money, property and other things we earn are being offered in part to God and the society made by Him. We will not use His blessings selfishly.

When sandalwood paste is applied on the forehead, it symbolises that just as sandalwood gives its fragrance freely and cools the mind, our life must be such that we spread fragrance and happiness throughout. We must learn to serve others. Whoever can be like sandalwood is dear to God.

213

Offerings of flowers saying *pushpam samarpiyum* is akin to saying that our life should be like a flower. It must blossom, be colourful, fragrant and spread contentment. Like flowers we must unite and wholeheartedly spread fragrance everywhere and live a life of service for the welfare of mankind.

A lamp can only be kindled when we have a lamp, oil (or *ghee*) and a wick. Together the three teach us to be worthy, loyal and dedicated. Just as a lamp is necessary to hold the *ghee* we need to be worthy of God's love and blessings. Like *ghee*, we must be devoted, willing to be consumed to spread light. Like the wick, we must surrender ourselves at the feet of God. When we are endowed with the spirit of the lamp, we spread light to dispel darkness and brighten the path for the weak and misguided. We surrender ourselves to God as we pray for His blessings.

The burning of incense and *dhoop* sticks generates positive magnetic vibrations that destroy negative feelings and promote health. These also symbolise that wherever we go, like the fragrance we must spread goodwill and contentment.

The use of turmeric-lime mixture for tilak is good for the skin and helps in developing harmony within the nerves. Turmeric is a good blood purifier, brightens skin and helps healing. It dispels many diseases, has medicinal properties and helps concentrate during prayers.

Your questions answered...

Some pray to Shiva, some to Vishnu, or Ram, or Krishna. Some pray to Durga. Do all prayers ensure similar benefit?

When we pray, we surrender ourselves to a force that is more powerful and superior. When we pray before an idol, we are really praying before the ideal that idol symbolises in our mind. All idols are symbolic of the Supreme Spirit. The benefit that accrues from prayer is not because of our presence before the idol. The benefit is in proportion to the faith and devotion we have for God in whatever form we may perceive Him.

Why do Hindus consider a conch shell auspicious?

Every Hindu who visits a temple is well acquainted with the use of a conch shell, a part of the prayer paraphernalia in every temple. Many householders too like to use one as part of their worship. Even if not used regularly, many like to keep it in the place of worship, since it is considered auspicious.

A majority of conch shells open on the left side, i.e., they are formed anti-clockwise. In contrast, those that open on the right side, i.e., formed clockwise, are rare, but very auspicious to keep in homes. These are expensive. It is believed that Goddess Lakshmi resides permanently in white conch shells that open on the right side. Both, Goddess Lakshmi and the right-sided conch shell have their origin in the sea and are believed to have the same father. A right-sided conch shell is considered the younger brother of Goddess Lakshmi.

The glory of a right-sided conch shell has been described thus:

दक्षिणावर्तेशंखायं यस्य सद्मनि तिष्ठति ।
मंगलानि प्रकुर्वन्ते तस्य लक्ष्मीः स्वयं स्थिरा ॥
चन्दनागुरुकपूरैः पूजयेद् गृहेऽन्वहम् ।
स सौभाग्ये कृष्णसमो धने स्याद् धनदोपमः ॥

In whatever home you find white right-sided conch shells, happiness and well-being shall always be there. Goddess Lakshmi lives there. In whatever home one uses sandalwood, camphor, flowers, rice and other items to offer prayers regularly that home shall be fortunate and prosperous like Krishna.

215

In the **Brahmvaivartpuran**, the white right-sided conch shell has been described thus:

शंख चन्द्रार्कदैवत्यं मध्ये वरुणदेवतन् ।
पृष्ठे प्रजापति विद्यादग्रे गंगा सरस्वतीम् ॥
त्रैलोक्ये यानि तीर्थानि वासुदेवस्य चाज्ञया ।
शंखे तिष्ठन्ति विप्रेन्द्रतस्मा शंख प्रपूजयेत् ॥
दर्शनेन हि शंखस्य किं पुनः स्पर्शनेन तु ।
विलयं यान्ति पापानि हिमवद् भास्करोदये: ॥

This conch shell is divine like Chandrama (moon) and Surya (sun). In the fore part, Ganga resides. In the middle, Varun resides, followed by Brahma. With Vishnu's permission all holy pilgrimages reside within this conch shell, which is like Kuber, the God of Wealth. Prayers must be offered to it everyday. Simply by looking at it reverently, all defects and disorders vanish just as ice melts when the sun rises. Its touch imparts divinity.

It is believed that whoever owns a pair of right-sided conch shells shall always hold exalted positions and be successful in whatever he does. Misery and failure keep away. Daily reverence and methodical offering of prayers to it shall bring success and fulfilment. When it is placed in a shop, it promotes success in business. At home, it attracts wealth and happiness. Placed with foodgrains, it promotes prosperity. It is truly a symbol of glory and prosperity.

When water is filled in a right-sided conch shell and sprinkled in the home on possessions and family members, the effect of curses, misfortune, evil thoughts and bad planetary influences are neutralised. When milk is filled in it and offered reverently to Lakshmi *yantra* (into which life has been infused through *pran pratishtha*) and to Lakshmi, one receives great wealth.

Religious texts say repetition of the mantra…

ॐ ह्रीं श्रीं क्लीं ब्लूं सुदक्षिणावर्त शंखाय नमः ।

108 times, along with methodical offering of prayers to the conch shell, bring honour and fame to a person. It is also believed this helps childless couples have a baby.

The conch shell that has its origin in the sea, and is blessed by the moon, symbolically has air, the universe and the planetary system within it. This outstanding conch shell promotes longevity, weakens enemies, and dispels disease, poverty and lack of knowledge. It is particularly recommended for worship. When placed near the ear, one hears melodious celestial sounds.

In the **Pulstya Samhita**, Maharishi Pulstya has said that to welcome Lakshmi and ensure that she resides permanently in one's home, only the use of a right-sided conch shell is effective. It has unbelievable qualities of attracting wealth. Using it one can get rid of loans, poverty and need. It ushers prosperity.

In the **Lakshmi Samhita**, it is described as capable of attracting wealth and success. Maharishi Vishwamitra notes that to attract prosperity and happiness, this conch shell is incomparable.

216

Shankaracharya has emphasised that if one had a right-sided conch shell and never used it, this is unfortunate. It is great fortune to have one, as it encourages one to perform noble deeds.

In the **Goraksh Samhita**, Guru Gorakhnath has explained that for tantrik use, it is unfailingly effective. He confirms its use, as do his followers, all having achieved great success with it.

Maharishi Markanday has explained that on all occasions when one prays to Lakshmi, the right-sided conch shell gives ample testimony of its ability to attract wealth and prosperity.

Your questions answered...

Do rituals actually have any effect on an individual?

Yes. Every action has a reaction. When a young man receives his degree, which of the two situations would create an impact upon his mind: when an office clerk hands him the degree in the college office, or when he receives it from the Vice-chancellor at the University convocation? Rituals are formal ceremonies that create an impact on an individual and the family.

Why are Hindus possessive about the rosary they use for prayers?

A rosary – a string of beads put together – to keep count of the number of times a person has repeated a mantra is an important prayer item in most Hindu homes. Commonly referred to as a *mala*, it typically has 108 beads. The source of beads could be *rudraksh* (seeds of the tree *Elaeocarpus ganitrus*), *tulsi*, *vajyanti* (the garden of Lord Vishnu), coloured glass, pearls or even precious or semi-precious gems. A rosary made of *rudraksh* is considered best. *Rudraksh* possesses germicidal and magnetic qualities.

In the **Angira Smriti**, the importance of a rosary has been described thus:

विना दमैश्चयकृत्यं सच्चदानं विनोदकम् ।
असंख्यता तु यजप्तं तत्सर्वं निष्फलं भवेत् ॥

Just as no religious ceremony is complete without kush, no charity is complete unless one gives it with one's hand, praying without a rosary has no count and will bring no results.

Why are there 108 beads in a rosary?

In the **Yogchudamani Upanishad** it is said:

षट्शतानि दिवारात्रौ सहस्राण्येकं विंशति ।
एतत् संख्यान्तितं मन्त्र जीवो जपति सर्वदा ॥

108 beads are stringed together to make a rosary because it is related to the frequency of our breath. In 24 hours, one breathes 21,600 times. 12 hours are spent in the daily routine.

That leaves us 12 hours for devotion to God. This means that each day 10,800 times breathing should be utilised for devotion to God. However, since this is not practical, the two zeroes have been removed. Therefore, breathing 108 times is appropriate during prayers.

Another explanation pertains to the sun. In relation to the earth, in one year the movement between the sun and the earth is 216,000 degrees. Since for six months the northern part of the earth faces the sun, and for the other six months the southern part of the earth faces the sun, the number is reduced to half, that is, 108,000 degrees. When three zeroes are omitted, the remainder is 108. Each of the 108 beads in the rosary is symbolic of each degree of change.

The third explanation is based upon astrology. The entire universe is divided into 12 segments. Each represents a sign of the zodiac. In Hindu religious texts, there are principally *Navgrah* (nine planets) that affect us. With 12 segments and 9 planets, when the two are multiplied we get the figure 108. Therefore, the number 108 represents the universe and controls our success.

As per another explanation, Hindu sages located 27 constellations, each of 27 stars. Since each constellation has four steps, 27 multiplied by 4 is 108.

This number exudes purity. Hindus use the prefix Sri followed by 108 (i.e., Sri 108) with the name of a religious head or a teacher who has wide influence, or those who have contributed to promote the knowledge and understanding of Hindu religious texts. Since these religious leaders are referred to as Sant, Mahant, Mandaleshwar or Mahamandaleshwar, depending upon their stature, they are addressed as Sri 108 Mahant... (name).

What is the best way to use the rosary?

The use of a rosary enables one to keep count of the number of times a mantra or prayer has been repeated. Each rosary denotes 108 times. On the top of each rosary there is a bigger bead called *Someru* – a name derived from a mountain of the same name that allegorically represents being composed of gold and gems. This mountain is accorded a coveted position in the universe. The same coveted position is accorded to the *Someru* in a rosary.

One begins using the rosary from the *Someru*, and when one reaches it again on completing one round of the rosary, crossing it is not recommended. Instead, one reverses the rosary and continues praying, moving one bead at a time. Irrespective of the number of times the rosary is rotated, one does not cross the *Someru*. Each time one reaches the *Someru* after completing one round of the rosary, one must think reverently of the god to whom prayers are being offered. At this point, the *Someru* is brought in contact with the forehead with the same reverence offered to God.

In the **Shivpuran**, Panchakshar Mantra, *shloka* 28, it is said that when using a rosary if one uses the thumb one achieves salvation. If one uses the forefinger it enables conquer of foes. When one uses the middle finger, prosperity is achieved. By using the ring finger one finds peace.

In the **Shivpuran**, Panchakshar Mantra, *shloka* 29, it is said:

अष्टोत्तरशतं माला तत्र स्यावृत्तमोत्तमम् ।
शतसंख्योत्तमा माला पञ्चाशद्भिरस्तु मध्यमा ॥

A rosary with 108 beads is the best. One with 100 beads is good. One with 50 beads is moderate.

Why do many Hindus wear a rosary around the neck?

Besides being acknowledged as an important accessory in prayer, a rosary made of beads of *rudraksh, tulsi* and other divine gifts of nature is useful when worn around the neck or other parts of the body. During prayer, the use of the tongue, the vocal cords and the larynx are under greater stress than in normal everyday use. Their continued use can cause problems pertaining to the throat and the adjoining glands. Use of a rosary around the neck helps prevent the occurrence of these problems.

Rudraksh beads come in many forms. They could be anything from one to fourteen faced. Their effectiveness varies with quality. It is customary to use a 26-bead rosary around the head, one with 50 beads near the heart, and one with 16 beads around the arm. One with 12 beads can be used as a wristband. It is believed that wearing a 108-bead rosary around the neck ensures fulfilment and success. It has been equated with the *ashwamedh yagya* – a celebrated sacrifice performed only by an emperor. The *Shivmahapuran, Padampuran* and other religious texts say that the virtuous wear a 108-bead rosary and find a place in heaven.

In the **Shivpuran** it is said:

यथा च दृश्यते लोके रुद्राक्षः फलदः शुभः ।
न तथा दृश्यते अन्या च मालिका परमेश्वरि ॥

220

A rosary made of no other item can be as blessed and fruitful as that of rudraksh.

In the **Shrimaddevibhagwata** it is said:

रुद्राक्षधारणाच्च श्रेष्ठं न किञ्चिदपि विद्यते ।

Nothing could be nobler than wearing rudraksh on one's body.

In *shlokas* 65 to 66, describing the qualities of a 108-bead *rudraksh* rosary, it is mentioned that benefits of the *ashwamedh yagya* accrue every moment to one who adorns the rosary around his neck and one finds a place in heaven. This benefits 21 generations.

One should wear a *rudraksh* rosary with devotion as directed in religious texts. This helps one grow spiritually, become free of worldly obstacles and problems, benefits the mind and heart, keeps blood pressure within control, banishes imaginary fears, ensures mental peace, calms and balances the flow of bile, and protects the wearer from sudden death. Whoever uses it to pray benefits ten-fold.

Hindu scriptures accord great religious importance to *tulsi*. It protects against disease, promotes longevity and has special magnetic qualities. Using it imparts its qualities to the person who wears it around his neck. One develops greater confidence and a magnetic personality. Fame and popularity grow and one feels blessed and content.

When wearing a *tulsi* rosary around the neck, contact with the skin helps prevent cough and cold, headache, skin disease and blood disorders.

In the **Shalgram Puran**, it is said:

तुलसीमालिकां धृत्वा यो भुक्ते गिरिनंदिनी ।
सिक्थेसिक्थे स लभते वाजपेयफलाधिकम् ॥
स्नानकाले तु यस्यांगे दृश्यते तुलसी शुभा ।
गंगादिसर्वतीर्थेषु स्नातं तेन न संशयः ॥

Wearing a tulsi rosary is very beneficial during mealtimes. A bath with tulsi rosary around the neck is equivalent to a bath in the holy Ganga and other holy rivers and streams.

Your questions answered...

While praying, I find it hard to concentrate upon God. What can I do?

Just as a child does not start running soon after birth, do not expect to be able to concentrate for long periods in prayer. You will learn concentration gradually. Many begin by participating in group prayers. In reality, God has no form. He is present in all things at all times. Until you reach the stage where you can perceive God everywhere, concentrate on whatever you find convenient. Concentrate on one who is kind and benevolent to you. To you he is God. Do it for whatever time that suits you. Your concentration will improve as you begin to enjoy these short experiences.

What is the effect of prayer on an individual?

Prayer lifts an individual to unparalleled glory. No other experience in life can be compared to it. Once a person is involved in it, it gives pleasure akin to reciting a melodious, heartfelt poem. It attracts prosperity and glory. One begins to experience peace and happiness.

Our religious texts cite innumerable examples of individuals who achieved this – outstanding devotees like Narad, Bhakta Prahlad, Dhruva, Jatayu, Ajamil, Kewat, Shabri and many more. These devotees achieved salvation through their devotion to the Almighty. Lord Shankar achieved immortality. It is devotion and prayer that ensures peace and contentment to saints and sages.

In the Vedas, Puranas and other religious texts, and also through the writings and discourses of the learned saints, the importance of prayer to God is repeatedly emphasised. Those who dutifully remember and offer prayers to God are transformed from simple people into an exalted state where the attributes of godliness become a part of them. In Kalyug, the fourth part of the worldly cycle where acts of sin predominate, the best form of achieving salvation is through devotedly praying to God. There is no other alternative but to remember the Almighty.

In the **Ramcharitmanas**, 1/22/8, Sant Tulsidas has said:

नाम निरूपन नाम जतन तें ।
सोउ प्रगटत जिमि मोल रतन तें ॥

Just as only one who knows gems well can evaluate their true value, one who knows the real worth and value of devotion to God achieves godliness through reverence and prayer.

In the **Shrimadbhagwat**, 6/2/14-15, it is said:

सांकेत्यं पारिहास्यं वा स्तोत्रं हेलनमेव वा ।
वैकुण्ठनाम ग्रहणमशेषाधहरं विदुः ॥
पतितः स्खलितो भग्नः संदष्टस्तप्त आहतः ।
त्वामनुबध्नामि हरिरित्यवशेनाह पुमान्नार्हति यातनाम् ॥

It does not matter how you remember God. You may mention Him in conversation. You may remember Him when narrating a joke. You may even remember Him with disrespect. The simple act of remembrance cleanses one's sins. Whoever thinks of Him on the occasion of a failure, a fall, in loss, on being hurt or when distressed and disabled, and utters His name, shall not suffer.

In the **Brihnnardiyapuran**, Vedavyas has said:

हरेर्नाम हरेर्नाम हरेर्नामैव केवलम् ।
कलौ नास्त्येव नास्त्येव नास्त्येव गतिरन्यथा ॥

In Kalyug multifarious maladies can be controlled in the initial stages by remembering God. None can offer as much support as God.

In the **Yogdarshan**, 2/44, Patanjali has said:

स्वाध्यायादिष्टदेवतासम्प्रयोगः ।

By offering prayers one comes face to face with God.

In the **Padampuran** it is written that whoever offers prayers to the Almighty everyday shall be free forever.

In the **Shrimadbhagwat**, 12/3/52, Vedavyas has said that whatever virtues one earns through meditation to Lord Vishnu in Satyayug, through *yagya* in Tretayug and through prayers and offerings in Dwaparyug, can be achieved in Kalyug just by remembering the name of God.

In the **Ramcharitmanas**, Uttarkand, 102A, Tulsidas has also said that in Kalyug one achieves salvation just by repeating the name of God. In Satyayug, Tretayug and Dwaparyug this had to be achieved through meditation, sacrifice, *yagya* and prayer. Tulsidas is emphatic about repeating the name of Ram.

भाव कुभाव अनख आलसहू ।
नाम जपत मंगल दिसि दसहू ॥

In the **Bhagavad Gita**, 8/5, Lord Krishna has said:

अन्तकाले च मामेव स्मरन्मुक्त्वा कलेवरम् ।
यः प्रयाति स मद्भावं याति नास्त्यत्र संशयः ॥

Whoever remembers Me at the time of his death shall come to Me. There should be no doubt about it.

The importance of repeating the name of God is evident from the life of Ajamil. He was a great sinner. Unintentionally, he had named his younger son Narayan. Just when he was about to die, the fear of death parched his throat and he called out to his son Narayan. According to *Shrimadbhagwat*, uttering the four syllables 'Na-ra-y-an' was equivalent to remembering the name of God. He was immediately absolved of all his sins. Just as fuel turns to nothing when fire embraces it, all the sins are pardoned by repeating the name of God. It is said that hearing His name being called, Narayan sent His messengers who snatched Ajamil from the hands of death, and carried Him to heaven.

Again in the **Bhagavad Gita**, 8/6, Lord Krishna said:

यं यं वाऽपि स्मरन्भावं त्यजत्यन्ते कलेवरम् ।
तं तमेवैति कौन्तेय सदा तद्भावभावितः ॥

Whatever are the last thoughts of a person when his soul departs from the body, those thoughts accompany the person to the next life. Whatever thought predominates in one's life at the end, irrespective of whether one is a saint, a common householder, an animal, a bird, a plant or any living thing, is reborn wherever the last thoughts were focused.

Your questions answered...

How can one live a complete life?

You can live a complete life by looking at and living life in totality. In life, beside oneself, one has responsibilities towards the family, at work and in society. All responsibilities are important even when they do not appear to be so. Only the priority varies from one time to another. To ensure you get your priorities right, let the Supreme Spirit guide you when you pray. When you have faith and devotion, you will be guided to the right path.

Why do Hindus chant a variety of mantras during prayer?

The word *mantra* is derived from Sanskrit and literally means *instrument of thought*. It could be a word, a phrase or sound recited or sung repeatedly. It aids concentration when meditating.

The syllables in a mantra are linked in a definite order. When recited or sung as recommended, they convey a significant meaning and have a definite effect. It is also said that a mantra gives protection and strength on recitation. The syllables that constitute a mantra when recited produce electrical ripples and waves that ensure magical effects. Different sounds and rhythms produce varied effects.

In the **Ramcharitmanas**, Arunyakand, 35/1, it is said:

मंत्र जाप मम दृढ़ बिश्वासा । पंचम भजन सो वेद प्रकासा ॥

A mantra is a medium that can arouse consciousness from slumber in an individual. The latent powers are activated and made effective.

Mantras are endowed with a variety of powers. Through these one can win the favours of gods and goddesses. It is said gods and goddesses are captivated by particular mantras.

The religious texts say:

मन्त्राधीनञ्च देवता ।

The gods and goddesses are dependent upon mantras.

225

When a mantra is recited the power of the words along with one's resolution and devotion is strengthened and intermingles with the divine consciousness. Together they create an extraordinary power in the inner body and outer space of the universe. An individual experiences success and contentment through the recitation of the mantra.

A curse and a blessing are both a result of the power of the word, or of a mantra. Religious texts are full of examples of such use of mantras. The greater the devotion, more intense the faith and confidence in God. Depending upon one's impatience to meet God, the devotion will be focused and the recitation of the mantra will be clear, profound and passionate.

People often question the power of the word. Are we not aware how words affect us in everyday life? A few words spoken kindly make us smile and respond positively. The words in a poem or a song motivate us. However, just a single word that hurts us can arouse anger and hatred. The words in a mantra are no different and specially selected for their influence and effect. They have the power to transform people.

In the **Bharadwaj Smriti**, 7/53, it is said:

अप्रतिष्ठितमाला या सा जपे विफला स्मृता ।
तस्मात् प्रतिष्ठा कर्तव्या जपस्य फलमिच्छता ॥

Before using a rosary to recite a mantra, it is necessary to 'infuse life' into it. This is done through recommended procedures and methodical recitation of mantras. The process is called pran pratishtha *or 'infusion of life'. The rosary then no longer remains a string of wooden beads. It becomes a divine vehicle to personal achievement.*

It is believed that when knowledgeable Brahmins recite mantras, they can convert a stone into a living symbol of God. This is the first step in establishing an idol in a temple. Only after this is done can one fruitfully offer prayers to the deity. In the same way, life must be infused into a rosary. Once this is done, it should not be treated as an ordinary string of beads. It possesses divine qualities and deserves the reverence and respect accorded to God.

What mantra would be ideal for a normal householder? Those who pursue religious knowledge under the guidance of a guru receive a mantra from him. The devotee then makes this mantra a part of his/her life. Those who do not have a guru and would like to chant a mantra may select any of these popular and time-tested ones. They are all very powerful and can be a source of great happiness and contentment to the devotee.

- ✦ Aum – recite it slowly with concentration.
- ✦ Aum Namo Narayana.
- ✦ Aum Namah Sivaya.
- ✦ Aum Namo Bhagavate Vasudevaya.
- ✦ Hare Krishna, Hare Krishna, Krishna, Krishna, Hare Hare.
  Hare Ram, Hare Ram, Ram, Ram, Hare Hare.
- ✦ The Gayatri mantra.

How many times should a mantra be recited?

This depends totally on an individual. In the beginning it may not be easy to concentrate. However, gradually through practice one learns to concentrate. The pleasure of reciting the mantra grows with practice. One begins to feel the benefits. There is a feeling of inner happiness, tranquillity and contentment. To begin with, one can repeat a mantra 108 times – that is, go through the rosary once. This can gradually be increased. There are people who go through the rosary as many as 20 times.

Your questions answered...

My Zodiac sign is Aries. Is there a mantra that I can chant?

Yes. There are mantras for all the 12 Zodiac signs. The details are given in the chart below. You can chant the mantra 108 times every morning. It will promote happiness and contentment.

Capricorn	*Makar*	ॐ श्रीं वत्सालय नमः
Aquarius	*Kumbh*	ॐ श्रीं उपेन्द्राय अच्युताय नमः
Pisces	*Minh*	ॐ क्लीं उद्धृताय उद्धारिणे नमः
Aries	*Mesh*	ॐ ह्रीं श्रीं लक्ष्मीनारायणाभ्यां नमः
Taurus	*Vrish*	ॐ गोपालाय उत्तरध्वजाय नमः
Gemini	*Mithun*	ॐ क्लीं कृष्णाय नमः
Cancer	*Kark*	ॐ हिरण्यगर्भाय अव्यक्तरूपिणे नमः
Leo	*Sinh*	ॐ क्लीं ब्रह्मणे जगदाधाराय नमः
Virgo	*Kanya*	ॐ नमो प्रीं पीताम्बराय नमः
Libra	*Tula*	ॐ तत्त्वनिरंजनाय तारकरामाय नमः
Scorpio	*Vrischak*	ॐ नारायणाय सुरसिंहाय नमः
Sagittarius	*Dhanu*	ॐ श्रीं देवकृष्णाय ऊर्ध्वषन्ताय नमः

Which mantra do Hindus consider most powerful?

There are innumerable mantras recited by Hindu devotees. None is as powerful as the Gayatri mantra. In the annals of time it is eternal. In the Puranas it is said that Brahma first received the mantra through a celestial call. He served as the creator of the world by virtue of the powers of reciting the mantra:

ॐ भूर्भुवः स्वः तत्सवितुर्वरेण्यं भर्गो देवस्य धीमहि धियो यो नः प्रचोदयात् ।

To give a better interpretation of the Gayatri, Brahma composed the four Vedas. Gayatri is therefore also known as Vedmata (mother of the Vedas).

Religious texts say:

सर्ववेदानां गायत्री सारमुच्यते ।

The Gayatri mantra is the essence of the Vedas.

In the **Brihadyogi Yagyavlkya Smriti**, 10/10-11, it is said:

नास्ति गंगासमं तीर्थं न देवः केशवात् परः ।
गायत्र्यास्तु परं जप्यं न भूतो न भविष्यति ॥

No pilgrimage is as holy as the Ganga. No God can equal Krishna. There is no mantra superior chanting the Gayatri mantra. There never will be.

In the **Devi Bhagwat**, 11/21/5, it is said that Narsinh, Surya, Varah, Tantrik and Ved mantras will be fruitless unless accompanied by the Gayatri mantra.

228

In the **Savitri Upkhyan Adhyay**, *shlokas* 14-17, it is said that if one were to chant the Gayatri mantra once, all sins for the day would be absolved. If one were to chant it ten times, the sins for the day and the night would be absolved. If it were chanted hundred times, sins for a month would be absolved. Chant it thousand times and sins for several years would be absolved. Chanting the mantra a lakh times would rid one of a lifetime of sins and ten lakh times would do away with sins of the past lives. If one were to chant it hundred lakh times it would absolve one of the sins of all lives. A thousand lakh times would qualify a Brahmin for salvation.

In the **Agnipuran**, 215/8, it is said that there is no better mantra for chanting than the Gayatri. However, it is not a mantra for oblations and offerings.

In the **Bhagavad Gita**, Lord Krishna has said:

गायत्री छन्दसामहम् ।

Amongst the mantras I am the Gayatri mantra.

It is believed that within the 24 syllables of the Gayatri mantra, the strength of 24 saints and gods is included. Therefore when the mantra is chanted the hidden strength within it creates vibrations in the body increasing the flow of blood and improving the intake of oxygen. Thus, all maladies in the body are destroyed.

Religious texts say that methodically chanting the Gayatri mantra removes obstacles affecting the body and the mind. It generates enthusiasm and positive activity, encourages noble thoughts, improves judgement, self-confidence, patience, compassion, peacefulness and contentment. Negative influences are eliminated. This promotes knowledge, creativity, insight, fame and longevity. It protects one from all kinds of problems and sudden death.

Your questions answered...

Can you explain the meaning of the Gayatri mantra in detail?

Yes. ॐ – *Om* refers to *the Supreme Spirit that sustains and protects everyone.* भूर् – *bhur* means *the land, the earth or the world that gives us life.* भुवः - *Bhuv* means *one who takes away everyone's suffering.* स्वः – *Sva* means *one who gives happiness and contentment.* तत् – *tat* refers to *the Supreme Spirit.* सवितुर् – *Savitur* means *the Creator of all things, the mother and father of the world.* वरेण्यम् – *varainium* is *that which is outstanding and welcome.* भर्गो – *bhargo* refers to *the purest form like the rays of the sun.* देवस्य – *Devasya* refers to *what belongs to the gods.* धिमहि – *dheemahi* means *contemplation.* धियो – *dheeyo* denotes *the mind and intellect.* यो – *Yo* refers to *the Supreme Spirit.* नः – *na* means *one's.* प्रचोदयात् – *prachodayat* denotes *to motivate us to be involved in good deeds.* In essence, the mantra means: *O Master of the universe, our Protector, One who takes away all our sufferings, One who gives happiness and contentment to everyone, we contemplate and meditate to the Creator of the universe in the form of knowledge and pure brilliance. Please motivate us to do good deeds.*

Besides the Gayatri mantra, which other mantra is very special to Hindus?

The Mahamrituanjaya mantra is very special. Chanting this mantra has helped people overcome incurable diseases and avoid early death. This mantra is devoted to Lord Shiva. When pleased with the devotee, Lord Shiva protects one from accidents, terminal diseases and death. One is able to get over the malefic effects of planets. It is customary to chant the mantra 125 thousand times over a period to promote long life. The responsibility of chanting the mantra can be entrusted to a responsible Brahmin priest.

It is believed that Shukracharya chanted the *Mahamritunjaya mantra* to revive the demon who had lost their lives during the churning of the ocean by the Gods and the asuras. Fo this reason, the *mantra* is also known as the *Mritsanjeevani,* meaning *one that revives from deatł*

In the **Rig-Veda**, 4/52/12, the *mantra* has been recorded as:

ॐ त्र्यम्बकं यजामहे सुगन्धिं पुष्टिवर्द्धनम् ।
उर्वारुकमिव बन्धनान्मृत्योर्मुक्षीय माऽमृतात् ॥

However, to give it the correct shape and homogeneity, the *mantra* is read as:

ॐ हौं जूं सः ॐ भूर्भुवः स्वः ॐ त्र्यम्बकं यजामहे सुगन्धिं पुष्टिवर्द्धनम् ।
उर्वारुकमिव बन्धनान्मृत्योर्मुक्षीय माऽमृतात् ॐ भूर्भुवः स्व सः जूं हौं ॐ ॥

We worship the three-eyed Lord Shiva, surrounded by fragrance. Please liberate us from the bonda of death, not for the sake of immortality, just as a ripe melon effortlessly severs itself from the stalk wi your blessings.

In the **Padampuran,** there is a mention of the *Mahamritunjaya mantra* as composed hymn form by Maharishi Markanday.

230

It is explained that Mahamuni Mrikandu did not have any children. To appease Lord Shiva both he and his wife underwent great penance and sacrifice.

Satisfied with their devotion, Lord Shiva appeared before them. He said, "You will be blessed with a son. However, if you want a capable, knowledgeable, renowned and religious son who is like a great ocean, then he will live only for 16 years. If you want an ordinary person as a son devoid of capability, he will live a hundred years. The choice is yours."

Mahamuni Mrikandu bowed before Lord Shiva and said, "I want a capable son even though his life may be short. I do not want an incapable son."

"So be it," Lord Shiva blessed the couple and left.

When the son was born Mrikandu named him Markanday. From birth he was devoted to Lord Shiva. He composed innumerable *shlokas* in his childhood. Amongst the more important ones was the Mahamrituanjaya mantra. When Markanday completed 15 years, Mrikandu remembered what Lord Shiva had said. He was worried. When Markanday asked the cause of the worry, Mrikandu revealed it. Markanday told his father that he would pray to Lord Shiva and seek his blessings to become immortal.

As Markanday completed his 16th year Yama, the God of Death, stood before him. Markanday explained that he wished to complete chanting the hymns of the Mahamrituanjaya mantra, and if he could wait a little. But Yama would not wait and shouted at him. The stubborn Yama prepared to squeeze the life out of Markanday. With Markanday chanting the Mahamrituanjaya mantra, Lord Shiva emerged from the Shivaling and stared at Yama in rage. Confronted with an angry Lord Shiva, Yama released Markanday from his grasp. To appease Lord Shiva, Yama blessed Markanday with immortality. Before Yama left, he declared that whoever chanted the Mahamrituanjaya mantra would never meet an unnatural death and would also be free from death-like suffering.

Thus, although Lord Shiva had himself confirmed that Markanday would die when 16, chanting the mantra pleased him into granting Markanday immortality.

Think it over...

As you grow in meditation, you will find how veil after veil is withdrawn, until a new revelation of what you are in the depths rises before you: a new consciousness of your hidden powers awakens within you. You become conscious of new reserves of life in your being: you have but to tap them and through you will flow *shakti*, energy, to others.

–T L Vaswani

How often do Hindus pray everyday?

In the religious texts and the code of recommended activities, praying at dusk has been accorded special significance. Therefore, sages and saints have been offering prayers thrice daily – at sunrise, midday and dusk, just as the sun dips below the horizon. Lord Ram and his guru Vashistha are also known to have offered prayers thrice daily. To develop personal magnetism, be progressive and successful and find personal fulfilment, prayers thrice a day are recommended.

In **Manusmriti**, 4/94, Manu has said:

ऋषयो दीर्घसन्ध्यत्वाद् दीर्घमायुखवाप्नुयुः ।
प्रज्ञां यशश्च कीर्तिं च ब्रह्मवर्चसमेव च ॥

It is only because of continuous offering of prayers at dusk for a long time that the saints and sages were blessed with intelligence, fame, goodwill, long life and divinity.

In the **Kurmpuran**, 18/26-31, the importance of offering prayers at dusk is explained. Dusk gives birth to a new period and leaves behind attachments and activities of another day. Born of three elements, it prepares one in advance for God's benevolence. Facing the east, with devotion and concentration a learned person must chant an eminent mantra like the Gayatri mantra during evening prayer. In the past, learned people have offered prayers at dusk and achieved salvation through single-minded devotion.

The three prayers – in the morning prior to sunrise, in the afternoon and at dusk – have been described as excellent, mediocre and ordinary.

In the **Devibhagwat**, 11/16/4-5, it is said that the morning prayer is excellent if offered when stars are visible, mediocre when stars are not visible, and ordinary when the sun has risen. The evening prayer is considered excellent when the sun can be seen, mediocre when the sun is setting and ordinary when the stars are visible.

According to Sage Vishwamitra, when offering prayers one must face the east or the north. In the evening one must face the west.

The best time to offer prayers in the morning is just before sunrise, in the day at noon and in the evening just before the sunset, extended until 10 minutes after it. Prayers, mantras, meditation and *kirtan* are virtuous and beneficial when offered at the appropriate time. The principal nerves of the body are particularly receptive and latent powers energised. Prayer thrice a day has a profound effect upon the physical, emotional and spiritual life of individuals.

Your questions answered…

- **There are thousands of temples with many deities all over India. Are there so many gods?**

There is only one God – Brahman, who created the world. He is manifested in many forms and known by many names as convenient to people. The many forms make it easier for a person to identify with one that is in harmony with personal thoughts. While one may see God as Vishnu, Ram or Krishna, others may see God as Shakti, Lakshmi or Saraswati. Others see Him as Sri Ganesh. There is but one God seen in many forms. People of learning revere Saraswati, businessmen revere Lakshmi and engineers and artisans pray to Vishvakarma. Those who seek a happy married life pray to Shiva and Parvati.

- **How does God guide us?**

God guides us through our conscience. When a person removes the impurities from the soul and becomes virtuous, God comes to reside in the conscience. The conscience guides one to do well and steer clear of evil. When we err and follow a wrong path, the conscience acts like a witness pointing its accusing finger at our faults.

Do all Hindus follow a complex procedure of prayer?

Every individual is unique and at a particular level of mental and spiritual development. Numerous recommendations in religious texts should not overawe a person. The details are merely meant to acquaint one with what has been said. Adopt what suits you. The Hindu way of life is liberal. If not, it would not have survived long periods of suppression and foreign rule.

Prayer is a simple way to uplift oneself physically, emotionally and spiritually. Just as a child does not start running soon after birth, one cannot expect a person who is new to Hindu customs and beliefs to adopt them with every minor detail. Begin in a small way. Learn to offer a simple prayer to God. Word it as you please. Begin and end with a few words of gratitude for everything He has blessed you with. It does not matter how long you pray. Your prayers could be brief or prolonged. Do what makes you happy.

You could offer prayers with some of the frills described earlier, or just sit quietly all by yourself and offer a few words in prayer. When you begin to enjoy your prayers, you will slowly find happiness and contentment and discover a new 'you'. Let this be the beginning of a higher life where you are more concerned about your family, friends and others than about yourself. This will be your first step in moving towards God.

A Simple Prayer

O God!
Lead me from the unreal to Real;
Lead me from darkness to Light;
Lead me from mortality to Immortality.
Aum – Peace! Peace! Peace!

How important is group prayer for Hindus?

Group prayers are common amongst all Hindus. Around the year there are many occasions when families or groups or even communities get together to pray, hear religious discourses and sing devotional songs. Religious discourses and activities have been practised since ancient times. Much of the knowledge has passed on by word of mouth. This is why, despite widespread illiteracy and foreign rulers who sought to curb Hindu religious activity, most of this knowledge is still available.

Hindus have a vast ancient religious literature rich in interesting stories. Even when psychology was unknown as a line of specialisation, our sages and saints used techniques that are now the norm in promoting knowledge, procedures, truth, love, justice, tolerance and good moral behaviour amongst the common man. They weaved convincing stories that are relevant even thousands of years later.

In every case good conquered evil. Every story has a moral and motivates people to stay away from evil and lead a good moral life. Stories about gods and goddesses are said to dispel fears, overcome problems, relieve pain and save people from ruin. Religious discourses are a common platform to narrate religious messages supported by appropriate stories.

In the **Shrimadbhagwat**, 2/8/5-6, Vedavyas said:

प्रविष्टः कर्णरन्ध्रेण स्वानां भावसरोरुहम् ।
धुनोति शमलं कृष्णसलिलस्य यथा शरत् ॥
धौतात्मा पुरुषः कृष्णपादमूलं न किंचति ।

235

God resides in the hearts of those that hear moral tales and enjoy the company of good pious people.
He cleanses all their shortcomings bit by bit just as the onset of winter cleanses the water of all the streams.

Thus, good people always remember God and keep him within their heart.

Vedavyas wrote **Shrimadbhagwat** so that the common man would know God through the medium of stories and model his life on the same moral pattern and greatly benefit by it. One does not need to wait until death to benefit from good deeds. The results become evident immediately. One begins to differentiate between good and bad, virtue and sin. Thereby, one can be more virtuous than sinful. One finds success in breaking bonds that are not beneficial and makes new links that take one towards final emancipation. By listening to stories one is also able to identify problems, find suitable solutions and overcome uncertainty.

Think it over...

It is not mere living together that makes a family. It is love and concern for each other that brings significant harmony and integrity to the family life.

−Swami Ishwarananda

How important is devotional prayer and singing to Hindus?

Group praying and singing of devotional songs and hymns is important to most Hindus. This brings people with a common aim of remembering God together. It helps people concentrate better. They find it inspiring and experience an inner peace that is superior to the pleasures of worldly possessions. Together the group achieves more than what each could independently.

In the **Ramcharitmanas** Sant Tulsidas has said that a devotee wins over the confidence of God through devotional songs and hymns. In response, God ensures success and happiness for devotees.

In the **Padampuran**, Uttarakhand, 14/23, it is said:

नाहं वसामि वैकुंठेयोगिनां हृदये न च ।
मद्भक्ता यत्र गायन्ति तत्र तिष्ठामि नारद ॥

O Narad! I reside neither in Vaikunth, nor in the hearts of devotees. I reside where my devotees form a loving companionship to sing devotional songs and hymns. I reside within their ultimate motive.

In the religious texts it is also said:

मुक्तिः ददाति कश्चित् न भक्तियोगम् ।

God makes salvation easily accessible to those who sing devotional songs and hymns. However, He does not give devotion to everyone.

In the **Bhagavad Gita**, 9/30, it is said:

अपि चेत्सुदुराचारो भजते मामनन्यभाक् ।
साधुरेव स मन्तव्यः सम्यग्व्यवसितो हि सः ॥

Even if a wicked sinner worships Me with pure devotion, he should be considered a saint because he has correctly resolved that there is nothing better than devoted worship of God.

Such a person has rightly resolved that there is nothing better than offering devotional songs and hymns to God. In a short period, such a person cleanses his soul and achieves happiness and contentment.

In the **Bhagavad Gita**, 9/33, it is said:

अनित्यमसुखं लोकमिमं प्राप्य भजस्व माम् ।

Having obtained this human life that is transient and devoid of joy, constantly worship Me.

The religious texts have laid great emphasis upon daily worship of God. Even the gods residing in heaven worship each other and Almighty God. What is good for the gods is still better for mankind.

In the **Brihadranyak Upanishad**, 1/3/27, it is said:

असतो मा सद्गमय तमसो मा ज्योतिर्गमय मृत्योर्मा अमृतं गमय ।

Take me from falsehood to truth, from the darkness to light and from death to immortality.

With worship one is able to establish a relationship with God. Thus, one attains supernatural powers that help overcome obstacles, hurdles, disease, suffering and grief.

In the **Rig-Veda**, 5/82/5, a prayer is offered to God:

ॐ विश्वानि देव सवितर्दुरितानि परा सुव। यद्भद्रं तन्न आ सुव ॥

O God, who has created this universe! Free us from the bondage of our sins. Bless us with thoughts that promote welfare. O benevolent God! Let our motives be pure, wise and sacred.

In the **Ramcharitmanas**, at different places the following thoughts are expressed:

मसकहि करइ विरंचि प्रभु अजहि मसक ते हीन ।	**Uttarkand**, 122 kha
जो चेतन कहं जड़ करइ जड़हि करइ चैतन्य ।	**Uttarkand**, 119 kha
तृन ते कुलिस कुलिस तृन करई ।	**Lankakand**, 34/8

God can make the impossible into possible. He can also make the possible into impossible. He does not lack anything. He is complete in every way. When we build a relationship with Him through worship, we begin to enjoy His benevolence and qualities.

In the **Chhandogya Upanishad**, it is said:

यदेव श्रद्धया जुहोति तदेव वीर्यवत्तरं भवति ।

Only those prayers offered with great devotion bring results.

It is imperative that when one worships through prayer, devotional songs or hymns, the feelings are honest, sincere and spontaneous. The results are then fruitful. One must call out to God truthfully, speaking from the heart. One finds happiness and contentment immediately.

When Draupadi was in sheer distress because of Duryodhan and none could protect her, it was a sincere call to God that protected her modesty. Lord Vishnu took the incarnation of Narsinh to protect Bhakta Prahlad. When Uttara felt her pregnancy was at risk due to an attack by Ashvatthama, she called out to God and was duly protected. Markanday's worship to Shiva saved him from death. There are innumerable examples when prayers have shown immediate effect. Mira, Surdas, Sant Tulsidas, Chaitanya Mahaprabhu, Tukaram and many more benefited from the benevolence of God.

Worship of God through prayers, meditation, devotional songs and hymns brings immediate results. They protect one from disease, sickness, sorrow and grief, and help absolve sins. One gains emotional and spiritual strength. Prayer is truly a tonic for emotional and spiritual well-being.

Your questions answered…

• Spiritual growth is something personal. How does group prayer help?

Although spiritual growth is personal, everyone is not aware of the need for spiritual growth from within. Very often group praying helps in kindling the flame within a person to introspect, think more deeply about God, and grow spiritually.

• Many times, prayer groups are too big. Can one still benefit from it?

Yes. A very important aspect of group praying is the presence of positive vibrations that everyone radiates on such occasions. With vibrations coming from a group, they become strong and influence all participants. Positive vibrations help neutralise the negative vibrations of some people and the spark kindles the desire to grow spiritually.

• Do many people strive to realize God?

No. One amongst thousands of human beings strives to realize God. Even amongst these, there are few who really understand the reality of God. Self-realization is a gradual process beginning with self-purification, becoming virtuous, and using prayer and meditation to seek God.

Why do Hindus clap when singing devotional songs?

It is customary to clap as one sings devotional songs and hymns in groups. Sri Ramakrishan too recommended clapping during morning and evening prayers. This helps cleanse one's sins. Just as birds fly away when one claps standing under a tree, ignorance vanishes when one sings devotional songs clapping to maintain the beat and rhythm. One feels pure and invigorated.

Clapping while singing devotional songs has been popular in temples, special gatherings and even homes. Besides spiritual benefits, it helps physically too. When the palms hit each other during clapping, the mounts in the palms are pressed. Since they are connected with the internal organs through nerves, the pressure during clapping stimulates the organs, improving blood circulation and breathing. Thereby, the whole body is benefited.

Regular clapping is akin to physical exercise. The quick movement of arms stimulates the whole body. The heart, lungs and kidneys function better. With improved circulation of blood, waste products are washed out faster.

Clapping has an equally important effect upon the emotional well-being of a person. It improves concentration by steadying the mind, which in turn enhances efficiency. The senses and the mind are better controlled, which is the beginning of one's path to salvation. Indeed as you worship God, clap your way to good health and happiness.

Your questions answered...

Does God ignore those who do not pray to Him?
God cares for everyone. But God is always closer to those who surrender to Him.

Who is a good devotee?
A good devotee is one who accepts and surrenders to the Supreme Spirit.

Why do Hindus accord great importance to the name of God?

*R*am Naam simply means *the name of God.* All Hindus believe there is magic in the name of God and this magic can transform their life.

When Ram and Lakshman along with Sugriva and his army reached the point from where it was necessary to cross the sea to reach Sita, who was in Lanka, the only option available was to build a bridge to cross over. Nala and Nila were entrusted the responsibility of building the bridge. However, when they began building the bridge, every stone brought to the waterfront sank into the sea. Then it was suggested that the name of God – 'Ram' – be written on every stone. When this was done, the stones did not sink. Soon the bridge was built.

When an inanimate stone with 'Ram' written on it did not sink, would the name of 'Ram' written within the heart of a devout person not ensure happiness and salvation?

In the **Ramcharitmanas**, Balkand, it is said:

नहिं कलि करम न भगति बिबेकू । राम नाम अवलंबन एकू ॥

In Kalyug one cannot depend upon deeds alone, nor can one depend upon devotion and knowledge. Only the name of God – Ram – can support you.

In the **Padampuran**, Patal Khand, 20/80, it is said:

रामेति नाम यच्छोत्रे विश्रम्भादागतं यदि । करोति पापसंदाहं तूलं वहिकणो यथा ॥

Even if one were to accidentally hear the name of Ram, it would absolve one of all sins just as a spark from a fire would burn cotton.

In the **Padampuran**, Uttarakhand, 71/20-21, it is said:

राम रामेति रामेति रामेति च पुनर्जपन् ।
स चाण्डालोऽपि पूतात्मा जायते नात्र संशयः ॥
कुरुक्षेत्रं तथा काशी गया वै द्वारका तथा ।
सर्वतीर्थं कृतं तेन नामोच्चारणमात्रतः ॥

Ram, Ram, Ram, Ram – One who chants Ram repeatedly becomes a pure soul irrespective of whether one was a depraved person. There is no doubt about it. Only through chanting the name one can gain the benefits as from pilgrimages to Kurukshetra, Kashi, Dwarka and other important places.

In the **Skandpuran**, Lord Shiva tells Parvati:

रामेति द्वयक्षरजपः सर्वपापापनोदकः ।
गच्छंस्तिष्ठन् शयनो वा मनुजो रामकीर्तनात् ।
इड निर्वर्तितो याति चान्ते हरिगणो भवेत् ।

'Ram' – chanting the two-syllable mantra absolves one of all sins. Whoever chants and sings 'Ram Naam' when moving, sitting or sleeping, or whenever possible, finds fulfilment and eventually a place with Lord Hari.

Without doubt, there is great strength in God's name. The vibrations generated through repetition of God's name reach deep within the individual and purify the mind and soul. The physical self grows stronger. One attains wisdom. All sins are absolved and all desires fulfilled. Obstacles and fears vanish. Devotion to God is strengthened and one moves towards salvation.

Think it over…

One who knows how to give love is a living god upon earth. To gain this mastery is the highest achievement in life.

–Swami Chinmayananda

Why do Hindus revere the *Sunderkand*?

To all Hindus the *Ramayana* is an important religious text. It describes the life of Sri Ram, the seventh incarnation of Lord Vishnu. It is divided into seven parts. Of these, *Sunderkand* is considered the most important. The reading of *Sunderkand* helps people find happiness and fulfilment. Therefore, when it is not possible to have a complete narration of the *Ramayana*, on all auspicious occasions people have a community prayer where *Sunderkand* is narrated.

Sunderkand concludes with the following verse:

सकल सुमंगल दायक रघुनायक गुन गान ।
सादर सुनहिं ते तरहिं भव सिंधु बिना जलजान ॥

Sunderkand sings the praises of Sri Ram. It helps achieve all that is good and auspicious, both worldly and spiritual. Whoever hears it with devotion shall without any means be able to cross the ocean of life.

The seven parts of the *Ramayana* have been equated with seven pilgrimages that lead to salvation – Ayodhya, Mathura, Maya, Kashi, Kanchi, Avantika Puri (Ujjain) and Dvarvati (Dwarka). Thereby, *Sunderkand* is equated with the fifth pilgrimage of Kanchi. Kanchi is again divided into two parts – Shiv Kanchi and Vishnu Kanchi.

Sunderkand is a beautiful, rhythmic verbal description of Sri Ram. It comprises three *shlokas* (hymns of praise), six *chhand* (metres), 60 *dohe* (couplets) and 526 *chaupai* (Hindi poetic metre). Of the 60 couplets, the first 30 pertain to the description and character of Sri Hanuman and the other 30 pertain to the qualities of Sri Ram. The word *sunder* meaning beautiful, handsome, virtuous, and good appears in 24 *chaupai*. Sri Hanuman is the chief character in *Sunderkand*. Within *Sunderkand* there are several stories that encourage those with mental uneasiness to achieve peace and harmony.

Sunderkand gives a beautiful description of Sri Ram's ambassador Hanuman's strength, knowledge and wisdom. With the blessings of Sri Ram he is able to cross the ocean in one leap. When faced by Lankini, guarding the gates to Lanka, he successfully overcomes her and gains entrance. Although a bachelor, Hanuman conveys an emotionally charged description of Sri Ram's longing for her that helps Sita forget her own pangs of loneliness due to separation from her husband. On meeting Vibhishna, he uses the policy of winning him over to his side by causing dissension. On meeting Ravana, he uses the policy of differentiation and discrimination. He also employs the policy of force to inflict punishment and attain sway in his favour. At the same time, he explains to Ravana how he could win the favour of the Supreme God. After obtaining Sita's blessings, he returns to Sri Ram to free him also from the longing of separation and motivates him to prepare for war. Besides the beauty and inspiration of the verses, *Sunderkand* directs one towards attaining spiritual knowledge and is attractive to all from the worldly and spiritual points of view.

Devotees chant the *Sunderkand* as an unfailing ritual and seek the favours of Sri Hanuman. Through its regular chanting one overcomes poverty and sorrow and is protected from obstacles and hurdles, besides being blessed with success and happiness. Faith and devotion are the key factors.

Think it over...

Do you seek God? Then see Him in man; His divinity is manifest more in man than in any other object. Man is the greatest manifestation of God.

—**Sri Ramakrishna**

Why do many Hindus perform the *Satnarayan katha* periodically?

The word *katha* pertains to a religious discourse. *Satnarayan katha* is, therefore, a religious discourse on Lord Satnarayan. It is popular with a large number of Hindus. Some organise it occasionally, but many have it in their homes every month on the full moon day. Individuals also fast on this day.

Satnarayan comprises two words – *sat* and *Narayan*. Whereas *sat* means *truth*, *Narayan* is a name of Lord Vishnu. Truth is Narayan. This thought emerges from the *katha*. Accepting truth as God is the principal aim, which is encouraged through this religious discourse. Acceptance of truth in everyday life ensures happiness and contentment.

Constituted of a series of stories, the *Satnarayan katha* aims at motivating people to live by truth, since it ensures happiness and contentment in this world and the next. By forsaking truth one suffers in many ways.

Once when Narad asked Lord Vishnu how mankind could be protected from sorrow and suffering, Lord Vishnu said:

व्रतमस्ति महत्पुण्यं स्वर्गे मर्त्ये च दुर्लभम् ।
तव स्नेहान्मया वत्स! प्रकाशः क्रियतेऽधुना ॥

My son! Not only in the abode of the dead, but also in heaven, there is a pure and virtuous fast that manifested by me.

When the *Satnarayan katha* is performed ceremoniously, it also prepares one for salvation. Accepting truth as a form of God, whoever performs this *katha* and fasts is greatly benefited through the blessings of God. God is always happy with truth and the truthful. He blesses them with happiness and mental peace.

One needs to be aware that truth should not be restricted to what one thinks or says. Unless truth is practised in the real sense it is of no avail. Truth must protect the righteous and bring about the welfare of mankind. Without it, truth is not truth. A resolution to be truthful is valid only with good and virtuous behaviour and sincere devotion to God.

In the **Mundak**, 3/1/6, it is said:

सत्यमेव जयते नानृतम् ।

Truth is ever successful, not falsehood.

By adopting truth in everyday life one achieves success and prosperity and the problems and sorrows of life do not affect such people. Their life is without obstacles and they achieve what they set out to do. Like the gods, such people find mental peace and happiness.

Your questions answered...

People pray to gain wealth and prosperity. Is it the right thing to do?

There are two kinds of wealth – perishable and imperishable. The riches that one has through personal effort, gift, or inheritance are perishable. They can be stolen and destroyed. They can be a cause of dispute. This wealth is not without limitations. It is short-lived. The treasure of the love of God is imperishable. It is a source of continuous happiness. One should pursue this wealth.

What are the essentials in religious ceremonies conducted by Hindus?

Religious ceremonies have an important role to play in the lives of most Hindus. A Brahmin priest usually conducts these ceremonies. He must be well versed with the *shlokas* and mantras recommended for specific ceremonies. Many of these are from the old religious texts, most of them in Sanskrit. If the ceremonies are done personally, it is necessary to understand their basic procedures.

Before any special ceremony a bath is very important. In the **Kurmpuran**, 18/6-9, it is said that everyone must take a bath early every morning. This has both tangible and intangible benefits. A mouth that is foul with stale saliva gets cleansed. Laziness, the effect of bad dreams, thoughts and actions are washed away. Nothing cleanses the body better than a good bath. It is a must before all religious activities.

Sanctity, purity and cleanliness are qualities that uplift mankind. Cleanliness plays an important role in keeping the body healthy, the mind content and the soul peaceful. A good bath does all this and prepares one for religious activity.

One must be pure both externally and internally. External purity is attained with the use of water, soap, shampoo and other cleaning agents. It is also affected by the food one eats. Internal purity comes only with control over passion, anger, greed, selfishness, attachment, pride, jealousy, deception, envy and other like activities. One must overcome these bad habits to become pure and tranquil.

In the **Bhagavad Gita**, it is said that a true devotee of God transmits pure vibrations. The character of the person becomes so pure that meeting, conversing and even touching him positively influences another immediately. Wherever such pure people live, the residence, environment and atmosphere becomes pure.

Explaining the benefits of a daily bath, religious texts assert that the body with nine openings is dirty. Excrements from all nine openings make the whole body dirty. These are cleared after visiting the toilet and having a bath. Without cleaning the body no religious activity must be undertaken.

In the **Vishwamitra Smriti**, 1/86, it is said:

गुणा दश स्नानकृतो हि पुंसो रूपं च तेजश्च बलं च शौचम् ।
आयुष्यमारोग्यमलोलुपत्वं दुःस्वप्ननाशं च तपश्च मेधा ॥

One who regularly bathes in the morning is blessed with good looks, brilliance, strength, purity, health, generosity and intellect. The effects of bad dreams are destroyed.

In the **Bhavishyapuran**, Uttarakhand, 123/1-3, it is said:

नैर्मल्यं भावशुद्धिश्च विना स्नानं न युज्यते ।
तस्मात् कायविशुद्ध्यर्थं स्नानमादौ विधीयते ॥
अनुद्धतैरुद्धतैर्वा जलैः स्नानं समाचरेत् ।

Without a bath the mind does not attain clarity. Feelings do not become positive. Therefore for purification of the body a morning bath is recommended. One must bathe in a river or with water drawn out with a pump.

In the **Devi Bhagwat**, Rudraksh Mahatam, 7, it is said:

अस्नातस्त क्रियाः सर्वा भवन्ति विफला यतः ।
तस्मात्प्रातश्चरेत्स्नानं नित्यमेव दिने दिने ॥

Without a bath in the morning all the deeds of the day bring no results. A bath every morning is necessary.

In the **Kashikhand**, 6, it is said:

न जलाप्लुतदेहस्य स्नानमित्यभिधीयते ।
स स्नातो यो दमस्नातः शुचिः शुद्धनोमलः ॥

Washing the body with water is not a bath. Only one who has control over his mind and senses truly has a bath. One who has washed the dirt off his mind is pure.

Your questions answered...

How can one experience inner pleasure, peace and contentment?

When you selflessly do something for another, you experience inner pleasure. When you do not perceive it as a pleasure, you experience peace. When you accept peace as God's gift, you experience contentment.

Why is a coconut used in all Hindu religious ceremonies?

Amongst Hindus at all religious ceremonies, auspicious functions and activities the coconut plays an important part. The coconut is considered auspicious, symbolic of wealth, honour, progress and good fortune. Therefore it is customary to offer a coconut to all gods and goddesses.

It is customary to mark the coconut with five red dots and place it on a water vessel (*kalash*) or offer it in prayer. Some cover it partially with a red cloth. It is also customary amongst many people that when a person is honoured, along with a gift a coconut is offered as a symbol of purity. In many places on the occasion of *Sharad Purnima* (full moon), a coconut is offered to God Varun.

Customs vary about offering the coconut whole or broken during the ceremony. Most people offer the whole coconut at the beginning of the ceremony, and later break it and offer this as *prasad*. Many consider a coconut the favourite fruit of Lord Shiva because the three eyes in a coconut are symbolic of the three eyes of Lord Shiva.

It is said that offering a coconut is equivalent to the offering of a human to God, as the coconut resembles a human head. The offering of a coconut has also been equated with offering blood to God. The coconut is important even during tantric rituals.

It is believed that the Hindu triad – Brahma, Vishnu and Mahesh – reside within the coconut. Religious texts explain that a person should be like a coconut – hard and tough from outside, soft and generous from inside.

According to ancient stories whatever one asks of a coconut tree is soon granted. Therefore it is known as the *Kalpavrishka* (the evergreen wish tree). The coconut is principally grown along the seaside, but used for ceremonies all over the country. It is therefore considered a symbol of national unity.

Your questions answered...

When everything belongs to God, what good comes from offering a handful of flowers or other things to God?

God is present in all things. Everything is available to Him. Whatever can one offer Him? Making an offering to God is an expression of humility. Humility is an expression of surrender. That is something only you can offer.

Why is a *kalash* seen at all Hindu religious ceremonies?

When conducting religious ceremonies a *kalash* (water pot) takes the pride of place amongst other paraphernalia. It is mostly made of copper. Other metals used are brass or stainless steel. The *kalash* is filled with water and the top is closed by placing a coconut tied in a red cloth along with mango leaves. At the end of the ceremony the water is used as *charanamrit* and also sprinkled around the home. It is believed to bring good fortune.

A *kalash* is considered auspicious because the Hindu triad – Brahma, Vishnu and Mahesh – reside in it along with their consorts – Saraswati, Lakshmi and Durga. During the churning of the ocean amrit (celestial nectar) was found in a *kalash*. It is believed that Sita emerged from a *kalash* in mother earth. In older temples a common scene is that of Lakshmi seated on a lotus and two elephants on either side offering water for a bath from a *kalash* held in the tusk.

In the **Rig-Veda**, 3/32/15, it is said:

आपूर्णो अस्य कलशः स्वाहा सेक्तेव कोशं सिसिचे पिबध्यै ।
समु प्रिया आववृत्रन् मदाय प्रदक्षिणीदभि सोमास इन्द्रम् ॥

A kalash filled with pure water is offered to Lord Indra.

In the **Ramayana**, it is said:

कंचन कलस विचित्र संवारे । सबहीं धारे सजि निज द्वारे ॥

When Ram returned to Ayodhya after victory in Lanka, at his coronation lines of kalash *filled with water were placed.*

In the **Atharva-Veda** it is said that with the blessings of Surya mankind is prospering and enjoying good life since times immemorial, as though with an urn full of celestial nectar.

Of whatever substance it may be made, all Hindus consider the *kalash* auspicious. Irrespective of the occasion – a prayer, ceremony, coronation, entry into a new home, undertaking a long journey or pilgrimage, a wedding or any other auspicious occasion, it is customary to have a *kalash* filled with water, covered with red cloth, marked with a swastika, mango leaves and a coconut, coin, kumkum, rice and flowers. One prays to it as symbolic of the Hindu triad of Brahma, Vishnu and Mahesh, and seeks their blessings for success. One also prays to Varun, so that the *kalash* may be symbolic of the grandeur of the ocean.

Human life has been compared to an earthen pot filled with water, which is symbolic of life. Just as the body is useless or inauspicious without life, an empty *kalash* is considered inauspicious. Therefore, in any ceremony it is always filled with water, milk or grains to make it auspicious. On death an earthen pot filled with water is taken around the dead body, the water allowed to drain away and the earthen pot then destroyed.

In the **Devipuran**, it is explained that at the beginning of a prayer to Ma Bhagwati one must first fill a *kalash* with water and appropriately establish it. During Navratri, prayers are conducted in many Hindu homes and a *kalash* is an important part of the set-up.

Think it over…

"Unless a man is pure in body and mind, his coming into a temple and worshipping Shiva is useless. The prayers of those that are pure in mind and body will be answered. Those that are impure and try to teach religion to others will fail in the end."

—Swami Vivekananda

What is the importance of *kusha asana* for sitting at a religious ceremony?

It is customary to use an *asana* made of *kusha* grass for sitting during religious ceremonies, since time immemorial. During religious ceremonies, much energy is generated. Since people sit on the ground for ceremonies, there is likelihood of the generated energy being wasted by leakage into the ground. Since kusha has good insulation qualities, participants retain the energy generated in the ceremony. It is believed that mantras chanted sitting on a kusha mat always bring good results.

In the **Devi Bhagwat**, 19/32, it is said:

नास्य केशान् प्रवपन्ति नोरसि ताडमाघ्नते ।

By using mats made of kusha one does not lose hair. It also helps in preventing a heart attack.

In the Vedas, kusha has been described as a medicine that gives immediate results. It is credited with promoting long life, helps in clearing up a polluted atmosphere and prevents spread of infection and disease.

In certain religious ceremonies, it is customary to wear a ring made of kusha grass to insulate this finger from the other fingers in the hand and prevent energy generated in this finger from leaking into adjacent fingers. It is believed that Surya resides in the ring finger. From Surya we get life energy, brilliance and fame, which must not be wasted.

253

This kusha ring also helps in preventing loss of energy by leakage into the ground through accidental touch. In such an event the kusha ring comes in between and prevents loss of energy. It is also believed that if the energy generated in the hand is not suitably protected it has a detrimental effect upon the mind and heart.

Your questions answered...

Why are some people attracted towards God and not others?

Those who understand they are incomplete seek God. Others live under the illusion that they are complete and are therefore not attracted to God.

What is the purpose of sprinkling water at the beginning of a ceremony?

When the person who is to perform the religious ceremony is seated the priest sprinkles water on him and chants the following mantra:

ॐ अपवित्रः पवित्रो वा सर्वावस्थां गतोऽपि वा ।
यः स्मरेत् पुण्डरीकाक्षं स बाह्याभ्यन्तरः शुचिः ॥

One may be in a pure or an impure state. In any situation if one remembers Lord Vishnu, one becomes pure.

Normally everyone who joins in a religious ceremony does so after a bath. After chanting the mantra and sprinkling water, the performer's attention is immediately focussed on the ceremony. Sprinkling water is symbolic of purity.

Lord Vishnu was sleeping on Kshirsagar (the ocean). A lotus bloomed from his navel. Brahma emerged from this flower and created the world. This means we too emerged from water. The sprinkling of water reminds us of our origins.

The lotus comes out of water, but is impervious to water. This makes it symbolic of detachment. Sprinkling of water again symbolises that the person performing the ceremony should learn to live a detached life.

Water is symbolic of life. One cannot do without it. Therefore at every religious ceremony the importance of water is acknowledged by sprinkling it. Water is acknowledged as a cleansing medium that is said to destroy all sins. Water that can end fire is also known to attract wrath. Sprinkling of water scares away poisonous and disease-causing elements. Water filled in a conch shell becomes pure and is capable of destroying harmful germs.

Your questions answered...

Is there need for so many rituals and ceremonies? Can't we reduce these?

When you understand the purpose and benefits of a ritual or ceremony, you will feel inclined to follow them. Nobody forces them on you. Are people forced to celebrate birthdays, anniversaries, Valentine's Day, Father's Day or Mother's Day? Do what ensures you happiness.

Why is lighting the lamp important at all religious ceremonies?

In India there is a tradition of lighting a lamp at the beginning of a religious, social or cultural ceremony in the belief that the presence of Agni (fire) ensures success. Fire is one of the five elements that form the human body. Fire is also a transformed form of Surya. For this reason before praying and making offerings to gods and goddesses it is customary to focus the energy by lighting a lamp.

Furthermore, a flame is symbolic of wisdom, through which the darkness of ignorance is dispelled. Offerings to the flame are equated with ones made to God. In places of worship, lamps are for *arti* to ask the Supreme Spirit to dispel the darkness in our mind and light it with knowledge and wisdom. We seek to be led from darkness to light, from death to immortality.

In the **Rig-Veda**, 7/4/4, it is said:

अयं कविरकविषु प्रचेता मर्त्येष्वग्निरमृतो नि धायि ।
स मा नो अत्र जुहुरः सहस्वः सदा त्वे सुमनसः स्याम ॥

O God in the form of light! You reside as a poet in one who is not a poet and as the celestial nectar in death. O God in the form of light! May you never give us unhappiness. May we be happy always.

A lamp teaches one to be upright, rise upwards and dispel darkness. The flame destroys sin and enemies. It ensures good health, purity, happiness and long life.

It is believed that lamps should be lit in odd numbers. An even number neutralises and wastes energy. If the flame of the lamp points north, it promotes health and contentment. When it points east, it promotes long life. West invites sorrow and south causes loss.

During continuous reading of the *Ramayana* the lamp is lit for 24 hours and during Navratri it is lit for nine days. In many temples lamps are lit continuously as an offering to God in the belief that as long as the lamp is lit, God continues to be present. One's desires are soon fulfilled. It is kept lit until one's purpose is not fulfilled. It is considered inauspicious if it blows out by itself. Therefore, one should resolve to keep a lamp continuously lit only after due consideration.

Amongst Sikhs during the continuous reading of the Guru Granth Sahib that takes 48 hours, a lamp is lit continuously.

The Badrinath temple situated deep in the Himalayas at a height of over 10,000 feet above sea level is covered with snow for more than six months in the year. Every year when it is closed before the onset of severe winter, the *Akhand Jyoti* (continuous lamp) is filled with ghee to last more than six months. When the temple gates are re-opened at the onset of summer, people gather from faraway places to witness and offer prayers to the *Akhand Jyoti*.

Your questions answered...

Do a person's good and bad deeds balance each other?

No, they do not balance each other. A person is rewarded for good deeds and punished for bad ones.

What is the purpose of tying a red thread on the wrist at the beginning of a religious ceremony?

It is customary for Hindus to tie a red thread – commonly called a *mauli* or *kalava* – on the wrist at the beginning of a religious ceremony. The thread is tied on the right wrist of men and the left wrist of women.

Thereby, one invokes the blessings of the Hindu triad Brahma, Vishnu and Mahesh and their wives Saraswati, Lakshmi and Durga. With Brahma's blessings one is compassionate, with Vishnu's blessings one gains strength to protect oneself and the blessings of Mahesh ward off bad influences. Blessings of goddesses are also obtained when Lakshmi showers prosperity, Durga imparts strength and Saraswati bestows wisdom.

येन बद्धो बलीराजा दानवेन्द्रो महाबलः ।
तेन त्वामनुबध्नामि रक्षे माचल माचल ॥

The red thread is also believed to protect one from the ill effects of disease by improving immunity. The practice of tying the thread dates back to the time when Vaman Bhagwan tied his holy thread on the wrist of the progressive King Bali to grant him immortality. The literal meaning of *mauli* is 'above all'. Here the reference is to the head that stands high. With the moon perched on top of Shiva's head he is referred to as *Chandramauli*.

What is the purpose of the resolve made at the beginning of a ceremony?

The role of devotion and a firm resolve in achieving success is well known. *To resolve* means *to be determined.* Without this firm determination success cannot be achieved. *Resolve* also indicates *a definite aim.* Once the aim exists, the ability to achieve it is generated from within the individual. Nothing is difficult for a determined person.

At the beginning of a religious ceremony the priest asks the person to make a firm resolve to achieve the purpose of the ceremony. It is customary to take a little water in one's hand and make the resolve. The water indicates that God Varun resides there and seeks his blessing.

A firm resolve is explained in many ways. It refers to the strength from one's desires, the determination of mutual discussion, and a project to achieve one's desires or as a motivate to act. It is also referred to as the basis of desire and action.

Devotion, self-confidence and concentration in conducting a religious ceremony emerge from the strength one gains from making a firm resolve. Even when giving charity or conducting a yagya, one must first resolve for its success.

In the **Manusmriti**, 2/3, it is said:

संकल्पमूलः कामो वै यज्ञाः संकल्पसंभवाः ।
व्रतानि यमधर्माश्च सर्वे संकल्पजाः स्मृताः ॥

A desire is the basis of a personal resolution. A yagya can be conducted only by a firm resolution, fast, yagya or other religious ceremonies are based upon a resolve.

Making a resolve also creates awareness amongst people about their family background, religious attachments and sentiments. This arouses pride within an individual and dissuades one from bad activities.

260

Why is *tilak* applied on the forehead in a religious ceremony?

A*tilak* is an ornamental or religious mark on the forehead, also called *tika*. According to Hindu religious texts, applying *tilak* or *tika* is necessary at all religious ceremonies, without which no Hindu ceremony is complete. From birth till death *tilak* is a part of life. All gods, goddesses, yogis, saints, sages and mahatmas apply *tilak* on their forehead. Some householders also apply *tilak* daily, although generally it is customary to apply *tilak* at the beginning of the religious ceremony.

According to tradition, applying *tilak* is a symbol of honour being extended to the person. Guests are welcomed or seen off with *tilak*. Even when householders leave on long travel or pilgrimage, they are seen off with a *tilak* and good wishes.

In the **Brahmvaivartpuran**, Brahmparv, 26, it is said:

स्नानं दानं तपो होमो देवतापितृकर्म च ।

तत्सर्वं निष्फलं याति ललाटे तिलकं विना ।

ब्राह्मणास्तिलकं कृत्वा, कुर्यात्संध्यान्यतर्पणम् ॥

If tilak is not adorned on the forehead at the time of a holy bath, yagya, prayer or religious ceremony, effort bears no fruit. The Brahmin priest must have a tilak when performing prayers, tarpan and other ceremonies.

The **Skandpuran** explains with what fingers *tilak* must be applied for best results:

अनामिका शांतिदा प्रोक्ता मध्यमायुकरी भवेत् ।
अंगुष्ठः पुष्टिदः प्रोक्ता तर्जनी मोक्षदायिनी ॥

When tilak is applied with the ring finger it brings peace, with the middle finger it prolongs age, with the thumb it promotes health and with the forefinger one attains salvation.

It is customary to apply *tilak* on the entire forehead with three fingers. Devotees of Vishnu use a *tilak* of two thin upward lines, devotees of Shakti (Shakti and Shiva) use two dots, and devotees of Shiva use three horizontal lines. Some religious texts suggest that those using a *tilak* of three horizontal lines during *shraddh*, yagya, meditation or prayers overcome death.

The *tilak*, *tika* or *bindiya* (for women) is applied in the centre of the forehead because the entire body is controlled from this point. Maharishi Yagyavalka said that this position is appropriate because Shiva's third eye is located here. After the application of *tilak* pure thoughts are said to emerge.

The conscious and subconscious minds are located here and a constant flow of thoughts and activities affect the whole body. These can make a person a god or a demon, wise or foolish. A person's sixth sense, or the third eye, is located here. Applying *tilak* here prepares a person for the upward spiritual movement to salvation.

The soul is also said to reside in this region. Applying *tilak* ensures a person always feels cool, comfortable and peaceful, does not suffer from headaches and is self-confident. A mentally tranquil person is better able to follow the right path and take better decisions. It also helps balance the hormones.

It is customary to use sandalwood, kumkum (vermilion), clay or ash from yagya for applying *tilak*. Saffron is used on special occasions. Sandalwood absolves one's sins, attracts prosperity and protects one from obstacles. It promotes wisdom and keeps the mind cool and peaceful. A mixture of kumkum and turmeric is germicidal and keeps the skin healthy, while helping the sinews and ligaments function naturally. Pure clay or soil helps destroy infectious germs. The use of ash from a yagya brings good fortune.

Your questions answered...

• **What is meant when Hindus talk of mental impurities?**

Mental impurities include feelings and emotions like lust, anger, greed, jealousy, pride, arrogance and a variety of fears. These separate an individual from God within just as layers of dust cover a mirror rendering it useless to see oneself in it.

• **Where do impurities of the mind come from?**

The impurities of the mind arise from desires. When a desire is fulfilled, we feel happy temporarily. This happiness gives birth to more desires. This way the impurities accumulate. When a desire is not fulfilled we feel disheartened and frustrated. This too gives rise to other kinds of impurities.

What is the purpose of *aachman* at the beginning of a ceremony?

At the beginning of every religious ceremony it is customary for the priest and the person conducting the ceremony to take water in the right palm thrice and drink it. This water is termed *aachman.*

Religious texts direct that *aachman* be taken thrice because:

प्रथमं यत् पिवति तेन ऋग्वेदं प्रीणाति ।
यद् द्वितीयं तेन यजुर्वेदं प्रीणाति यद् तृतीयं तेन सामवेदं प्रीणाति ॥

By taking the aachman *thrice all the three Vedas, Rigveda, Yajurveda and Samaveda, become content and grant whatever one desires.*

In the **Manusmriti**, 2/60, it is said:

त्रिराचामेदपः पूर्वम् ।

In the beginning aachman *must be taken thrice.*

Aachman helps clear the throat and voice, helping one can chant the mantras with clarity. During all prayers, begin by taking the *aachman* thrice. If the prayers are lengthy, *aachman* can be taken again thrice in between to soothe a parched throat.

It is also believed that by taking the *aachman* one is absolved of physical, mental and oral sins and is able to achieve intangible results that, though not visible, are beneficial all the same.

In the **Manusmriti**, different ways of taking *aachman* are described. In the Brahmtirth way, it is taken from under the thumb. In the Prajapatyatirth way, it is taken from under the big finger. In the Devtirth way, it is taken from the forepart of the fingers. *Aachman* from between the thumb and index finger is prohibited because this procedure is used to offer tarpan to forefathers.

A method for taking *aachman* is also described in the **Bodhayan**, suggesting that the hand must be curled to look like a cow's ear. Then *aachman* is taken thrice.

Your questions answered...

Why do responsibilities towards others appear difficult to fulfil?

Anything with which we are not in harmony appears difficult. When we accept something as a part of us it appears easy. Everyone is comfortable with what appears easy.

Why are offerings made to the *Navgrah* at the beginning of all religious ceremonies?

Amongst Hindus it is customary that before doing anything auspicious or religious, after first making an offering to Sri Ganesh, offerings are made to the *Navgrah*, or the nine planets – Surya, Chandrama, Mangal, Budh, Brihaspati, Shukra, Shani, Rahu and Ketu.

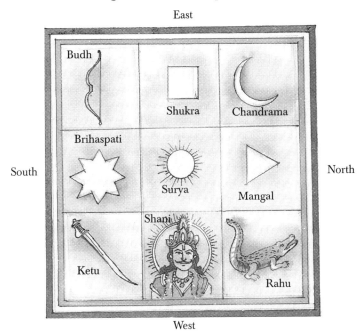

It is believed that these nine planets control everything in this world, and also the lives of every individual. The extent of the influence varies with the place and time of one's birth. Astrology is the science that studies and forecasts the effects of these planets on the lives of people. When something new is done, it is natural for everyone to desire success and for this, the blessings of all nine planets are sought through offerings and prayers. Even if the effect of any of the planets is malefic, through prayers this effect is considerably controlled.

It is believed that the planets reflect some rays on earth, influencing the lives of people. Every little change in the position of these planets and stars affects individuals, by affecting different parts of the body and the flow of blood. The body derives energy from Surya. Therefore, every little change affects energy levels. The circulating blood transmits the changes to every part of the body immediately. Brilliant and illuminating, Surya is the storehouse of spiritual energy. Devotees of Surya are greatly blessed. Chandrama is known as the master of medicines. Since it controls the mind, it is also known as the king of the mind. Mangal is

265

symbolic of Kartikeya. He is the commander of forces, known to be stern, merciless, very powerful and strong. Budh is wise, intelligent and sharp. Brihaspati is the guru of gods and is known as Devguru. Eternally strong and powerful, he is the teacher among gods. Shukra is benevolent and brings honour and fame. He also promotes good health and virility. Shani is known to create most problems. Rahu is no better than Shani. Ketu is a copy of Rahu. Both Rahu and Ketu are always on the prowl creating problems whenever they can.

In the **Yagyavalkya Smriti** it is said:

श्रीकामः शान्तिकामो वा ग्रहयज्ञं समाचरेत् ।

Those people who desire wealth and peace must make offerings to the Navgrah.

By making offerings to the *Navgrah* they are appeased. Through prayer their malefic effects are reduced and the good effects enhanced. Thus, a happy environment is created and there is an auspicious atmosphere in the family.

It is also believed that in the human body Surya contributes the soul, Chandrama controls the mind, Mangal controls blood circulation, Budh gives the power to think, Shukra ensures virility, and Shani is responsible for happiness and sorrow. Together they control the entire body.

Considering these effects of the *Navgrah* on the body and mind, it is natural to make offerings to them before any auspicious or religious ceremony.

Once a curious woman asked Ramakrishna Paramahans, "Is it possible for priests to pray and make offerings to the planets and change unfavourable influences into favourable ones?"

Paramahans responded, "The planets are not so mean that without reason they should change course and create problems. They are also not so fickle that they can be content or discontent with simple rituals. Priests are not their representatives that they should dance to their tune for a price."

Is blowing a conch shell important at religious ceremonies?

A conch shell is an important part of religious ceremonies. Blowing the conch shell during a religious ceremony, wedding or important function is both important and auspicious. In temples it is customary to blow conch shells in the morning and evening prayers. Without the sound of the conch shell the prayer or ceremony is considered incomplete. The sound of the conch shell is considered auspicious in other religions also.

In the **Atharva-Veda**, 4/10, it is stated that a conch shell is a blend of space, the planetary system and gold. Its sound frightens enemies, controls demons and evil spirits, chases away ignorance, laziness and disease and promotes long life.

In the **Ranvir Bhaktiratanakar Skande** it is said:

यस्य शंखध्वनिं कुर्यात्पूजाकाले विशेषतः ।
विमुक्तः सर्वपापेन विष्णुना सह मोदते ॥

Whoever blows the conch shell during prayer is absolved of all sins and finds contentment with Lord Vishnu.

The conch shell is blown before sunrise and after sunset since the rays of the sun are believed to interfere with waves from the conch shell. The sound of the conch shell effectively clears pollution. Indian scientist Jagadish Chandra Bose conducted an experiment showing that as far as the sound of the conch shell penetrated, disease-causing bacteria became ineffective or died. Investigations at Berlin University confirmed that the sound of the conch shell was an effective and cheap way of destroying bacteria in the atmosphere. It is said that it also helps control cholera and malaria and is useful amongst patients of hysteria, epilepsy and leprosy.

Amongst Hindus there is a saying *Shankh .baje, bhoot bhage*, meaning 'when the conch is blown, ghosts flee'. Its continuous sound is said to ward off heart attack and it is also good for people who stammer.

It is customary to make small children wear little shells stringed together around their neck, as it helps them speak sooner and clearly. Blowing of the conch shell enhances lung capacity and protects one from lung ailments. It also helps in getting rid of mental tension, regulating blood pressure, controlling diabetes and preventing diseases affecting breathing and digestion.

It is customary to fill a conch shell with water and leave it at the place of prayer. This water is later sprinkled on devotees, since it is believed to have curative qualities and improves health. In some areas, ladies wear bangles made of conch shells.

Your questions answered...

Can a person really attain God? How?

A person can attain God through single-minded devotion. *Bhagwan* Krishna said that whoever performs his duties dedicated to Him, depends upon Him, is devoted to Him, has no attachment, and is free of malice towards all beings, attains Him.

What is the purpose of *Agnihotra* at Hindu religious ceremonies?

*A*gnihotra simply means *a sacrificial fire.* Amongst Hindus, there is a family name Agnihotri, derived from the fact that at one time these families maintained a perpetual fire in their homes. In many homes prayers are offered with fire, particularly amongst Arya Samaj Hindus.

In the **Valmiki Ramayana**, 1/6/12, it is said:

नानाहिताग्निनायज्वा ।

Everyone performed Agnihotra in Ayodhya everyday.

Lord Ram and Sita performed Agnihotra on the day of the coronation. It is also said the aggrieved Kaushalya did not miss out on Agnihotra even on the day Ram left home for 14 years of exile.

In the **Suttinipat**, 568/21, Buddha explained the importance of Agnihotra*:*

अग्गिहुत्त मुखा यंत्रा सावित्री छन्दसो मुखम् ।
राजामुखं मनुस्साणं नदीनां सागरो मुखं ॥

Just as the ocean amongst the rivers, a king amongst the people and Savitri amongst the verses, Agnihotra is amongst the yagyas.

In the **Atharva-Veda**, 19/55/3, it is said:

सायंसायं गृहपतिर्नो अग्निः प्रातः प्रातः सौमनस्य दाता ।
वसोर्वसोर्वसुदान एधि वयं त्वेन्धानास्तन्वं पुषेम ॥

May the fire in the home give us happiness and peace in the morning and evening, a happy temperament, resolve and good health. May it give us fame and honour. May we awaken you through yagya fire so that we may be robust and strong. Agnihotra promotes good health and mental contentment. It is a ladder to spirituality.

In the **Atharva-Veda**, 9/2/6, it is said:

अग्नेहोत्रेण प्रणुदे सपत्नान् ।

Agnihotra destroys enemies.

Agnihotra promotes mental peace and gives contentment. It clarifies the air in the home, spreads fragrance, purifies the atmosphere and thus helps householders. It gives them energy and the power to concentrate. It releases mental tension. Through a cleaner environment it promote good health for everyone and has innumerable benefits.

What is the purpose of a *yagya* and offering *ahuti*?

A huti is *an oblation or offering*. It can also refer to *a sacrifice*. However, when conducting a *yagya* it is customary to have a *havan* or *fire sacrifice*. The fire is ceremoniously lit, symbolic of inviting Agni, the fire God. Thereafter as mantras are chanted an offering in the form of ghee or *havan samagri* (a mixture of herbs and ghee) is offered to the fire at the end of the mantra. While making the offering, the word *Swaha* is uttered loudly.

In the **Matsyapuran**, it is said that when the five essential constituents – gods, havan fluid or offering, Veda mantra, the divine law and a gift to the Brahmin – are there, it is a yagya. Any good activity done for universal welfare is a yagya.

Sages and saints have identified three purposes of a yagya – prayer to gods, developing harmonious company and charity. Prayers to gods are used as models to shape our lives. Harmonious company is having relatives and friends who share similar thoughts and are motivated towards togetherness and mutual support. Charity is to share one's blessings, extend support to society and create a feeling of universal brotherhood.

Through a yagya one attains physical, mental and internal peace, purification of the self, spiritual progress and protection from sickness. The yagya fire has five qualities – it is always hot or active; it is exemplary; it is attractive to all that come to it; it is generous because it gives rather than store its benefits; the flame is always high, symbolising concern, character and self-respect.

In the **Kalikapuran**, 23/7/8, it is said:

यज्ञेषु देवास्तुष्यन्ति यज्ञे सर्वप्रतिष्ठितम् ।
यज्ञेन ध्रियते पृथ्वी यज्ञस्तारयति प्रजाः ॥
अन्नेन भूता जीवन्ति यज्ञे सर्वप्रतिष्ठितम् ।
पर्जन्यो जायते यज्ञात् सर्वयज्ञमयं ततः ॥

Yagyas please the gods. It was through a yagya that the entire world was established. Yagya supports the whole world. Yagya protects people from sin. People live on grain. Grain is produced from clouds that bring rain. Clouds emerge from the yagya. The whole universe depends upon yagya.

Religious texts say:

श्रीकामः शांतिकामो वा ग्रहयज्ञं समारभेत् ।
वृष्टि आयुः पुष्टिकामो वा तथैवाभिचरन पुनः ॥

All those who desire prosperity, peace, a long life, happiness, rain and physical and mental well-being must perform a yagya.

In the **Bhagavad Gita**, 3/15, it is said:

तस्मात्सर्वगतं ब्रह्म नित्यं यज्ञे प्रतिष्ठितम् ॥

The universal Supreme Spirit is always present in a yagya.

In the **Mahanarayaniya Upanishad**, it is said:

यज्ञेन हि देवा दिवंगताः यज्ञेनासुरानपानुदन्तः ।
यज्ञेन द्विषन्तो मित्रा भवन्ति यज्ञेन सर्वप्रतिष्ठितम् तस्माद्यज्ञं परमं वदन्ति ।

Through yagya the gods attained heaven and overcame the demons. Through yagya even enemies become friends. Therefore outstanding people consider a yagya a special activity.

In the **Agnipuran**, 380/1, it is said:

यज्ञैश्चदेवानाप्नोति ।

Through a yagya the gods grant one's wishes.

In the **Padampuran Shristhikhand**, 3/124, it is said that pleased by a yagya the gods bless mankind with well-being.

In the **Manusmriti**, 3/76, it is said that an oblation dutifully offered to the fire is received by Surya.

In the **Samaveda**, 879, it is said that whoever offers oblations to the fire is blessed with good children, wisdom, wealth and prosperity.

When Brahma created mankind man visualised that his life would be full of need, problems and sorrow. He complained to Brahma, "Lord! Who would nourish and protect insecure mankind?"

Brahma responded, "Dear son! Through a yagya offer oblations to the gods. They will bless you with wealth, prosperity, well-being and fame."

In a yagya, after chanting the mantra it is customary to say *Swaha* when making an oblation to the fire. *Swaha* is the name of Agni's wife. It is customary to invoke her name during an offering to make her the medium of the oblation. *Swaha* literally means *good speech*.

Your questions answered...

What is the difference between a devotee, a saint and a seer?

A devotee seeks spiritual growth. A saint seeks the truth, and has attained purity of speech and character. A person who has attained freedom from attachment to worldly possessions and sees all as a part of God is a seer.

Why is it important to chant mantras loudly?

It is believed that during a yagya the gods come down and grant the wishes of a person performing the yagya. The power of Vedic and yagya mantras is such that the gods become helpless and are persuaded to come down. When mantras are ceremoniously chanted and offerings made, powerful vibrations are generated. These dispel feelings of hatred, dishonesty, impropriety, selfishness and other negative actions amongst those present, resulting in the elimination of many problems, worries and fears.

It is believed that in an environment dominated by the sound of Vedic mantras, children are blessed with noble qualities and thoughts. Wherever there is a divine influence, good people emerge, endowed with love, goodwill, honesty and good thoughts.

Religious texts describe several kinds of yagyas. Besides daily yagya, there is provision for special kinds too. Thousands, hundreds of thousands or more mantras may be chanted at the yagya. Eventually the blessing is attained. The sound of mantras being chanted, combined with the power of the resolve made by the person performing the yagya, reaches the divine power that converts the chants into the desired blessing.

Once Maharaja Prathu resolved to perform hundred Ashvamedh yagyas. After he had completed 99 yagyas and was already feeling the beneficial effects, Lord Indra felt demoralised and was worried about losing his kingdom. During the hundredth yagya, Indra changed form and took away the horse in order to create an obstacle. However, Prathu's son forcibly had the horse released.

273

Enraged by Lord Indra's wicked intentions, Prathu picked up his bow and arrow and announced that he would kill Indra. When the rishis heard the announcement they were alarmed. They went to Prathu and said, "O Monarch! With your dreadful arrow you will not only destroy Indra but also the whole of Devlok (abode of gods). You have the intention to kill Indra only. By destroying us needlessly along with him your achievement will be reduced. Permit us to control the proud Indra by chanting mantras and offering him to the yagya fire as an oblation."

Maharaja Prathu responded emphatically, "Through his unprovoked action this knave has hindered my achievement. For such time as you take to attract him through your mantras and offer him as oblation, and until I see him burn in this *agni kund*, I will not let go of my bow."

To satisfy Maharaja Prathu, the rishis chanted mantras and made oblations to the fire. When Indra was attracted to the fire and was about to be burnt, Brahma intervened. He requested the rishis to let Indra go. Lord Indra asked Maharaja Prathu for forgiveness. On everyone's request, Maharaja Prathu forgave him.

It is evident that mantras are very powerful. But they must be chanted in a balanced note and rhythm. They soothe and clear the mind of undesirable things.

Your questions answered...

Life is dynamic. We change everyday, as does everything around us. If God exists in everything, with such changes how can God be eternal?

A chameleon changes colours. By changing colours does a chameleon cease to be a chameleon? Likewise, the changes we see are manifestations of God. But God is changeless and undoubtedly eternal.

What is the importance of *charanamrit* in religious ceremonies?

The word *charanamrit* comprises two words, *charan* and *amrit*. *Charan* means *feet* and *amrit* is *the celestial nectar that makes one immortal*. Together the words mean *nectar of God's feet*.

In all temples after the morning and evening *arti*, *charanamrit* is given. Even after a religious ceremony, *charanamrit* is served to all present. *Charanamrit* is normally kept in a copper vessel, as copper has many curative qualities. Ayurveda and homoeopathic practitioners have confirmed this. Copper cures spasmodic pains. It is believed that drinking water stored in a copper vessel improves intellect, memory and wisdom. When served in temples a few crushed leaves of tulsi are added. Tulsi too has great medicinal qualities.

Devotees accept *charanamrit* in the palm of the right hand supported by the left.

In the **Ramayana**, Ayodhyakand, Doha 101, Tulsidas has said:

पद पखारि जलुपान करि आपु सहित परिवार ।
पितर पारु करि प्रभुहि पुनि मुदित गयउ लेइ पार ॥

When Kewat washed the feet of Sri Rama and accepted the water as charanamrit, *not only did he attain salvation, but his forefathers also attained it.*

In the **Ranvir Bhaktiratanakar Brhnna**, it is said:

पापव्याधिविनाशार्थं विष्णुपादोदकौषधम् ।
तुलसीदलसम्मिश्रं जलं सर्षपमात्रकम् ॥

275

To absolve oneself of sins and get rid of disease God's charanamrit *is like medicine. If tulsi leaves are added the qualities are enhanced.*

In the **Ranvir Bhaktisagar** it is said:

अकालमृत्युहरणं सर्वव्याधिविनाशनम् ।
विष्णुपादोदकं पीत्वा पुनर्जन्म न विद्यते ॥

Charanamrit *protects one from untimely death. It destroys all kinds of diseases. It breaks the chain of death and rebirth.*

Charanamrit has great qualities and benefits a person physically, emotionally and spiritually. Therefore, always accept *charanamrit* with grace and humility.

Your questions answered…

Why do good people suffer and bad people prosper many times?

Both are being punished or rewarded for past deeds. Once the account is settled, they will begin with a new account.

What does *Panch Mahayagya* mean?

Religious texts say the householder must perform *Panch Mahayagya.*

In the **Manusmriti**, 3/70, it is said:

अध्यापनं ब्रह्मयज्ञः पितृयज्ञस्तु तर्पणम् ।
होमो दैवो बलिभोतीनृयज्ञोऽतिथि पूजनम् ॥

The five mahayagyas include Brahmayagya – teaching of Vedas, Pitrayagya – devoted to forefathers, Devyagya – devoted to the gods, Bhootyagya – devoted to charity, and Nriyagya or Atithiyagya – devoted to guests.

Details of the recommended five yagyas for householders are given briefly:

Brahmayagya pertains to reading the Vedas and other religious texts and teaching them to others. The study increases wisdom, and discussion during teaching helps one have a better interpretation of intricate details. This motivates one to go into deeper study. Reading religious texts and chanting the Gayatri mantra fulfils the need for Brahmayagya.

Pitrayagya pertains to *tarpan, pind daan* and *shraddh.* Religious texts assert that it is the duty of everyone to make these offerings to their forefathers. It makes them happy and content and they bless successors with wealth, wisdom, happiness and a long life.

Devyagya pertains to making offerings to gods and performing *havan.* The *havan* helps clear the home of all kinds of pollution. Pleased with the offerings, gods bless the householder and his family with good fortune and happiness. Therefore, gods and goddesses must always be remembered.

Bhootyagya pertains to sharing whatever one has. God has blessed everyone with many material comforts. If one sets a small part of this aside for the needy the purpose is served. Nobody is so poor that he cannot give. In the **Manusmriti**, 3/92, it is said that one should give to a dog, a depraved person, a lowborn person, or one who is sick or a leper. One should also give to crows, ants and insects by placing some food in a clean place. In this way all kinds of living things are served. This charitable and compassionate work prepares one for salvation.

Nriyagya pertains to the love, affection and service extended to guests. A householder must first offer meals to the guest and only eat after the guest has eaten. Religious texts describe a guest as god. The **Mahabharata**, Shantiparv, 191/12, says that if a guest departs hungry and thirsty the householder faces misfortune.

In the **Vishwamitra Smriti**, 1/15-16, it is said:

नित्यकर्माखिलं यस्तु उक्तकाले समाचरेत् ।
जित्वा स सकलाल्लोकानन्ते विष्णुपुरं व्रजेत् ॥

Necessary duties must be done everyday at the right time. Whoever does it attains the best and eventually reaches the abode of Vishnu. Therefore every householder must devotedly perform the Panch Mahayagya *at the appointed time. Only then he can be happy and peaceful.*

Your questions answered...

It is natural for a person to desire something. But when the desire is fulfilled, why is the pleasure shortlived?

This is because the pleasure derived from fulfilment of a desire is momentary. It is human nature to desire things. But once we have it, the object of desire does not attract us any longer. Fulfilment of a desire leads to another one. This is an unending process. Therefore, joy derived from fulfilment of a desire is illusory and momentary.

How can one find longlasting fulfilment?

One finds contentment when in control of desires. The lesser the desires, the greater the fulfilment and happiness.

Do Hindus practise animal sacrifice?

In the **Mahabharata**, Shantiparv, it is said:

सुरा मत्स्याः पशोर्मांस द्विजातीनां बलिस्तथा ।
धूर्तैः प्रवर्तितं यज्ञे नैतद् वेदेषु कथ्यते ॥

Knaves and rascals initiated the offering of liquor, fish, animals and human sacrifice in a yagya. They had a demonical temperament and desired to eat meat in a yagya. In the Vedas eating of flesh has not been recommended.

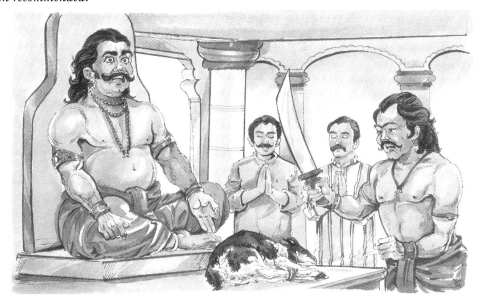

To please Bhairav, Bhawani and other gods and goddesses, some Hindus who were greedy for meat began offering animal sacrifices. During Mughal rule, meat eating became popular. It said that some greedy priests wrote certain *shlokas* that claimed the goddess desired animal sacrifice, and the flesh would be served as *prasad*. These *shlokas* were mischievously included some religious texts. All Hindu religious texts forbid the eating of meat and consider it food for demons. No religious text permits meat eating. If gods and goddesses were greedy for meat, they would motivate one into savage acts rather than towards compassion. Would they even have been different from demons? Killing innocent animals in the name of religion and offering them to gods and goddesses to fulfil selfish desires cannot be justified in any way. With such sinful acts one cannot expect to be blessed with prosperity, good fortune and happiness. Such sacrifices do not please any god or goddess. If one does find happiness sometimes, it is temporary. Bad deeds only ensure sorrow and hell.

In the **Shrimadbhagwat**, Vedavyas says that whoever offers animal sacrifice and prays to demons and evil spirits will be worse than animals. Hell is certain. In the end, such people roam about in the utter darkness of ignorance and sorrow.

In the beginning of mankind, the gods asked once the rishis, "According to the Vedas in the yagya today there should be *ajbali. Aj* means a *goat* and *bali* means sacrifice. Why do you not offer the sacrifice?"

The rishis responded, "A seed is also known as *aj. Aj* denotes cereals. The Vedas direct us to use cereals. Killing of animals is forbidden in a yagya and is irreligious."

Your questions answered...

Why is it that many do not find happiness through charity?

When one gives what has been acquired by wrong means, it cannot bring more than momentary satisfaction. A person who gives his time to guide a young person benefits more than one who gives some money that has been wrongly earned. Besides, when a person gives to receive acclaim, appreciation and praise, he cannot find happiness through it because he has already been paid for what he has given.

What is a *yantra* that's used by Hindus in religious ceremonies?

A *yantra* as used in prayers is a *drawing* or *diagram*. It is believed that commendable results are attained when specific *yantras* are used for different gods and goddesses. It is believed that gods and goddesses reside in *yantras*. Therefore like mantras, *yantras* too show their effect. It can also be said that *yantras* are a graphic form of mantras.

A *yantra* is intended to be a medium to arouse consciousness and awareness about the purpose of a prayer. A *yantra* comprises geometrical shapes. These may be square, triangular, circular, conical, five-sided or eight-sided. The movement of planets is circular and forces in the universe affect it. By offering prayers to the *yantra* everyday, one pleases the gods and also attains the desired fruit. These *yantras* have been designed for the benefit of the common householder. However, *yantras* are effective only after *pran pratishtha* or the infusion of life.

In the **Bhuvaneshwari Kram Chandika**, it is written that Lord Shiva tells Parvati, "Dear Parvati! Just as a living thing needs a body and a lamp needs oil, gods need the *yantra*."

This statement is repeated in the **Kularnvatantra**:

यन्त्रमित्याहुरेतस्मिन् देवः प्रीणातिः ।
शरीरमिव जीवस्य दीपस्य स्नेहवत् प्रिये ॥

A brief description of some of the popular yantras is given below.

Shri Yantra: Through this *yantra* one attains the favour of Lakshmi and is never short of money. By praying to it everyday one attains all benefits.

281

Shri Mahamrityunjay Yantra: This *yantra* protects one from destructive influences like accidents, crises, sickness, epidemic and similar life-threatening calamities.

Baglamukhi Yantra: This is to overcome enemies or obstacles and gain favourable verdicts in legal cases.

Bisa Yantra: God helps those who have the *Bisa yantra* in all endeavours. All difficult things become easy. By praying to it every morning obstacles are overcome and one attains success and honour.

Kuber Yantra: This *yantra* makes Kuber, the god of wealth, benevolent.

Shri Kanakdhara Yantra: It helps in attaining wealth and dispelling poverty and ensures many blessings.

Shri Mahalakshmi Yantra: With prayers to this *yantra* one is assured of perpetual prosperity.

Surya Yantra: It promotes good health and well-being, protects one from diseases and promotes intellect.

Panchadashi Yantra: This *yantra* has the blessings of Lord Shiva and ensures morality, wealth, family happiness and salvation.

Of all *yantras* the one that brings astonishing results in the shortest period is the *Shri yantra*. In Kalyug, *Shri yantra* is like Kamadhenu, the celestial cow. With successful prayer and offerings, all the four basic human pursuits *dharma* – discharge of duty, *artha* – acquirement of wealth, *kama* – gratification and *moksha* – final emancipation are attained. The Vedas say that 33 crore gods and goddesses reside in the *Shri yantra*. This *yantra* can eliminate Vaastu shortcomings. The origin and development of the universe is depicted in this *yantra*.

The **Durga Saptshati** says:

आराधिता सैव नृणां भोगस्वर्गापवर्गदा ।

With worship the primordial power gives happiness, enjoyment and pleasures of heaven.

There is a story pertaining to the origin of the *Shri yantra*. Once at Kailash Mansarovar, Adi Shankaracharya underwent great penance and pleased Lord Shiva. When Lord Shiva offered one blessing, Shankaracharya inquired whether universal welfare could be attained. In response, Lord Shiva gave him the *Shri yantra*, an embodiment of Lakshmi, along with the *Shri Sukt mantra*.

Shri yantra is the place of worship of goddess Bhagwati Mahatripur Sundri, an embodiment of Brahma. She resides in the circles. Her chariot as well as subtle form and symbol is there. Any prayer offered to Rajeshwari (a monarch), Kameshwari (one who grants wishes) and Mahatripur Sundri without the *Shri yantra* brings no results. All gods and goddesses dependent upon Mahatripur Sundri reside in the *Shri yantra*.

Mahatripur Sundri has been referred to in religious texts with names like Vidya (knowledge), Maha Vidya (best knowledge) and Param Vidya (ultimate knowledge).

The **Vamkeshwar Tantra** says:

सर्वदेवमयी विद्या ।

In the **Durga Saptshati**, the same thing is said:

विद्यासि सा भगवती परमा हि देवी ।

Hey Devi! You are the ultimate knowledge.

There is a story about the effectiveness of the *Shri yantra.*

Once, unhappy with her visit to earth, Ma Lakshmi returned home to Vaikunth. Due to her absence, many problems emerged on earth. Maharishi Vasishth sought the help of Lord Vishnu to pacify Ma Lakshmi, without unsuccess. Then Devguru Brihaspati explained that the best way to attract Lakshmi to the earth was through the *Shri yantra.* With worship of the *Shri yantra*, Ma Lakshmi immediately returned to earth and said, "*Shri yantra* is my foundation. My soul resides in it. Therefore, I had to return."

Worship to *Shri yantra* after *pran pratishtha* ensures happiness and salvation. The best occasions to establish *Shri yantra* are Diwali, Dhanteras (two days before Diwali), Dashera, Akshay Tritiya (the third day of the lunar fortnight) and Pratipada (the first day of the lunar fortnight) and other auspicious days. At the time of worship one must face the east and pray with devotion and concentration.

Think it over...

When we turn towards God, we become thoughtful towards others. We see what is good in them, and ignore their weaknesses and mistakes. This, in turn, gives birth to generosity. Generosity serves both, the person we serve and the self. When we share ourselves with others, God compensates us manifold through love, peace and happiness.

Why are all Hindu religious activities entrusted to Brahmins?

In Hindu religious texts, Brahmins are accorded high position. This is primarily because a Brahmin is expected to endeavour to build a good society through his good qualities and knowledge. It is the responsibility of a Brahmin to study and teach, perform yagyas and other important ceremonies. It is desired that people tread a common path, make progress and adopt a positive lifestyle. Compared to others, a Brahmin is supposed to be more sacrificing, tolerant and devoted. A Brahmin needs to survive amongst both the poor and the rich. Either way, he needs to live a balanced life where he can serve all kinds of people in society. The Vedas mention the qualities of a Brahmin.

In the **Yajur-Veda**, 31/11, it is said:

ब्राह्मणोऽस्य मुखमासीत् ।

A Brahmin is the mouthpiece of Brahma.

A Brahmin first attains knowledge and then disseminates it through speech. He never keeps things only to himself. He is responsible for showing people how to live a noble life.

In the religious texts, the qualities of a Brahmin are described as:

देवाधीनं जगत्सर्वं मंत्राधीनश्च देवता ।
ते मंत्रा विप्रं जानन्ति तस्मात् ब्राह्मण देवताः ॥

The world depends upon the gods. The gods depend upon mantras. Brahmins know the use, the meaning and the way to chant mantras. Therefore Brahmins are like gods.

In the **Mahabharata**, Shantiparv, 11/11, Vedavyas has said:

284

चतुष्पदां गौः प्रवरा लौहानां कांचनं वरम् ।
शब्दानां प्रवरो मंत्रौ ब्राह्मणो द्विपदां वरः ॥

Amongst four-footed animals, the cow is the best. Amongst minerals, gold is the best. Amongst words, mantras in the Vedas are the best. Amongst the two-footed, Brahmins are the best.

The *Mahabharata* also mentions that since birth a Brahmin is the master of the earth. As a living being, he is responsible for looking after and protecting religious texts.

In the **Atharva-Veda**, 5/19/10, it is said:

न ब्राह्मणस्य गां जग्ध्वा राष्ट्रे जागार कश्चन ।

Wherever a Brahmin is shown contempt and disrespect, happiness vanishes.

Religious texts also say that wherever Brahmins are not accorded respect, brave or intellectual people are never found there and the community is ruined. A Brahmin is not a person born in the home of a Brahmin, but one who has the qualities of a Brahmin.

In the **Brahmvaivartpuran**, chapter 85, the importance of a Brahmin has been explained. Just as Ganga is important amongst rivers, Pushkar is important amongst pilgrimages, Kashi amongst cities of deities, Shankar amongst the most knowledgeable, Vedas amongst religious texts, Peepal (the bo tree) amongst trees, prayers amongst offerings, a fast amongst vows, in the same way, amongst all people a Brahmin is outstanding. All virtues, pilgrimages and vows reside within the Brahmin. One must seek their blessings.

A Brahmin is known for his good qualities through which it is natural for him to do good deeds. Since his mind is in harmony with what is good and proper, a Brahmin does not experience problems in normal life. He is worthy of respect and reverence.

In the **Bhagavad Gita**, 18/42, Lord Krishna explained it thus:

शमो दमस्तपः शौचं क्षान्तिरार्जवमेव च ।
ज्ञानं विज्ञानमास्तिक्यं ब्रह्मकर्म स्वभावजम् ॥

Control of the mind and the senses, willingness to endure hardships to fulfil sacred responsibilities, purity from within and without, forgiving the faults of others, simplicity in the use of the mind, the senses and behaviour, belief in the Vedas and other religious scriptures, in God and life after death, study and teaching of the Vedas and religious texts and realisation of the truth relating to God – these are the natural duties of a Brahmin.

It is because of the good qualities and deeds of a Brahmin it is directed that he must conduct all religious ceremonies. With such qualities, any person who entrusts the Brahmin with the performance of a ceremony does not find it difficult to trust and depend upon him.

In the **Manusmriti**, 10/76, it is said:

षण्णां तु कर्मणामस्य त्रीणि कर्माणि जीविका ।
याजनाध्यापने चैव विशुद्धाच्च प्रतिग्रहः ॥

The teaching of religious philosophy, performing yagyas and accepting charity from virtuous castes – these are the ways of livelihood of a Brahmin.

In the **Manusmriti**, 1/88, it is also said that when charity comes unasked, it is like celestial nectar. When it is demanded, it is condemnable.

In the **Rig-Veda**, 1/125/6, it is said:

दक्षिणावतामिदिमानि चित्रा दक्षिणावतां दिवि सूर्यासः ।
दक्षिणावन्तो अमृतं भजन्ते दक्षिणावन्तः प्रतिरन्त आयुः ॥

Those who give dakshina *(honorarium) are bright like the stars; those who give* dakshina *shine like the sun; those who give* dakshina *receive nectar; those who give* dakshina *live a long life.*

In the **Mahabharata**, Shantiparv, 313/84, it is said:

मृतो यज्ञस्त्वदक्षिणः ।

Without dakshina *(honorarium) a yagya is like a dead person.*

When a Brahmin offers his services in conducting religious ceremonies it is only appropriate that he must be paid an honorarium for the services. Conducting a ceremony is a specialised work. One cannot conduct it satisfactorily without a Brahmin priest.

Your questions answered...

Is it necessary to partake of the *prasad* offered after a religious ceremony?

Most people take *prasad* to mean whatever eatable is offered after the religious ceremony. In reality, *prasad* is meant to represent the blessings of the Supreme Spirit invoked during the religious ceremony. *Prasad* is symbolic of purity, joy, happiness, contentment and peace. We should think of God and these virtues as we partake of the *prasad* offered to us.

Why are temples and deities important to Hindus?

Of all living things only mankind has established places of prayer. It is immaterial in what country an individual lives or to what class, community or religion one belongs. It also does not matter whether an individual calls the place of prayer a temple, mosque, church or gurudwara. The purpose of all is one – to remind mankind of the Supreme Spirit. They are places where mankind finds the comfort of spiritual support and is taken away from the turmoil and tribulation of everyday life. The building of new places of worship confirms that mankind finds solace within them and uses these places as stepping-stones to personal fulfilment.

All places of prayer are worthy of reverence and offer an atmosphere of spirituality and inner peace. With a deity installed, it attracts special attraction. One can pray individually or in groups. One can chant mantras, sing devotional songs, pray, meditate or perform *arti*. With an established deity, regular offering of prayers and oblations, use of incense sticks and other religious activities, the environment in a place of prayer is strongly charged with positive vibrations. There is no place for negativity. The positive vibrations counteract any negative vibrations that individuals may bring in. Therefore, on entering a place of worship one can feel the flow of peace within. One goes to a place of worship with optimism. In such an environment one is ready for special rituals, offering prayers and expressing faith. The benefits are felt immediately and one finds fulfilment.

Once Seth Manik asked Jagatguru Shankaracharya, "Learned Sir, you know the Vedas as well as you know yourself. You know that God has no form and is omnipresent. Why then do you support deity worship in temples?"

Jagatguru replied, "Son, not everyone is capable of perceiving the divine omnipresence. In a temple, prayers are offered from sunrise to sunset, conch shells are blown and bells rung. In that environment, perception of God is easier. Such an environment is not available in many homes. In the positive environment in a temple everyone can pray. One can get a glimpse of moral and ethical behaviour and faith in a temple. This is very important for the common man."

The dome in a temple is of special significance keeping in view the needs of good acoustics and architecture. Mantras chanted or devotional songs sung before the deity strike the dome of the temple and ricochet on the deity. The top of the dome is narrow and converges to a centre point. It is so constructed that it aligns with the point where the deity stands.

The words in a mantra are creative, eternal and contain divine energy. When this energy is reflected via the dome in the temple it arouses the deity. Thereby, a devotee finds fulfilment in proportion to his devotion and offering. The mantra and manner of chanting influence the deity accordingly. One achieves whatever is in harmony with the mantra. Deities in temples where meaningful mantras are regularly chanted turn extremely benevolent. These temples become famous and crowds throng there regularly.

The temple dome is a scientific application of the pyramid technique. Sages and saints were aware of these benefits. The pyramid technique aims at creating a dome-like structure that has a focussed area where a thing is protected from negative external influences of the earth.

Within the pyramids of Egypt one can find dead bodies and things preserved over thousands of years. Special magnetic energy is generated within the pyramids that act as a protective force. Against this scientific background, one can appreciate the significance of temple domes, which focus the emotions of devotees towards the deities, and help find fulfilment.

Think it over...

Kindness is the foundation of all religions; pride the parent of all sins.

—Sant Tulsidas

288

Is it true that Hindus have innumerable gods and goddesses?

It is said that Hindus have innumerable gods and goddesses. This is an erroneous statement based upon appearances, not facts. Who can qualify to be a god or goddess? Only one who has the ability, ethical behaviour and generous temperament along with the ability to fulfil the desires of devotees can be said to be a god or goddess.

In the **Brihadranyak Upanishad**, chapter 3, Yagyavalkya has said that in reality there are only 33 gods and goddesses. Of these 8 are Vasu, 11 Rudra, 12 Aditya and Devraj Indra and Prajapati. The 8 Vasu include fire, earth, air, sky (space), sun, Dyau, moon and the planets. Entire mankind depends upon these. The five *gyanindriya* (the five senses of perception, namely the eye, ear, nose, tongue and skin), the five *karmindriya* (the five organs of action, namely hands, feet, larynx, organs of reproduction and the anus) and the soul comprise the 11 Rudra. The 12 months of the year are referred to as the 12 Aditya. The clouds are Devraj Indra and nature or the will of the Supreme Being, referred to as Prajapati.

The whole universe depends principally upon six divine forces – fire, earth, air, sky, Aditya and Dyau. When the religious texts have said that there are only 33 gods and goddesses, or forces that govern this universe, the words 33 *koti* as used in the original text have been misinterpreted to mean 33 crores (330 million) gods and goddesses, instead of 33 categories of divine forces.

In the **Rig-Veda**, 1/164/46, it is said:

इन्द्रं मित्रं वरुणमग्निमाहुरथो दिव्यः स सुपर्णो गरुत्मान् ।
एकं सद्विप्रा बहुधा वदन्ति अग्निं यमं मातरिश्वानमाहुः ॥

An embodiment of truth, knowledgeable persons know the Supreme Being in different forms and different names. The Supreme Being is known by names like Agni, Yama, Matrishva, Indra, Varun, Divya, Suparn, Gurutman and many more.

The religious texts are full of such narratives. Yet, the truth is that there is **only one God**. We see Him in different forms and with different names.

All Hindus believe in the supremacy of the Hindu triad – Brahma, Vishnu and Mahesh. Amongst goddesses, their wives – Saraswati, Lakshmi and Parvati – are most revered. All others are their forms and incarnations.

Once there was a discussion amongst the sages as to who amongst Brahma, Vishnu and Mahesh was the most important. To resolve the issue, the sages decided to appoint Bhrigu, the son of Brahma, to inquire and report to the sages.

Bhrigu decided to first visit Brahma, who was happy to see his son. However, when Bhrigu did not greet and offer reverence to Brahma, he felt hurt and infuriated. He left without talking to Bhrigu.

Next Bhrigu went to Mount Kailash to meet Shiva, who was happy to see Bhrigu and wanted to embrace him in welcome. But Bhrigu responded rudely saying, "I will not meet you. You have contravened the rules of simple courtesy and good manners." This statement offended Shiva, who chased Bhrigu with his *trishul* to punish him.

Bhrigu then went to Vaikunthlok to meet Vishnu. At that time, Vishnu was sleeping. Bhrigu stood near Vishnu's bed in the hope that he would wake up. When he did not wake up for a long time, Bhrigu was infuriated and kicked Vishnu in the chest. Vishnu woke up and saw the enraged Bhrigu before him. Vishnu stood up, touched Bhrigu's feet and gently said, "Honoured sage, my chest is hard. Your feet are delicate. Have I hurt your foot?" When Bhrigu witnessed Vishnu's kind and courteous behaviour, he felt ashamed. Vishnu offered Bhrigu a comfortable chair to sit on. Bhrigu was flattered and content.

When Bhrigu returned to the sages, he said, "Bhagwan Vishnu is most outstanding amongst the gods."

Your questions answered...

Why are there many temples devoted to Vishnu (and his incarnates) and to Shiva, but hardly any to Brahma?

It is human nature to seek what we do not have. We can create thoughts, but cannot sustain good thoughts and intentions. To enable us to do so we seek the help of Vishnu, the sustainer. He helps us in our effort. Similarly, we create negative thoughts in our minds but cannot easily destroy them. We seek the help of Shiva to destroy them. So, we repeatedly need Vishnu and Shiva. Since creation is not a problem, we do not seek the help of Brahma, the creator.

Why do Hindus ring a bell when they enter a temple?

Temples where bells keep ringing are ones where the deities are awake to the call of devotees. Bells are hung at the entry of the temple and rung to inform the deity of the devotee's arrival. The use of bells during *arti* is to tell all those living nearby that it is time for prayers. During prayers and *arti*, both at sunrise and sunset, all kinds of bells, small and big, are used. Between them, a definite beat and rhythm is employed for greater effectiveness.

It is believed that the ringing of bells arouses the divinity within deities into which life has been infused. If bells are not used, there is the likelihood that the deity may be in meditation and the prayers or offerings may not be accepted. It is also believed that the sound of bells protects one from harmful effects of problems. According to the **Skandpuran**, the ringing of temple bells absolves man from sins committed over hundred births.

Mankind was created in the presence of a musical sound. The same sound is generated when a temple bell rings. The same musical sound is also generated when one chants *Om*. It is significant that the bull Nandi is considered symbolic of the same musical sound.

A bell also symbolises death. When taking a dead body for cremation, one rings the bell. It is believed that when this world ends, there will be a similar sound of ringing of bells.

Your questions answered...

Why is *pran pratishtha* important before an idol becomes a deity?

Pran pratishtha means *infusing life into an idol*. Without breath – *pran* – a human body is nothing. Similarly, an idol is a piece of metal, wood or stone until life is infused into it. This is done through a detailed ceremony by chanting mantras requesting God to reside in the idol. Once this is done the idol becomes a deity. Thereafter, it must be bathed, clothed, given ornaments, food, incense sticks and articles of prayer, followed by *arti* in the morning and evening.

Does idol worship by Hindus promote religious feeling?

Hindus are often criticised for their overwhelming belief in idol worship. In every Hindu home one finds pictures and small idols of gods. When Hindus believe in one Supreme Being and the omnipresence of God, what's the need for idol worship?

This question is convincingly answered by modern psychology. To have faith in God it is necessary to have pictures or idols before an individual. When one sees a picture or idol, one is able to relate to it much faster. Visualisation plays an important role in identifying with God. A devotee cannot benefit from prayer or offerings to God unless the mind is under control. The picture or the idol helps focus attention, concentrate and gradually control the mind. Thus, an individual gradually develops a relationship with the Supreme Being and is able to find personal spiritual growth from within.

When one is face to face with an imposing idol of a deity, one is reminded of its many virtues and is able to concentrate better. In due course, one can concentrate *without* a picture or idol. Therefore, through a picture or idol, one moves from reality to a much higher plane that is not visible. Besides, in a temple, an idol has an aura of its own. Offering prayers there ensures fulfilment.

In the **Shrimad Bhagwat**, it is said:

अहं सर्वेषु भूतेषु भूतात्मा अवस्थितः तं अवज्ञाय मां मर्त्यः कुरुते पूजाविडम्बनाम् ।

I am present within every living being in the form of a soul. It is sheer hypocrisy and mockery when people disregard this fact and follow unnecessary rituals of offering prayers.

Pictures and idols help focus attention and concentration. For that reason they are useful. Hinduism has survived thousands of years because of their use.

Why don't Hindus perform auspicious ceremonies during *Chaturmas*?

Every year beginning with the 11th day of the moonlit period of Asadh (fourth month in the Hindu calendar) until the 11th day of the moonlit period of Kartik (eighth month of the Hindu calendar), i.e., a period of four months, it is believed that Hindu gods and goddesses are at rest. This period is referred to as *Chaturmas – four months.*

Since gods and goddesses at rest can get enraged if disturbed during this period, it is customary not to organise auspicious occasions like weddings, moving into a new house, establishing a temple, organising a community prayer or other auspicious activities. These activities are renewed only after the gods and goddesses have completed their rest on the 11th day of Kartik.

In the **Padampuran, Shrimad Bhagwatpuran** and other religious texts, this rest period is referred to as *yognidra*, a term that describes the rest Vishnu took after annihilation of the world. This term is also used when Vishnu is in deep meditation and cannot be disturbed. The inability to be available to devotees is termed as sleep or rest.

The sun, moon and air are also forms of Vishnu. During these four months when the weather is disturbed because of rains, the sun and the moon are not at their prime because of clouds and rain. It is therefore considered a period of rest for them. During rains the weather is hot, humid and uncertain. This affects health, as during this period the activity of bile, symbolic of fire, is not at its best. This reduces physical activity.

It is narrated in the **Vishnupuran, Padampuran** and **Shrimad Bhagwatpuran** that during his incarnation as Vaman, in response to a boon, Vishnu had asked Devraj Bali for land that he could cover in three steps. Transforming himself into an extraordinary form in response to a promise, Vishnu took one step to cover the whole earth, the sky and the adjacent area. In the second step, Vishnu covered the whole of heaven. Preparing for the third step, Vishnu asked Bali where he could place his foot. To fulfil his pledge, Lord Bali had no option but to surrender and offered his head for Vishnu's foot. Vishnu was pleased with Devraj Bali's sacrifice, generosity and charitable disposition. He honoured him as a charitable person and let him rule over Patal Lok and gave him a boon.

To redeem the boon, Devraj Bali asked Vishnu to reside in his palace. Vishnu granted the boon. When Lakshmi found that her husband had become bonded to Devraj Bali, she tied a *raksha bandhan* and made Bali a brother. When Bali asked her what she desired as a gift, she requested that Vishnu be freed from the boon he had granted. It is said that since then the three gods Brahma, Vishnu and Mahesh have been taking turns of four months each to reside in Bali's palace.

Therefore, Vishnu resides there during the four months of divine rest. Thereafter, Shiva takes over until Mahashivratri. Brahma is there for the next four months. According to the Puranas, Vishnu's real self goes to *yognidra* on Sheshnaag, while his physical body resides in Devraj Bali's palace.

Your questions answered...

There are a large number of temples. Do we need any more?

A Hindu temple is not only a place to offer prayers. That is just one need. A temple is intended to be a place of learning and for discourses, exchange of views, celebrating festivals, organising musical and artistic concerts. For many it is a place of retreat where they can introspect. For society, a temple should be a place for expression of faith and devotion to God. Through this devotion society should grow spiritually. A temple is basically a community centre. The need for such centres will continue to grow.

Why do Hindu gods and goddesses use different animals as vehicles?

It is said that all gods and goddesses have vehicles that make up for any deficiency they may have. For this reason, all gods and goddesses have different vehicles amongst birds and animals. The religious texts describe the different vehicles of gods and goddesses. The **Devi Bhagwan** mentions that Lakshmi uses an owl as a vehicle and Durga uses a lion. The **Shivpuran** mentions that Sri Ganesh used a mouse as a vehicle and Shiva used the bull Nandi. There are reasons for the choice of a vehicle.

Gods	Vehicles
1. Shiva	Bull Nandi
2. Vishnu	Sheshnaag
3. Saraswati	Swan
4. Durga	Lion
5. Laxmi	Owl
6. Ganesh	Mouse

A mouse is self-willed, unrestrained and uncontrollable. These qualities are symbolic of the mind. In this situation, instability is obvious. If we can control the mind just as Ganesh controls the mouse, we can concentrate upon the Supreme Being and achieve much. With knowledge of the inner soul, one can control the unstable mind. It is the mind that binds a person, or takes one towards salvation.

In the **Ganeshpuran** it is said that Conch Gandharv once offended Rishi Saubhri, who was enraged and cursed him to become a mouse. When Gandharv beseeched that he be absolved from the curse, it was modified so that he could become the vehicle for Ganesh and be entitled to live in heaven. Since the mouse was frisky and created problems for everyone, Ganesh controlled him with his mantras. Pleased with the mouse's devotion, Ganesh made him his vehicle.

Shiva uses the bull Nandi, who perceives religious knowledge well. His white colour is symbolic of his capabilities. His four legs are symbolic of the four religious pillars – compassion, charity, austerity and purity. Through these four qualities one can attain salvation.

Saraswati has a swan as her vehicle. Therefore, the swan is revered amongst birds. It is symbolic of water and milk – good judgement. It is known to pick up pearls from water. With such qualities, one can find one's way to God.

Lakshmi uses an owl as a vehicle. An owl is day-blind and can see only at night. When Lakshmi is remembered individually without her consort Vishnu, she travels at night on her vehicle. When she travels with Vishnu, they use Vishnu's vehicle Garuda. Since Lakshmi travels alone at night, those obsessed with wealth and prosperity operate in darkness. They are unaware of the light of the Sun that is symbolic of self-knowledge or self-realisation.

Durga uses a lion as a vehicle. The lion is symbolic of strength and virility and is a ferocious animal. Devotees of Durga gradually develop the qualities of a lion. They develop strength through their devotion, but often get intoxicated with it. They are capable of overcoming foes.

Vishnu's vehicle Garuda is the king of birds, well known for its farsightedness. With divine powers, it is capable of flying long distances. Garuda is symbolic of the Vedas. It has great capacity for rejuvenation.

Yama, the god of death, travels on a male buffalo. With its black ferocious looks, it is often equated with an evil spirit and considered inauspicious.

Both Shani and Ketu use a vulture as their vehicle. Both create problems for people. The vulture too is a bird that is forever looking for the dead.

Think it over...

Even as satisfaction of hunger is the perceptible result of eating, cheerfulness of mind and a sense of peace are the tangible result of devout worship.

—Swami Tapovan

Why do Hindus walk around the deity in a temple?

When in a temple, it is customary to circumambulate the deity. This practice is not based upon blind faith but has a scientific basis.

When a temple is established and life is infused into the deity through a proper *pran pratishtha* ceremony, divinity enters the deity. This divinity is in the form of magnetic waves starting from the central point of the base of the deity. This spreads around in a circle. The vibrations are the strongest near the deity and gradually weaken, as the circle becomes larger. The positive vibrations influence a person walking around the deity.

The divine halo always moves clockwise. Divinity too moves clockwise. It is therefore essential that one walks around the deity clockwise. By moving along the magnetic field of the deity one can benefit from the positive vibrations one receives. These vibrations are a blessing that add to one's strength and protect one from all kinds of problems and calamities. After completing prayers and offerings, it is therefore customary to walk around the deity.

It is believed that the longer one walks around the deity, the greater the benefit from the vibrations. It is customary to walk around the deity of Lord Krishna thrice. For Durga, one round is customary. In general, it is customary to walk 5 to 11 times around a deity.

Religious texts direct that when going around the deity of Shankar one should not cross the line where the offering of milk and water flows. For this reason, one takes only half a round around Shankar. One returns and then does the other half. It is also believed that the vibrations around Lord Shankar move both ways, clockwise and anti-clockwise.

When one walks anti-clockwise, the divine vibrations that move clockwise counter the individual's personal vibrations, gradually destroying them. Therefore, the anti-clockwise movement is prohibited, which is equivalent to committing a sin. The harmful effects caused depend upon the deity. Whatever the consequences, one has to bear them.

Your questions answered...

Many religions criticise idol worship. Even amongst some Hindu sects, idol worship is not practised. What is your opinion?

When praying, if you have an idol that you can see, touch and feel, the mind is influenced sooner and can concentrate better than if one were only to describe the idol. The reactions are faster and better. In the field of entertainment from still black and white pictures we moved to silent black and white movies. Then sound was added. Next colour was added. With greater scientific development, a wide screen and special sound effects emerged. Why? To influence a person better. Anything that influences the human senses better does so sooner and deeper. One is free to choose what makes one happy. In praying the objective is always the same. How one achieves it is a personal choice.

What is the importance of *Vanprasth* in Hindu life?

Vanprasth is the third of the ashrams or stages of life as suggested in the Hindu way of life. After a person crosses the age of 50, the children are grown up, married and have their own children. At this stage, it is customary to pass on responsibilities of the household to the children and step into *vanprasth*.

This is the stage of gradual detachment from a householder's life to a wider sphere of service and spiritual growth. *Vanprasth* is the soul of Hindu religion and culture. After living a householder's life, raising a family, setting up each of the children on their own, this is the time to repay the debt to one's nation through positive thinking and service.

The greatest asset of a person now is the experience of a life well lived. This experience can show the path to others. Just as a river keeps flowing, *vanprasth* too means *keep flowing, keep moving*. This is the time to give freely of one's positive experience to society.

In the **Harit Smritikar**, 6/2, it is written:

एवं वनाश्रमे तिष्ठन् पातयश्चैव किल्विषम् ।
चतुर्थमाश्रमं गच्छेत् संन्यासविधिना द्विजः ॥

After living a householder's life one must move on to vanprasth. *This helps overcome mental pressures and ensures tranquillity. It prepares one for sanyas (renunciation).*

In the **Manusmriti**, 4/257, it is said:

299

महर्षिपितृदेवानां गत्वाऽऽनृण्यं यथाविधिः ।
पुत्रे सर्व समासज्य वसेन्माध्यस्थमाश्रितः॥

As you grow older, pass on the responsibilities of the household to the son. Accept vanprasth *as a way of life. Now is the time to repay the debt to your forefathers, saints and to God.*

Vanprasth is the time to live a life based upon high ideals, the time to propagate goodwill, good thoughts and a positive outlook on life. One should oppose wrong beliefs and practices and support what is good for society. This is the time to gradually grow spiritually.

In the **Chhandogya Upanishad**, 3/16/5, it is written that the detached life as commended in *vanprasth* starts when one turns 48. Life is a *yagya*, an offering. In *vanprasth*, one sets out to do the third *yagya* of life.

In the **Atharva-Veda**, 9/5/1, there is a call for mankind to carry forward the soul. It calls for an entry into *vanprasth*. It says that the soul should move forward to find the company of great people and commends that one cross the sea of ignorance and find happiness in the third stage of life.

Your questions answered…

If I am a soul and part of the Supreme Spirit, why do I feel detached from God?

You feel detached from God because you are not aware of the reality. You are looking at things that are illusory, not real. When you perceive reality, you will come closer to God.

How can I be reunited with God?

God is omnipresent. You can reunite with Him by perceiving Him in everything around you. He will not be visible immediately. As your faith and devotion grow, you will begin to feel and sense Him.

What does a Hindu achieve through *sanyas*?

The fourth and last stage of life is *sanyas* – a very significant period of life. According to Hindus, there are four basic aims of human existence. The first, *dharm* relates to discharge of one's duty. The second, *arth* relates to acquiring of wealth. The third, *kam* relates to gratification. And the fourth, *moksha* relates to final salvation. *Sanyas* is the stage to achieve *moksha*.

Moksha aims at giving up desires and attachment. Whatever one needs to do to achieve this aim is *sanyas*.

In the **Manusmriti**, 6/33, it is said:

चतुर्थमायुषो भागं त्यक्त्वा संगान्परिव्रजेत् ॥

In the fourth stage of life one must give up all kinds of attachments and accept sanyas.

After living a householder's life from 25 to 50 years age, when one's activities are greatly influenced by the senses, it is not easy to rise above passion and desires. Therefore, the third stage of life from 50 to 75 years, *vanprasth* is devised to gradually detach oneself from desires. At this time, the wife continues to give company to a man even while desires are gradually controlled as one prays and conducts *yagyas*. One makes efforts to repay the debts of society. After success at this stage, one is ready for *sanyas*.

In the **Manusmriti**, 6/35-36, it is said:

ऋणानि त्रीण्यपाकृत्य मनो मोक्षे निवेशयेत् ।
अनपाकृत्य मोक्षं तु सेवमानो व्रजत्यधः ॥
अधीत्य विधिवद्वेदान्पुत्रांश्चोत्पाद्य धर्मतः ।
इष्ट्वा च शक्तितो यज्ञैर्मनो मोक्षे निवेशयेत् ॥

After repaying debts to your forefathers, saints, sages and God, prepare for emancipation. One who seeks emancipation without repaying debts goes to hell. Only after reading the Vedas, when one begets sons and performs yagyas according to one's ability should one try to concentrate on the fourth stage of life.

At this stage, no responsibilities are assigned to one who has adopted *sanyas*. Now, the aim is to renounce everything so that one gets completely detached from worldly things and can look forward to emancipation.

In the **Manusmriti**, 6/49, it is said:

अध्यात्मरतिरासीनो निरपेक्षो निरामिषः ।
आत्मनैव सहायेन सुखार्थी विचरेदिह ॥

One who has taken sanyas should reflect upon the soul. One must be detached from the materialistic world and partake of vegetarian food only to sustain the body that is the medium of the desired emancipation when one leaves this world.

In the **Narad Parivrajkupanishad**, it is explained that one who is peaceful, calm, pure, truthful, content, kind, courteous, without ego and free from pride and conceit is worthy of *sanyas*.

In the **Bhagavad Gita**, Lord Krishna explains the provisions of *sanyas* in the chapter on Karmyoga and Sankhyoga, saying that one who acts without the desire for the fruit of action is a true *sanyasi* and *yogi*.

The system of *sanyas* to seek emancipation is founded on scientific principles. To understand this, one must have basic knowledge about religion. Hinduism is based upon two important principles of the immortality of the soul and rebirth. Depending upon the balance of good and bad deeds, one is reborn in different places. Of all kinds of births, birth as a human is most outstanding. However, this birth is not free from the shackles of happiness and sorrow.

Beyond the happiness and sorrow of human life there is the severe torture of living in a womb for over nine months. If bad deeds predominate, there is the possibility of being born amongst evil spirits. To protect oneself from such eventualities, there is only one hope – avoid sinful acts. If one does commit a sin due to ignorance, one must seek forgiveness to balance the good and bad deeds. When there are no deeds to be accounted for, there will be no birth. The soul will become free to return to the Supreme Spirit to find eternal peace and contentment.

The purpose of *sanyas* is to achieve a state where all deeds are balanced and the soul is free to return to its eternal abode.

Rebirth is based upon the balance of good and bad deeds. The soul needs a body to move further. The father and mother provide the body that is the vehicle of the soul. Therefore, the first debt upon anyone is that of the parents. The parents are only instrumental in providing a body for the soul. The body is nourished by nutrients provided by nature, or through the gods who supervise the work of the Supreme Spirit. Therefore, one becomes indebted to the gods for their benevolence and it is necessary to repay this debt.

The human body is born of the sperm and ovum provided by the father and mother. However, the characteristics that the sperm and ovum carry have come down from the forefathers of the father and mother. The forefathers may not be alive, but their temperament, culture and knowledge pass on to the newborn. This is known as the debt to rishis or saints.

Every human being is burdened with three debts. The first one is to the parents. The second debt is to the gods. The third debt is to the rishis or forefathers. One cannot find emancipation unless one is free from all three debts. This is possible only through *sanyas* in the fourth stage of life.

With life divided into four ashrams or stages, the first – *brahmacharya ashram* is devoted to learning to become a good individual. Through a religious temperament one enjoys all the pleasures of life in the second – *grihast ashram*. After that, 25 years of *vanprasth* begins and one learns to control the senses. Finally, one strives for salvation during *sanyas*.

Think it over...

The Vedic scriptures amply prove that in the past it was householders, more than renunciates, who worked in the field of philosophical thought. Indifference to worldly pleasures is the chief requisite for spiritual advancement.

–Swami Tapovan

303

Why do Hindus cremate the dead?

Whoever is born must die. Amongst Hindus it is customary to do the last rites by consigning the body to fire. On this occasion, all relatives, friends and acquaintances get together to mentally convey a farewell to the departed soul. Their presence on this occasion reminds everyone of the ultimate truth – everyone has to die some day. It also reminds them of the futility of living only for oneself.

In the **Chudaman Upanishad** it is said that Brahma gave birth only to the flame-like soul. From the soul, the sky was born. From the sky, air was born, from air fire, from fire, water and from water the earth was born. These five elements united to form the human body. When a dead body is cremated in fire, the elements return to nature from where they came initially.

In the **Atharva-Veda**, 18/2/56, the cremation of a dead body is explained thus:

इमौ युनज्मि ते वह्नी असुनीताय वोढवे ।
ताभ्यां यमस्य सादनं समितीश्चाव गच्छतात् ॥

O Departed Soul, your lifeless body is offered so that the two fires may unite for your salvation. set the body on fire. Through these two fires you may go in your best state to Yama, who controls death.

In the **Atharva-Veda**, 18/3/71, it is said:

आ रभस्व जातवेदस्तेजस्वदूहरो अस्तु ते ।
शरीरमस्य सं दहाथैनं धेहि सुकृतामु लोके ॥

O Fire! Accept this dead body. Give it refuge. May your acceptance of the body bring you glory. O God in the garb of fire, burn this body and deliver the person to the abode of righteousness.

In the **Yajur-Veda**, 40/15, it is said:

वायुरनिलममृतमथेदं भस्मान्तं शरीरम् ।
ओ३म् क्रतो स्मर क्लिबे स्मरकृतं स्मर ॥

O industrious person! At the time of leaving the body chant the principal and outstanding name of God, Om. Remember God. Remember your past deeds. The air that goes in and out of the body is like celestial nectar. However, the end of the physical body is ash. It will end as ash. The dead body is worthy of being turned to ash.

There is a belief amongst Hindus that after death the soul continues to hover around the dead body due to its earlier attachment with it. When the body is consigned to the flames and burnt to ashes the relationship between the soul and the body ends.

It is customary amongst Hindus that the son of the deceased performs the cremation ceremony. This is to prepare the son to accept that his father or mother is dead. It also prepares him emotionally to take over the responsibilities of the household and also fulfil his duties towards society.

During the cremation ceremony when the dead body is set on fire, an important part of the ceremony is *kapal kriya*. The significance of this is explained in the **Garudapuran**. During *kapal kriya*, the skull is broken with a bamboo pole because it consists of very hard bone that cannot be burnt easily even by fire. When broken, it burns with the rest of the body and is converted to the five elements that constitute the body and becomes a part of the ashes.

There are other beliefs about this practice also. Since the soul resides in the forehead, with the breaking of the skull the residence of the soul is destroyed. For the soul, this begins the search for a new birth. There is another belief that unless the forehead is broken and burnt a portion may remain without burning. This is said to affect the development of the forehead in the next birth.

Why do Hindus immerse ashes of the dead in holy rivers like the Ganga?

The remnant of the dead body after burning is left behind in the form of ashes. Hindus respectfully call these ashes *phool* – literally *flowers* – to express devotion and respect for the departed soul. When children are symbolically referred to as 'fruit', it is appropriate to refer to the ashes of forefathers as 'flowers'.

It is customary to gather the ashes on the fourth day after death. They are then immersed in sacred rivers like the Ganga. If it is not possible to immerse them immediately, they are kept in a locker in the crematorium and immersed as soon as possible.

In the **Shankhsmriti**, page 7, the consigning of ashes to the Ganga is explained:

यावदस्थीनि गंगायां तिष्ठिन्ति पुरुषस्य च ।
तावद् वर्ष सहस्राणि ब्रह्मलोके महीयते ॥

As long as the ashes of the deceased person remain in the Ganga, the person continues to enjoy happiness in worthy places for thousands of years.

In the **Kurmpuran**, 35/31-34, it is said:

यावदस्थीनि गंगायां तिष्ठन्ति पुरुषस्य तु ।
तावद् वर्ष सहस्राणि स्वर्गलोके महीयते ॥
तीर्थानां परमं तीर्थ नदीनां परमा नदी ।
मोक्षदा सर्वभूतानां महापातकीनामपि ॥

सर्वत्र सुलभा गंगा त्रिषु स्थानेषु दुर्लभा ।
गंगाद्वारे प्रयागे च गंगासागरसंगमे ॥
सर्वेषामेव भूतानां पापोपहतचेतसाम् ।
गतिमन्वेषमाणानां नास्ति गंगासमा गतिः ॥

Whatever number of years the ashes remain in the Ganga, the departed soul is held in reverence in heaven for thousand times the number. Of all the pilgrimages and of all the rivers, Ganga is considered most holy. It grants salvation to all, including those that have committed gross sins. Although accessible everywhere to the common man, Ganga is unique at Hardwar, Prayag and Gangasagar. Those who desire salvation, including emotionally downtrodden sinners, there is no better place than the Ganga.

Religious writers also believe that the deceased person's journey towards the eternal home does not start until the ashes are consigned to the Ganga.

Another belief about consigning ashes to the Ganga and other sacred rivers is that the water from these rivers is used extensively to irrigate large tracts of land along the river. Since the rivers keep flowing and parting with nutrients that they carry in the water, the nutrient content reduces. Since bones are constituted of phosphates, the ashes consigned to the rivers increase the phosphate content of the water that irrigates fields. Phosphates are essential ingredients for growing grains. With the irrigation water, phosphates are passed on to the fields and the crops. The ultimate purpose of ensuring that the elements of the body return to nature after death is achieved.

Think it over...

The person, not larger than the thumb, dwelling within, always dwelling in the heart of man, is perceived by the heart, the thought, the mind; they who know it become immortal.

—**Svetasvatara Upanishad**

Is the soul really immortal?

Hindu religious texts assert that the soul is part of the Supreme Spirit. Therefore, like God, the soul too is eternal. However, in this world the soul has an entity. When the soul enters a body it is given the name of the person. The soul has no colour, form or sex.

In the **Rig-Veda**, 1/164/38, it is said:

अपाङ्प्राङेति स्वधया गृभीतोऽमर्त्यो मर्त्येना सयोनिः ।
ता शश्वन्ता विषूचीना वियन्तान्यन्यं चिक्युर्न नि चिक्युरन्यम् ॥

The soul is immortal. The physical body is destructible. The soul controls all the functions in the body. The body functions as long as the soul resides within it. The most learned people do not understand the mysteries of the soul. The principal aim of life should be to understand it to the best of one's ability.

In the **Brihadranyak Upanishad**, 8/7/1, it is said that the soul never sins. It never grows old. It is free from death and sorrow. It is never hungry or thirsty. It has no desires, but we should desire it. It does not dream of anything, but we should dream about it. It is an entity that we must try to understand better.

In the **Bhagavad Gita**, 2/20, there is a reference to the immortality of the soul:

न जायते म्रियते वा कदाचित्न्नायं भूत्वा भविता वा न भूयः ।
अजो नित्यः शाश्वतोऽयं पुराणो न हन्यते हन्यमाने शरीरे ॥

The soul was never born, nor does it die. It will not emerge again. It is unborn, eternal, everlasting and without age. Even when the body is destroyed, the soul remains untouched.

In the **Bhagavad Gita**, 2/22, there is further reference to the soul:

वासांसि जीर्णानि यथा विहाय नवानि गृह्णाति नरोऽपराणि ।
तथा शरीराणि विहाय जीर्णान्यन्यानि संयाति नवानि देही ॥

Just as a man discards his old clothes and takes on new ones, in the same way the soul discards the old body and enters a new one.

It is also said that weapons cannot cut a soul. Nor can fire burn it. Water cannot wet it, nor can air dry it. The soul is eternal, omnipresent, immovable, constant and everlasting.

It is believed that it takes 13 days for the soul to avoid going into an inauspicious form of a ghost or spirit. It is therefore customary to offer prayers and give charity to seek peace for the soul. It is only after 13 days that the soul moves on to meet the forefathers.

Think it over...

The Yaksh asked Yudhistra, "What is the strangest thing in the world?"
Yudhistra responded, "The strangest thing in life is that everyone sees someone or the other dying everyday. Yet everyone feels that they will live forever."

On what grounds do Hindus assert that the soul is reborn?

Hindu religious texts authoritatively assert about the rebirth of the soul. After death the physical body serves no purpose. It is consigned to the flames so that the five elements that constitute the body return to nature. However, the soul is immortal. According to spiritual belief, it is reborn.

There are innumerable instances when people have recounted their experiences in the last birth. These were confirmed to be true. This is scientifically called paranormal phenomena – something beyond the scope of normal scientific understanding.

According to Hindu religious texts, it is through religious rites and rituals after death that the soul proceeds to take rebirth. Many details related to this subject are available in religious texts.

In the **Mahabharata**, Vanparv, 209/32, it is said:

शुभैः प्रयोगैर्देवत्वं व्यामिश्रैर्मानुषो भवेत् ।

With good deeds a soul takes rebirth amongst the gods. With a mixture of good and bad deeds one takes rebirth as a human.

In the **Kathupanishad**, 2/2/7, it is said:

योनिमन्ये प्रपद्यन्ते शरीरत्वाय देहिनः ।
स्थाणुमन्येऽनुसंयन्ति यथाकर्म यथाश्रुतम् ॥

309

According to one's deeds and knowledge one may take rebirth in a special home. Another may take birth as an immovable living thing.

In the **Yogvashisth**, it is said:

एहिकं प्रोक्तनं वापि कर्म यदचितं स्फुरन् ।
पौरषोऽसो परो यत्नो न कदाचन निष्फलः ॥

The deeds performed in the last and the current births definitely show up as the fruit of actions. None of the deeds done by mankind pass without bearing fruit.

In the **Patanjali Yogsutra**, 2/12-13, it is said:

क्लेशमूलः कर्मोशयो दृष्टादृष्ट जन्मबेदनीयः ।
सतिमूले   तदिपाको   जात्यायुर्भोगाः ॥

If the accumulated deeds and rituals of the last birth are good, one is reborn in a good home and endowed with good abilities and a long life. When the soul leaves the body it takes with it the knowledge, deeds and the intellect with it. Based on these the soul takes rebirth. With time these show up in the new life.

Maharishi Vashistha said:

आशापाशा शताबद्धा वासनाभाव धारिणः ।
कायात्कायमुपायान्ति वृक्षाद्वृक्षमिवाण्डजा ॥

The mind of a man is engulfed by hundreds of desires and ambitions. After death, bonded to these desires and ambitions, the soul seeks to fulfil these just as a bird in search of fruit leaves one tree to find another to perch on.

In the **Bhagavad Gita**, 8/6, it is said:

यं यं वापि स्मरन्भावं त्यजत्यन्ते कलेवरम् ।
तं तमेवैति कौन्तेय सदा तद्भावभावितः ॥

Whatever the soul is thinking of at the time of death, having always been absorbed in it, the soul will attain the same in the next life.

There is reference to rebirth in many Hindu religious texts, explained through specific situations and stories. Both Maharishi Valmiki and Sant Tulsidas have given descriptions of rebirth in the *Ramayana*.

Once Shatrupa asked Manu, "Bhagwan! Why is it that a soul has to wander from one birth to another? Many times even after taking the human form the soul is demoted to lesser forms. Why is it so?"

Manu responded, "When the soul commits sins physically, it is born in the plant world. When one sins through speech, one is born as an animal or bird. Through

310

sinning by the mind a human is degraded. The sins of the last and present births express bad temperament and one takes rebirth in ugly monstrous forms."

When Maharaja Praduman died, there was uproar in his family. Everyone was devastated. Maharishi Kauts was an expert on rebirth. He was summoned and told that the family wanted to see the king in whatever form he was in.

The king had taken rebirth as a wood insect. He had a small family. When an effort to catch the insect was made, he screamed to be left alone. He was happy in his present life. With new attachments to the new family he had forgotten old attachments. Worldly attachments last only till the physical body exists.

One can find the basis of rebirth in religious, moral, psychological and philosophical explanations. Dr R Ruth has described the physical transformation of inanimate objects also as rebirth. It is explained that both objects and energy are capable of change. Energy cannot be destroyed. It only changes form. Many times the changed form is not visible.

It is also suggested that the DNA is passed in invisible form through the soul to the next birth. Past deeds are conveyed through the soul this way. Past memories, knowledge and past experiences have passed from generation to generation in this way. Our present knowledge is the accumulated form of past knowledge and experience. We know that characteristics from forefathers pass on through our genes.

> ## Your questions answered...
> **How can one be sure that one's actions are righteous and therefore good?**
>
> For any action to be classified as righteous, it must fulfil four basic requirements. First, the action must be legally permissible. Second, it must be morally right. Third, it must be acceptable to society. And fourth, the individual must find happiness in it.

Why do Hindus insist upon last rites being performed by the son?

According to Hindu religious texts, it is desirable that the son performs the last rites of a deceased. This is one of the main reasons why most Hindus are obsessed about having a son.

In the **Vashistha Smriti**, 17/3, it is said:

अपुत्रिण इत्यभिशापः ।

To not have a son is a curse upon a person.

Again in the **Vashistha Smriti**, 17/5, it is said:

पुत्रेण लोकाञ्जयति पौत्रेणानन्त्यमश्नुते ।
अथ पुत्रस्य पौत्रेण ब्रध्नस्याप्नोति विष्टपम् ॥

One who has a son is entitled to enter all regions of the universe, one who has a grandson is entitled to eternity and one who has a great grandson is entitled to the abode of Surya.

In the **Manusmriti**, 9/138, it is said:

पुंनाम्नो नरकाद्यस्मात् त्रायते पितरं सुतः ।
तस्मात्पुत्र इति प्रोक्तः स्वयमेव स्वयंभुवा ॥

In Hindi, a son is putra. *When 'Pu' symbolises* hell, *'tra' derived from 'tran' means* one who protects. *Together 'putra' means* one who protects a person from hell.

Brahma called a boy *putra*. Therefore, god-fearing people desire a son to protect them from going to hell. It is for this reason that the son does the last rites like cremation, *pind daan* and *shraddh*.

In the religious texts, it is also written that those blessed with a son need never worry about their last rites. Just by being available to be seen at the time of death the son becomes free of parental debt. One whose son offers *shraddh* goes to heaven. The last rites by the son protect the father or mother from birth in low places. According to Dharmraj, if one has several sons the elder one should perform the last rites. The other sons may be present, but must not perform the rites.

It is said:

भ्रातरश्च पृथक् कुर्युर्नाविभक्ताः कदाचन ।

Religious texts direct that the son should perform the shraddh *ceremony of a person. If there is no son, the wife/husband should perform it. If they are not available, then a real brother should do it. In their absence, the son-in-law or his son can conduct the ceremony.*

Your questions answered...

If God is present in everyone and at all places, then is God also present in sinners?

Yes. If God were not present in sinners how would He reform them? Life is full of many examples where thieves became saints.

What is the importance of *pind daan* for the deceased?

The custom of *pind daan* dates back to the time when the Vedas were written. The *pind daan* is performed after the death of a person. The word *pind* means *a body*. The word *daan* denotes *charity* or *giving*. Therefore, *pind daan* means *giving a body to the deceased*. Depending upon circumstances, the son or another person performs *pind daan*.

When a person dies, the soul leaves the body. To end the relationship between the soul and the body, the body is consigned to flames where it is converted into ashes. These ashes are consigned to a holy river like the Ganga. Thereby, nothing remains of the physical body, but the soul waits for a new body.

It is believed that it is the responsibility of the son to give the deceased a new body. How does one give a body to the deceased? This body is symbolically given to the deceased through *pind daan*. It takes ten days of *pind daan* to create the body. With the body ready, the appetite is aroused. On the 11th and 12th day the food offered at *shraddh* is eaten. It is believed that on the 13th day the messengers of death usher the deceased into Yamlok, the abode of Yama. When the last rites are performed with devotion the deceased enters Yamlok happily. To Hindus this is important.

In the **Yogvashisth**, 3/55/27, it is said:

आदौ मृता वयमिति बुध्यन्ते तदनुक्रमात् ।
बंधु पिण्डादिदानेन प्रोत्पन्ना इवा वेदिनः ॥

314

At this stage the soul is aware that the old body is dead and that it is through the pind daan *of the son or brethren that a new body has been created. This experience is conveyed through feelings and sentiments. The physical rites are only symbolic. These sentiments embrace the deceased.*

On receiving *pind daan* the soul feels happy and content and after giving blessings proceeds to Yamlok. A son who does not offer *pind daan* to the deceased can be cursed in retaliation.

It is believed that it was Brahma who first performed the *pind daan* ceremony in Gaya. Since then this tradition has continued. Offering *pind daan* during the dark fortnight of Ashvin is of special significance. Symbolically a *pind* is a round ball made of a mixture of wheat and rice flour with some sesame seeds mixed along with some milk and honey. Seven balls are made out of 100 grams of flour. Of these, one is offered to the deceased and the rest to others as desired.

Earlier *pind daan* was performed around the year. There were 360 platforms where *pind daan* was done with wheat and oat flour mixed with dried milk. *Pind daan* is also performed symbolically with mud balls. Presently *pind daan* is performed at Vishnu temple, Akshay, Vat, Phalgu and Punpun river, Ramkund, Sitakund, Brahm Mangalgauri, Kagbali, and with the five pilgrimages they together make 48 platforms where *pind daan* is performed.

In **Vayupuran**, according to a narration titled *Gaya Mahatam*, when creating mankind, Brahma created a demon named Gayasur. The demon went atop the Kolahal Mountain and offered great penance to Vishnu. Pleased with Gayasur, Vishnu asked him to seek one blessing. So, Gayasur requested that whoever came in touch with him – be it an angel or a demon, an insect, a sinner, a saint or a sage, or an evil spirit – should find salvation after having been purified of all sins. From that day everyone who came in touch with him found salvation and proceeded to Vaikunth (abode of Vishnu).

In the **Kurmpuran**, 34/7-8, it is said:

गयातीर्थं परं गुह्यं पितृणां चातिवल्लभम् ।
कृत्वा पिण्डप्रदानं तु न भूयो जायते नरः ॥
सकृद् गयाभिगमनं कृत्वा पिण्डं ददाति यः ।
तारिताः पितरस्तेन यास्यन्ति परमां गतिम् ॥

All forefathers appreciate a pilgrimage to Gaya by their successors. Once the pind daan *is performed in Gaya, one achieves salvation. One becomes free of rebirth. If one visits Gaya even once and offers* pind daan, *the forefathers become free from hell and other dreadful destinations and achieve salvation.*

In the **Kurmpuran** it is also said that whoever goes to Gaya for *pind daan* is blessed and seven generations from the paternal and maternal side are benefited along with the personal self who achieves salvation.

Only a son or another male relative is authorised to offer *pind daan*. However, in 1985, the Brahmins of Mithila authorised women relatives also to offer *pind daan*. It is said that once Sita too offered *pind daan* after Dasrath died.

It is said that when Ram, Lakshman and Sita reached the banks of the Phalgu River in Gaya to offer *pind daan*, Ram and Lakshman left Sita there so that they could collect the necessary items for *pind daan*. When they were away, there was a celestial call saying that the auspicious time for *pind daan* was passing away, and that Sita should proceed with *pind daan*.

Considering the situation, Sita proceeded to do *pind daan* with cows, Phalgu River, Ketaki flowers and fire as witnesses. She personally chanted mantras offering balls made of river sand to Dasrath. When Ram and Lakshman returned, Sita told them about what had happened. Ram and Lakshman found it hard to believe. When Sita asked witnesses to testify about what she had said, none besides the Vat tree did so.

Sita was enraged. She cursed the cows that they would eat impure things. She cursed the river Phalgu that it would be dry on the top and water would flow beneath the waterline. She cursed the Ketaki flower that it would never be used for auspicious occasions. She cursed the fire that whatever came in contact with it would be destroyed. She blessed the Vat tree that it would remain evergreen.

Think it over...

Just as a candle cannot burn without fire, men cannot live without a spiritual life.

—Gautam Buddha

What is the purpose of the *Shraddh* ceremony?

After 13 days of death it is customary to feed Brahmins, saints and sages in the fond memory of the deceased. This ceremony is called *shraddh*. It is believed that when Brahmins and others are offered food in memory of the deceased, one's devotion for the deceased remains steadfast. When the ceremony is performed as a gesture of gratitude to the deceased, it brings with it great inner peace and goodwill. It is believed that this makes the deceased happy and content. It is an important step towards salvation of the deceased.

In the **Manusmriti**, 3/275, it is written:

यद्ददाति विधिवत् सम्यक् श्रद्धासमन्वितः ।
तत्तत् पितृणां भवति परत्रानन्तमक्षयम् ॥

Whatever one offers ceremoniously and with devotion to the deceased reaches them in heaven in an imperishable and eternal form.

In the **Brahmpuran** it is said that in the dark fortnight of Ashvin, Yama frees all souls so that they can visit their children to accept the food they offer at the *shraddh* ceremony. Those who do not offer food to their forefathers during this period attract their wrath and may have to suffer if cursed by them. Coming generations may suffer on account of this lapse. It is also customary to perform *shraddh* on the death anniversary of the deceased. The ceremony aims at feeding Brahmins until they are content.

317

In the **Garudapuran** it is said:

आयुः पुत्रान् यशः स्वर्ग कीर्ति पुष्टिं बलं श्रियम् ।
पशुन् सौख्यं धनं प्राप्नुयात् पितृपूजनात् ॥

When shraddh *is performed to their satisfaction, the deceased bless successors with age, a son, fame, salvation, heaven, glory, stability, strength, prosperity, cattle, happiness, money, growth and eternal blessings.*

In the **Yamsmriti**, 36-37, it is said a father, grandfather and great grandfather desire the *shraddh* ceremony just as birds living on trees desire that the tree bear fruit. They expect that successors will offer honey, milk and *kheer* (rice-porridge) at the *shraddh* ceremony.

In the **Yamsmriti**, 40, it is said:

यावतो ग्रसते ग्रासान् हव्यकव्येषु मन्त्रवित् ।
तावतो ग्रस्ते पिण्डान् शरीरे ब्राह्मणः पिता ॥

Whatever number of morsels a Brahmin, expert in mantras, eats, that many morsels are accepted by the father of the person performing shraddh *by being present within the body of the Brahmin.*

In the **Atharva-Veda**, 18/3/42, another way of reaching food to the forefathers is explained. It says that while offering oblation to the fire, the person performing *shraddh* should pray as follows:

त्वमग्न ईडितो जातवेदो वाड्ढव्यानि सुरभीणि कृत्वा । प्रादाः पितृभ्यः ।

O admirable God of Fire! You know how and in whatever form or place my father resides. Whatever foods we present as an offering please reach it to him with your beneficence.

According to **Maharishi Jabali**, whoever performs *shraddh* in the dark fortnight of Ashvin will be blessed with a son, long life, good health, and glory and will attain whatever is desired.

In the **Vishnupuran** it is written that when *shraddh* is performed with devotion, it not only gives contentment to the forefathers, but also to Brahma, Indra, Rudra, Ashwini Kumar, Surya, Agni, Ashtvasu, Vayu, Rishi, mankind, birds, animals, reptiles and also the spirits.

In the **Brahmpuran** it is said that the family of the person who performs *shraddh* with devotion will be trouble free.

According to **Maharishi Sumantu**, in this world there is no other path to good fortune than performing *shraddh*. All wise people must devotedly perform *shraddh*.

In the **Markandeypuran** it is said that the nation and family where *shraddh* is not performed will never have brave and healthy men who live a hundred years.

In the **Mahabharata**, Vidur tells Dhritrashtra that whoever does not perform *shraddh* is termed foolish by wise people.

Your questions answered...

I live in a big city. The only Brahmins I can think of inviting for the annual *shraddh* are priests in temples. I have tried to invite them, but they are unable to come. What should I do?

You have two options. Give food items to Brahmin priests in a temple or in a Hindu religious educational institution. If you do not have access to Brahmin priests, you can give food or food items to needy people in institutions for the needy. Two important aspects of *shraddh* are one's emotional involvement for forefathers and giving of food, rather than any other item, in charity.

How does *tarpan* help please the deceased?

*T*arpan literally means *offering of water to the deceased*. It is customary to add milk, oats, rice, sesame seeds, sandalwood and flowers when offering *tarpan*. The mixture is offered in a small stream made with the use of kusha and offered while chanting mantras. When this offering is made with devotion, gratitude, goodwill, love and good wishes, it immediately ensures contentment for the deceased. This offering is made on the death anniversary of the deceased. If one does not know the date of the death, then the ceremony can be performed during the dark fortnight of Ashvin.

In the **Manusmriti** *tarpan* has been described as *pitra-yagya* – a yagya dedicated to the memory of forefathers. It is believed that it gives contentment to the deceased, and promotes comfort and happiness for successors. The ceremony is meant to remember the deceased, offer reverence and appease the hunger for remembrance. Forefathers look forward to this by their successors.

Among *shraddh* ceremonies, six kinds of *tarpan* are commended. Each has its own significance.

Devtarpan aims at making an offering to water, air, Surya, Agni, Moon, energy and the gods that work selflessly for the welfare of mankind.

Rishitarpan aims at making an offering to Narad, Charak, Vyas, Ddhichi, Sushrut, Vashistha, Yagvalkya, Vishwamitra, Atri, Katyayan, Panini and other rishis.

Divyamanavtarpan aims at making an offering to all who have made sacrifices for the welfare of mankind such as the Pandavas, Maharana Pratap, Raja Harishchandra, Janak, Shivi, Shivaji, Bhamashah, Gokhale, Tilak and other important people.

Divyapitratarpan aims at making an offering to those forefathers who left behind great moral values and wealth for successors.

Yamtarpan aims at making an offering to remember the God of Death, and to accept the principle of birth and death.

Manushyapitratarpan aims at making an offering to all those who are related to the family as relatives, teachers, friends and others.

In this way, through *tarpan* an individual makes offerings of goodwill for everything connected with the person. It ensures happiness and contentment.

Think it over...

No man who is fit to live need fear to die. To us here, death is the most terrible thing we know. But when we have tested its reality, it will mean to us birth, deliverance, a new creation of ourselves. It will be what health is to a sick man; what home is to the exile; what the loved one given back is to the bereaved. As we draw near to it, a solemn gladness should fill our hearts. It is God's great morning lighting up the sky. Our fears are the terror of children in the night. The night with its terrors, its darkness, its feverish dreams, is passing away; and when we awake it will be into the sunlight of God.

–Fuller

Epilogue

It is not surprising that people around the world are interested in the Hindu way of life. In appreciating the special attributes bestowed upon mankind by God, the Hindu way of life has not only recognised the four stages of life as a human being, but also prescribed duties relating to each. Through vision and experience, great saints, sages and philosophers have suggested positive ways to make life meaningful. Mankind has greatly benefited from their knowledge.

The Hindu way of life has not restricted itself only to spiritual growth. It has touched every aspect of human life. Beginning from the time a child is conceived to the time a person dies after living a complete life, every aspect has been covered. The recommendations have been proved by time and are worthy of adoption by modern society, just as they were thousands of years earlier when first proposed.

The modern generation may have an objection to the sense of exaggeration, particularly when old religious texts describe the benefits of a good deed, or explain the punishment for a wrong one. Perhaps, at that time it was necessary to exaggerate benefits to motivate people, as well as exaggerate the punishment to instil fear that would restrain people from committing bad deeds. Are modern marketing personnel not doing the same? To create a balance, one can make appropriate adjustments whenever required.

The greatest benefit of the Hindu way of life is that it can suit everyone. It is practical and flexible, appreciates the complexities of life, encourages one to be virtuous and explains that one need not go far to meet God. He is right within every individual – an invisible divinity. The more one learns to be truthful, honest and thoughtful towards all without exception, the faster that divinity emerges as a strong force leading one to spiritual attainment.

The Hindu way of life is no bitter pill coated with sugar to entice people towards God. It explains and accepts that every individual is unique. At birth, everyone begins with the good and bad deeds of the last life. At death, after making adjustments, one carries the balance forward to the next life. The Hindu way of life recognises that every human being is driven by four basic aims – *dharm, arth, kam* and *moksha*. When one understands the reality and lives a virtuous life based upon these simple rules, spiritual growth comes naturally.

Mystic Meanings of the Symbols and Weapons used to Depict Various Gods and Goddesses

Sword: The symbol of the sword indicates the power to remove fear and destroy ignorance and to help the Sadhak surmount all difficulties.

Shield: Provides the power to shield oneself against problems.

A Hatchet (Ankush): Symbolizes control of the elephant of desires and cutting away of the bondage of desires. The hatchet cuts the person away from the false identification of his self with his physical body.

Conch Shell: The sound of ocean waves, the pure sound that brings liberation to human beings. This sound resembles the sound of AUM.

Chakra: A symbol of Dharma which revolves on its own axis. It cuts through obstacles and destroys disharmony and imbalance. Vishnu and Krishna have the powers of using this chakra.

Wheel: The form of the chakra, represents time. Chakra wheel creates the cycle of time. Whatever is not in conformity with the cosmic rhythm must come to an end.

Club: The club is made of metal, an earth element and it is a tool for maintaining control over the earth.

Arrow: This arrow is shot to destroy lust and carnal desires.

Damru: The drum depicts the powers of rhythm of the heart beat.

Axe: The axe was the first weapon invented by human kind. It is used as a symbol to cut through all obstacles.

Thunderbolt (Wajra, Wand): Indicates the electrical energy of fire and physical heat that emanates from within the body.

Trident: Symbolizes the balance of the three forces of preservation, creation and destruction. Three aspects of consciousness—cognition, conation and affection. Three gunas of Prakriti. Modes of Nature Satva, Rajas and Tamas.

Rat: Rat is the vehicle of God Ganesha. It is the symbol of the intuitive intellect, which like a rat, cuts asunder the network of subtle desires, and burrows into the depth of the unconscious to level the glory of the self.

Lion: Lion is vehicle of Goddess Durga. It is used as symbol of immense spiritual strength which unfolds in a spiritual aspirant as he begins to discover the grace of the Goddess.

Swan (Hamsa): Swan is the vehicle of Goddess Saraswati. Mystical swan possessed the ability of separating water and milk and thus revealing the real milk that is the discerning knowledge that separates knowledge from ignorance, nonself. The pure mind is the vehicle of God.

Tiger Skin: Symbolic of the tiger of the mind that dwells in the forest of desires.

Elephant Head: Ganesha is shown with an elephant head. It is symbolic of wisdom and majesty.

Elephant Trunk: Symbolizes double consciousness which is characteristic of the state of spiritual liberation; the elephant uses its trunk as the organ of smell as well as an organ of action.

Tusk of Ganesha: God Ganesha is shown with only one Tusk. It symbolizes non duality of existence.

Garuda (Eagle): Garuda is the vehicle of God Vishnu. It is the symbol of Manvantra.

Peacock: Symbolizes multi aspected divinity.

Four Heads: Can see in four directions at once.

Lotus Flower: A symbol of purity, completely unaffected by its environment, and spiritual unfoldment.

Scripture: Knowledge. May impart sacred knowledge when God is properly invoked.

Vase: It contains Amrita, the precious fluid of vital potency.

Skull: Indicates surmounting or overcoming fear of death.

Laddu (Sweet): Symbolizes the most refined state of pure consciousness. It brings health and prosperity to the house-hold.

Raised Hand : It is a mudra of assuring protection.

Conch Shell: The sound of ocean waves, the pure sound that brings liberation to human soul

Ganga: Cooling and purifying stream of self knowledge and wisdom that cools the sufferings of the world process.

Snakes: Passions which have been tamed. Mental powers under the control of the Divinity.

Rosary (Mala): Acts as powerful centering device. Working the Mala removes nervousness and distraction and quietens the mind and facilitates interaction with God.

Four Arms: Symbolize super human glories and devine consciousness.

Matted Locks: Matted locks of God Shiva represent the mystic realms which are high, profound and inaccessible for those who lack spiritual strength and purity.

Moon: Symbolizes mind in a state of complete tranquility and purity.

Blue Complexion of Krishna: Symbolizes the infinite expanse of the consciousness of supreme knowledge.

Flute: Represents the devotee who has transcended his ego-self and has become an unobstructed medium for the music of the soul.

Vina: The musical instrument, symbolizes harmony and heavenly melody. Wisdom weaves the discordant notes of multiplicity and disharmony of the world into an effulgent unity and heavenly melody.

Holy Mother India

India is the only country in the world,
Always remained on the top of the spiritual world.
Ancient civilizations of Rome and Greece are no more,
But the ancient civilization of India is still intact as before.

Slavery of hundreds of years, could do it no harm,
It is still there, peaceful and calm.
No other country can match its rich spiritual heritage,
It gave the world many a true saint and sage.

Rama, Krishna, Buddha and Ram Dev,
Chaitanya, Ramakrishna and Nam Dev.
Shankracharya, Tuka Ram and Tulsidas,
Vivekananda, Sai Baba and Ram Das.

They gave the message of ultimate reality,
And showed the path for the world fraternity.
Buddhism, Jainism and Vedanta are parts of Hindu Dharma,
Which give a true message of Sanatan Dharma.

Ramayana, Mahabharata and Bhagwad Gita have messages,
Which have no parallel in the world literature of messages.
When other countries came to know our spirituality,
A few decided to visit us for a glimpse of our spirituality.

Mystic Significance of Hindu Gods and Goddesses

Hindu religion is a very unique religion,
Many Gods and Goddesses are worshipped in this religion.
Brahma, Vishnu and Shiva are their main Gods,
Others are the descendants of these Gods.

Though God is one, He is worshipped in different ways,
As Truth is one, but the wise speak of it in different ways.
God has infinite manifestations and aspects,
Each mind envisages a different aspect.

People are at different levels of evolution,
So they have different degrees of purity and devotion.
As a man is photographed in different poses,
Even so God has infinite poses.

Vishnu, Krishna and Rama are manifestations of one God,
All Gods and Goddesses are manifestations of the supreme God.
Deep mystic significance is hidden in all forms,
As all the Gods and Goddesses have different forms.

They are designed to awaken man's hidden powers,
One has to meditate deeply to develop those powers.
Every God and Goddess has an esoteric meaning,
Special knowledge is required to understand that meaning.